JONATHAN SWIFT

A CRITICAL INTRODUCTION

JONATHAN SWIFT

A CRITICAL INTRODUCTION

BY

DENIS DONOGHUE

Professor of
Modern English and American Literature
University College, Dublin

CAMBRIDGE
AT THE UNIVERSITY PRESS
1969

Published by the Syndics of the Cambridge University Press
Bentley House, 200 Euston Road, London N.W.1
American Branch: 32 East 57th Street, New York, N.Y. 10022

© Cambridge University Press 1969

Library of Congress Catalogue Card Number: 77-79053

Standard Book Number: 521 07564 5

Printed in Great Britain
by Alden & Mowbray Ltd at the Alden Press, Oxford

CONTENTS

INTRODUCTION

The English Tripos at the University of Cambridge includes a
'Special Author' Paper, designed to encourage the student to
study one major writer in some depth. The present book has
developed from a series of lectures I gave in 1965–66, when the
chosen Special Author was Jonathan Swift. In the lectures I
was concerned to question a certain assumption, dominant
then as now, that irony is the key to Swift. The first difficulty
in this assumption is that only a small part of Swift's work
satisfies the ironic requirement; though I acknowledge that
the ironic books are among the most powerful literary master-
pieces. *Gulliver's Travels* and *A Tale of a Tub* may be fruitfully
considered in terms of irony, but these terms are not particularly
useful when we are reading *Contests and Dissensions*, the political
tracts, the journalism, the sermons, many of the poems, and so
forth. It is difficult to rest content with a key which fits well
enough on two or three brilliant occasions but seems almost
irrelevant to the majority of Swift's writings. The fact that
Swift's sensibility is at once powerful and, in its general impression, unified is another version of the same problem. A further
difficulty may be felt in our tendency to read Swift as if he
were Samuel Beckett. We are often invited to think of Swift
as a modern, ironic, alienated figure, adept of dread, dancing
without any intimation of merriment on the bones of Lockean
orthodoxy. But the trouble with this image is that it exaggerates
the subversive element in Swift and ignores many other
elements, less modish but equally important. Swift Our Contemporary is merely a fraction of Jonathan Swift 1667–1745,
though it is a fraction especially congenial to twentieth-
century readers. I have tried to suggest a few of the missing

elements. In reading Swift we find some difficulty in naming the sources of his feeling. It is obvious that a certain sense of life is operative in his work, but it is hard to define that sense with any precision, or to locate it in contemporary attitudes. It is enough to say, at the beginning, that this sense issues in certain characteristic gestures; but it is too much if we go on to assert that these gestures certify a coherent body of attitudes, commitments, values. This idiom seems to imply certainty where there is none. To read Swift is to move in a context of feeling where the relation between directness and obliquity is peculiarly delicate. Still, the gestures are significant. I have tried to describe them.

While concentrating on Swift in this way, however, I have also taken the liberty of suggesting certain comparisons and contrasts. It seemed desirable not only to indicate a social and historical setting, but also to invoke a certain perennial context of ideas and images. Many questions in Swift may be answered by reference to history and society, but it is hardly necessary to restrict oneself too severely in this respect. Where a motif in his work seems particularly important, I have allowed myself to pursue it, even where it leads to other writers and other times.

D. D.

'ONE LASH THE MORE'

I notice a whiff of Swift in some of my notes. I too
am a desponder in my nature, an uneasy, peevish,
and suspicious man, although I have my moments
of volatility and *fou rire*.

Charles Kinbote in *Pale Fire*

I

The reception of Swift in the past twenty years or so has been
remarkably thorough; especially that sense of his achievement
which is registered in terms of irony, satire, parody, obliquity,
persona, and so forth. But it is possible to feel that this impression
of his work, its nature and force, is based upon certain assumptions which have passed too easily into common lore. It is
generally assumed, for instance, that Swift uses the *persona* in
ways entirely congenial to the novelist; that these are the ways
in which his imagination is exercised. But when we try to say,
somewhat more narrowly, what his use of the *persona* entails, we
find ourselves slipping into an idiom which is less appropriate
to a consideration of Swift than of Flaubert or James. It is not
certain that we are proceeding along the right lines. If the
use of the *persona* implies that Swift, in the relevant works, hands
over his fiction to a reliable narrator, a dramatic character, a
single voice; and that, having done so, he withdraws to watch
the drama from a distance; then it is necessary to remark
that Swift is not that kind of writer. He does not entrust the
work to a representative figure, in the modern sense; to a
perceiving consciousness or a qualified participant. He is not

I

Flaubert or James. He is not, in the sense implied by those names, a novelist at all.

It comes to a question of form. Modern readers have been schooled to a certain severity in this matter; as pupils of James, we are distressed in the presence of a 'loose baggy monster', any book which does not appear to maintain the high formal decencies. James's favourite form, it is commonplace to say, is one in which everything is consigned to a superbly qualified consciousness, a person who takes part in the drama and reports the choice results. Anything that may be deemed to lie outside that consciousness must put up with the disability and wait for another occasion, another novel. James was not always strict with himself in this principle; he did not despise the omniscient narrator in *The American*, for instance, though he excluded him from *The Ambassadors*. It is enough to say that he thought as well of form as of art itself and understood that they might be identified, without violence to either term. But Swift is something else again. When we address ourselves to *Gulliver's Travels* or *A Tale of a Tub*, we find that he is careless, casual, if Jamesian standards are recalled. He appears to do whatever he chooses when the humour takes him. Sometimes he seems to confine himself to the bounds of a fictional character, if we think of character in fairly loose terms; at other times, he ignores this restriction. In this modern light his art seems primitive, as if he never acquired the knack. But the final impression of these books is not like that at all. It is impossible to think of them as casual; rather, they seem monstrously sophisticated.

It is necessary to argue, perhaps, that in reading these books we should regard another notion of form; or at least we should advert to another tradition, in which Swift's versions of form, however odd, are well received and understood. Robert Martin Adams has invited us to recognise that there are certain works of literature in which the form is, to use his own term, 'open'. 'The open form', he writes, 'is literary form...which includes a major unresolved conflict with the intent of displaying its unresolvedness.' Such works appear to involve a certain 'humiliation of the mind'; the mind, which in art is always presumed to be a free agent, appears in these works somehow to court its own defeat.[1] Henry James said of his father that he only cared for virtue that was more or less ashamed of itself. There are writers of whom it may be said that they only care for form that is more or less in despair. It is the condition of their freedom that every choice is deemed to be, by definition, a choice among desperate measures. Freedom looks like whim, because it is circumscribed by necessity and its attendant despair. Often this despair is the source of wild humour, born for the gallows. We meet the figures of desperation in works as different in other respects as *A Tale of a Tub*, Ibsen's *Ghosts*, and Kafka's *Metamorphosis*; Mr Adams's list might be extended to Beckett and beyond. It may be said of the *Tale*, for instance, that its most subversive act is its first act, where Swift, we are told, entrusts the whole enterprise to a character whose competence is doubtful, whose limitations are inordinate. As soon as the book begins we are called into a world where no one can be presumed to see straight or to speak the truth; worse still, where truth, if sometimes uttered, is never reliably indicated. If we read on the assumption that the words are reliable, we run into delusion from the start. But we head in the same direction, I would argue, if we proceed upon the opposite assumption, that the speaker is merely a Grub Street hack, a fool, a Modern, and that everything he says has the effect of convicting him out of his own mouth. It is commonly assumed that Swift's speaker is nothing but a hack and that every word he speaks may be discounted as the voice of folly. But in practice this does not answer. Many of his sentences seem to require a different reading; they are, in some instances, so pointed, so demonstrably true, so intelligent—if the word

[1] Robert Martin Adams, *Strains of Discord* (Cornell University Press, Ithaca, New York, 1958), pp. 13, 180.

may be allowed—that they cannot be discounted. If we insist upon taking the speaker as a miserable hack, we have to admit that the wretch often speaks good sense. The account of King Henry IV of France which occupies some brilliant pages in section IX of the *Tale* is largely taken from Mezeray's *Abrégé Chronologique de l'Histoire de France* and is certainly meant to be enjoyed for its own sake, without ironic qualification: we are to laugh at Henry's folly, the nature of the speaker is not a relevant question while the laughter proceeds. The same applies to earlier citations from Pausanias and Herodotus; these are intrinsically ready, their relevance to the Church cannot be discounted because of any doubts about the speaker. In an easier work, the *Argument to Prove that the Abolishing of Christianity...May be Attended by Some Inconveniences*, there are similar problems. The speaker is a nominal Christian, and the insecurity of his position is part of the irony. But if we discount everything he says we throw away a lot of sense as well as some folly; a stance as rigid as this, on either side, works against the book. It is more prudent to assume in the *Tale* that the *persona*, if it is held at all, is held very loosely indeed, that Swift makes no promise to restrict himself to the absurdities of a hack. It may emerge that our concern with the nature of the speaker is beside the point.

There is a well-known passage in the 'Digression concerning Critics' where the writings of critics are acknowledged as mirrors of learning:

Now, whoever considers, that the Mirrors of the Antients were made of Brass, and *sine Mercurio*, may presently apply the two Principal Qualifications of a True Modern Critick, and consequently, must needs conclude, that these have always been, and must be for ever the same. For, Brass is an Emblem of Duration, and when it is skilfully burnished, will cast Reflections from its own Superficies, without any Assistance of Mercury from behind.[1]

[1] *A Tale of a Tub*, edited by A. C. Guthkelch and David Nichol Smith (Clarendon Press, Oxford, 1920), p. 103.

Irvin Ehrenpreis quotes the passage, mentioning that mercury formed the backing of glass mirrors and that, figuratively, it meant wit. Reflections are, in modern idiom, aspersions. Mr Ehrenpreis says that the tone 'suggests the cocksure arrogance of one who has taken over wholesale the opinion of others'.[1] This comment is just, in a sense, and it would be sufficient if we were concerned only with the words in their bearing upon the speaker. If we were pondering a man's character by attending to his diction, we would read the passage somewhat as Mr Ehrenpreis reads it. But I would argue that this reading confuses the issue. When we meet this paragraph we are meant to take it as it comes, to enjoy its ingenuity, the persistence with which it traces the implication of its figures. I am not sure that we are meant to laugh at the cocksure 'author' at all, at this point. We laugh at his victims, the critics, for the usual Augustan reason, their self-engendered glitter; it makes little difference, for the moment, what view we take of the speaker. That the jibe is common does not detract from its force; most jokes are common, that is to say, old. Mr Ehrenpreis reads the words so that he may restore them to their speaker; reflecting then upon the speaker's nature. His reception of the words depends upon his sense of their speaker, a sense already largely formed, though it may still be marginally altered. His interpretation always moves in that direction. But I am not sure that Swift encourages us to read the words in that way. It may be that we are to take them for what they are worth as events of language, sentences which depend as much upon the resources of language as upon the presumed character of the speaker. We may not be wise in reading the words merely for the satisfaction of seeing their speaker gulled by his own eloquence. It may be more profitable to attend to the medium. In the present passage, even if we insist on ascribing the words to a cocksure author,

---

[1] Irvin Ehrenpreis, *Swift, The Man, His Works and the Age. Vol.* 1: *Mr. Swift and His Contemporaries* (Methuen, London, 1962), p. 206.

we are still allowed to enjoy a joke aimed, with notable accuracy, at critics; just as we are allowed to relish the pun on mercury and the latent meaning of brass. 'Superficies' may be a hint to the reader, nudging him to look out for superficiality; or it may not. The word may be used as a neutral term, as in the passage in *Gulliver's Travels* about the word-machine. My argument is that it is better to postpone referring the words to their speaker, at least until we have taken their measure as words on a page. In the first instance we are to attend to the skill with which language is used. The interest of the passage is, to begin with, intrinsic; our reception of the medium is far more important than our sense of the speaker's character. It is strange that we are prepared to attend to Shakespeare's plays in this way; to the medium as such. It is universally agreed that considerations of 'character' are relevant but only as part of the dramatic economy; not as all in all. But we are still encouraged to read *A Tale of a Tub* as if the question of the Hack's character were the first and only question.

I shall look at another passage from the *Tale* and argue against Mr Ehrenpreis's reading once again. We shall never agree. The passage is a famous moment in the 'Digression on Madness':

And therefore, in order to save the Charges of all such expensive Anatomy for the Time to come; I do here think fit to inform the Reader, that in such Conclusions as these, Reason is certainly in the Right; and that in most Corporeal Beings, which have fallen under my Cognizance, the Outside hath been infinitely preferable to the In: Whereof I have been farther convinced from some late Experiments. Last Week I saw a Woman flay'd, and you will hardly believe, how much it altered her Person for the worse.

Mr Ehrenpreis reads this passage by turning every ostensible plus into a minus. 'The real proposition here', he says, 'is that man's moral essence or reason—his inside—is infinitely

more important than his physical accidents—the outside.'
He continues:

Reason and judgment are therefore analytical or introspective
while the senses, passions, and imagination (when divorced from
the understanding) may be tricked by appearances. It is better
to be sadly wise and know oneself, Swift really says, than to be
complacently self-deceived. . . . Swift says with a straight face that
surface counts for more than substance, but means ironically that
it is worth nothing by comparison. He says with contempt that
reason is mistakenly occupied with internals, but he means seriously
that reason is correct in its business.[1]

Now it is not my brief to maintain that every ostensible plus is
a real plus; but Swift gives us no warrant, here or elsewhere,
to despise the evidence of the senses or to think ourselves well
employed peering into the depths. Mr Ehrenpreis writes of this
passage as if he were reading Nietzsche or Dostoevsky; we are
to leap into the destructive element. But the force of the passage
is the force of detachment. There is abundant evidence that
Swift feared the depths and detested the urge to challenge
them: he did not despise the prudence which sustains commonsense and limitation. Mr Ehrenpreis is so concerned to discount
the 'author' of the *Tale* that he drives himself into perversities
of interpretation. There were many aspects of life which Swift
was content to leave to God; there were many things beyond
man's reason, and he was willing to leave them there. He was
not, after all, one of the great questioners: he asked questions
only when there was a reasonable hope of answering them.
I would argue that the rhetorical force of the passage implies
and endorses the merit of prudence; implies that it is better,
by and large, to take things as they come and leave them as
they are. Anything else is mere Pride, a destructive force.
If this rhetoric is a plus sign, we have no warrant to write
minus. Reason, as qualified by this passage, is the attribute
of the curious anatomist; it has already been rebuked for its

---

[1] Ehrenpreis, *Mr. Swift and his Contemporaries*, pp. 222–3.

destructive power. Its conclusions are valid, subject to the qualification that the same conclusions might have been reached, without cost, by that other form of reason which is common sense. The experiment upon the woman's body has issued in the right conclusion. The difference between Right Reason and Rationalism is the cost of their respective operations: in the first case, no cost; in the second, every cost, every harm done. The shock of the last sentence is caused by the reader's sense of the inhumanity attendant upon the logic of the experimental mind; as if the activity of that mind caused the death of every relevant human feeling. Shock is more extremely registered because of its ostensible rejection; the speaker—who is certainly in evidence now—is not shocked, he has witnessed the experiment in the spirit in which it was conducted, brainwashed by the rationalists.

But these effects are local. We should not assume, reading the *Tale*, that the words are primarily designed to carry the voice of a single identifiable speaker. We are reading words on a page; implying rather things being said than a voice saying them. The distinction is a matter of emphasis, but it is real, nonetheless. The unity of a single voice is not present. Rather, the 'author' is the anonymous slave of print; 'he' is as servile as the printed page. We can say, for the moment, that he changes, literally, from paragraph to paragraph, as one paragraph differs from another on a sheet of paper without announcing the change. But merely to surround the speaker with this qualification is not enough. To advert to 'him' at all is largely to concede Mr Ehrenpreis's case; accepting his rules. Hugh Kenner has remarked in *The Stoic Comedians* that the *Tale* parodies the nature and structure of books as such. But there is more to be said. The 'author' of the *Tale* is anonymous: if we insist upon giving him a character, a role, or a name, he is not the Grub Street Hack, he is Anon. We have then to cope with the fact that one anonymous speaker differs from another but there is no known way of telling the difference. If

8

the 'author' makes fun of L'Estrange or Dryden, it is primarily for the sake of the fun; these passages are defined by the nature of their victims. So we have Anon. capitalising upon the promiscuous vagaries of anonymity, writing a book to make fun of books. The irony here is, like comedy elsewhere, intrinsic; there is no need to send the words back to a presumed hack before enjoying them. The situation is like a narrative with a good joke inserted: we relish the joke without questioning too strictly its relation to the speaker or the situation. Mr Ehrenpreis takes the words in one sense only, as the transcript of a man's speech, so he can do nothing with them except, moment by moment, trace them back to their presumed origin. He does not allow for the fact that words are exerted upon their object, regardless of their mere source. The critical force is deployed through the words; the crucial question is the direction the force takes. These words are bullets: the important consideration is their end, not their origin. This implies that words may be independent of their origin, once they are released. It is my impression that Swift wrote, very often, upon that understanding. In *Gulliver's Travels* the crucial words are often aimed outside the book altogether; their work is not done until some hated thing in contemporary England has been killed. Or at least until external damage is done. This applies to the Lilliputian rope-dancers, Flimnap's recourse to the King's cushion, the faction of High Heels and Low Heels, the war between Lilliput and Blefuscu, Big Ends and Little Ends, the consideration of virtue as an essential qualification for jobs in Lilliput, Gulliver's panegyric of England in his conversation with the King of Brobdingnag. Clearly, the King's denunciation of England is more important for the critical force it exerts upon its object than for whatever light it throws upon his own character. Mr Ehrenpreis's account of the *Tale* does not allow for these considerations. He neglects one of the wilder discoveries of Gutenberg culture, that one can do very strange things with words by treating them as black marks on a white page, ascribing them to Anon. or, indeed, to Nobody. Words alone become certain good, in their weird way. A book is a very odd thing if it is treated as an object among other objects. The first peculiarity is that words, released in this way, have no responsibility towards a speaker; they live their own lives. *A Tale of a Tub* has always been considered a difficult book, perhaps a subversive book, because the victim of its attack is hard to place. In fact, it is a far harder book than we have allowed; its problems are indefinitely extended if, as I would argue, we have to take its anonymity seriously. Anonymity is the nearest state we can recognise as corresponding to the irresponsible motions of print: we describe it negatively by saying that the words are not necessarily bound to a particular speaker; the continuity between one paragraph and the next is virtual and arbitrary. The chief characteristic of these words is not that they transcribe sound; they may do this, or they may not. Their chief characteristic is that they occupy space. The dots, the fracture of discourse, the *caetera desunt*, and so forth do not mean that a speaker has lapsed into silence. In a world of sound, silence may be neutral, a pause between one breath and another, a form of transition; but in the spatial world of the book, a break in the text is a gap in the universe. The *Tale*, then, is a direct result of the discovery, on the part of the Gutenberg culture, that words acquire a different kind of life, a peculiar 'character', when they are cut loose from a speaker and fixed independently in space. Grub Street is a trope of the printing press. The press locks words in space: imprisoned, they lead a monstrous life, no visitors allowed. The *Tale* is the result of this discovery, and a parody of the culture which made it possible. This does not mean that Swift was an example of Oral Man lost in silent space. That he was uneasy in his time is obvious. By parodying the Gutenberg age he tried to take the harm out of its arrogance, so that he might live in peace. But meanwhile, even in the *Tale*, he would not be prevented from writing whatever he wanted to write: no formal demands could be accepted which tied his hands.

I am suggesting that the *Tale* should be taken as an example of 'plural form', a kind of literature which makes nonsense of *decorum personae* because it takes advantage of every available licence. It is characteristic of works written in this spirit that they defeat their readers; if the works are, broadly speaking, fiction, they take pains to secrete the narrator in the words themselves. They delight in secrecy and confusion. Now you see the author, now you don't. The only indisputable fact is that words are visible on the page; but what is going on behind the words, we may go read in the stars. The crucial question concerns the source of the words: if we think of them as the narrative voice attending to its proper business, we are sometimes consoled and often frustrated; because voice implies someone to whom the voice belongs. This is still the first and easiest way of receiving words. But there are works which do not disclose themselves in these terms. Some years ago John Peter, interpreting *The Waste Land* as a monologue, tried to describe a body of presumed experience from which the words of the poem would naturally arise, offering a biography of 'the speaker'.[1] But the poem defeats this infringement: it is not a monologue, so the words cannot be referred to a single body of personal experience. There is no 'speaker', in that unified sense. If there is a narrator in the *Tale*, most of his energy is devoted to concealing his identity. So we are better advised to think of the words as issuing from a printing press. *A Tale of a Tub* is distinctly the work of a press: the point about print is that every paragraph looks continuous with the one that precedes it, but this appearance may conceal deceit. The press has promised nothing, except to keep our eyes engrossed.

To establish the case, it is necessary to show that in treating words in the cavalier fashion implied, Swift wrote within a well-

[1] John Peter, 'A New Interpretation of *The Waste Land*', *Essays in Criticism*, vol. II, pp. 242–66.

authenticated tradition. Or at least it is necessary to prove that there are other works which call for similar reception. According to this tradition, the works allow us to receive some parts in one spirit, some parts in another, but labels are never reliably fixed. The easiest example is the Bible; a sacred text throughout, but some parts may be read literally, other parts figuratively. Two seventeenth-century readers might differ in choosing the occasions when a literal reading was required; but they might well agree upon the plural principle involved. Rosemond Tuve has pointed out that in the development of allegory the principle was readily accepted that 'narratives would necessarily be intermittently capable of allegorical reading'; and she remarks that modern readers of allegory 'are often much more unwilling than earlier writers of it to allow some characters or some portions to serve simply and only the story-or-historical reading'.[1] Unnecessary difficulties are caused by assuming that works which are allegorical in some parts are allegorical from start to finish.

But we must be specific. In More's *Utopia*, that blessed place is nowhere, but Utopian ideals are not 'nothings': they are as real as Plato's Ideas; possibilities of the mind, operative in the degree of their force. This force is operative as rebuke, for contrast; as when Coleridge proposed to consider Church and State according to the Idea of each; that is, according to the most complete figure of its possibility. So the Houyhnhnms are Ideas, operative in the degree of their critical force. Bentham said that pleasures and pains may be comprehended under one phrase: 'interesting perceptions'. Houyhnhnms, Yahoos, Brobdingnagians, More's Gulikians are interesting Ideas; their main interest is the moral pressure they exert upon man. More's basic irony is the demonstration that 'barking Scyllas, ravening Celaenos, and Laestrygonians, devourers of people, and such like great and incredible monsters' are

[1] Rosemond Tuve, *Allegorical Imagery* (Princeton University Press, Princeton, 1966), p. 222 n.

commonplaces; the really incredible things are 'citizens ruled
by good and wholesome laws'. So he treats these citizens as
Ideas, poetic figments, operative also in the degree of our
need. The gap between Fact and Idea is demonstrated by
More's pretence that it does not exist. Raphael Hythloday is
a Holy Fool, we are knaves, More is a rueful man of affairs;
but it is never clear when Raphael is to be taken seriously or
when we are meant to smile at his words, as the fictive Cardinal
smiles at the jester. The jester is sent off, in the interests of
peace. More leads Raphael to supper, postponing indefinitely
whatever reply he wishes to make. Irony is silence. Again, in
the *Moriae Encomium* Erasmus often ascribes to Stultitia appropriately foolish sentiments (in keeping with the Horatian
principle of *decorum personae*) but some of the things Stultitia
says are not at all foolish; they often embody Erasmus's deepest
convictions. The common explanation is that Stultitia shifts
her ground again and again, so that it is often hard and sometimes impossible to know where we stand. We find ourselves
in this predicament if we have relied upon the ostensible nature
of Folly. In fact, the *Encomium* is a Hall of Mirrors, often
distorted mirrors which, receiving distortions, send further
distortions on their distorted way. The final effect of the book,
as of Swift's *Tale*, is to impede the arrogance of judgment:
this is how Pride is tamed. Arrogance of judgment is to be
rebuked, but judgment itself is not to be disowned. Again
it is entirely proper, within the tradition of plural form which
I would describe, that the author of the *Anatomy of Melancholy*
is given as 'Democritus Junior' and that when we hunt him
through byways and digressions we recall with increasing
frustration his first warning, 'I would not willingly be known.'
In *The Rehearsal Transpros'd* Marvell defends the King's Declaration of Indulgence to Non-Conformists, so he finds it convenient to write, in some parts, as if he were a court wit and,
in other parts, as if he were a sober spokesman for the Non-
Conformists themselves. At one point he asks pardon for this

breach of formal decorum, but clearly the breach was already commonplace. Horace had not prevented sixteenth- and seventeenth-century writers from shifting ground, within the work, as often as they wished. Indeed it might be argued that it was necessary to play fast and loose with *decorum personae* if the full possibilities of print culture were to be fulfilled.

Readers of *Gulliver's Travels* are often led to conclude that the Houyhnhnms are objects of Swift's satire just as much as the Yahoos; that the cool, passionless existence they have devised is monstrous, rationalist, Deist. This may or may not be true: my own reading of the book suggests that, far more than we have allowed, the life of the Houyhnhnms embodies Swift's desire for ease and rest. To be relieved of passion he was prepared to pay a high price. At one point we read:

As these noble Houyhnhnms are endowed by Nature with a general Disposition to all Virtues, and have no Conceptions or Ideas of what is evil in a rational Creature; so their grand Maxim is, to cultivate Reason, and to be wholly governed by it. Neither is Reason among them a Point problematical as with us, where Men can argue with Plausibility on both Sides of a Question; but strikes you with immediate Conviction; as it must needs do where it is not mingled, obscured, or discoloured by Passion and Interest.[1]

It is perverse to discount the implications here, either because they apply to the invalidated Houyhnhnms or because the words come from the equally suspect Gulliver. Whatever we have made of Gulliver or the Houyhnhnms up to this point, the fact remains that a situation in which reason operates by instinct would be a happy situation and one particularly congenial to Swift. It is not fanciful to assume that Swift's feelings are accurately implied at this point, regardless of Gulliver's limitation. For the moment, it seems fair to say, Gulliver's sentiments and Swift's have coincided: there is no discernible irony. This does not mean that, as an invariable

[1] *Gulliver's Travels*, edited by Herbert Davis (Basil Blackwell, Oxford, 1959) p. 267. All quotations are from this edition.

rule, Swift endorses Gulliver; nor does it mean that in every respect and in every consideration he endorses the Houyhn-hnms. In plural form we have to accustom ourselves to live from moment to moment. Even in the passage on instinctive reason it is better not to take the words as attaching them-selves to the Houyhnhnms, in the sense that a trait of character attaches itself to the man who possesses it; but rather as a relevant sentiment, locally pointed for contrast. The fact that the sentiment is invoked at that moment is more important than that it is attached to the Houyhnhnms. The words have more to do with human limitation, by reflection and contrast, than with Houyhnhnm merit. Certainly it is possible to detach the sentiment easily enough from Gulliver: we are to apply it to ourselves rather than to him. The force which connects it to Gulliver is not of primary importance; its bearing upon us, upon the rational sense of mankind, is far more significant.

The King of Brobdingnag has a long conversation with Gulliver:

He wondered to hear me talk of such chargeable and extensive Wars; that, certainly we must be a quarrelsome People, or live among very bad Neighbours; and that our Generals must needs be richer than our Kings. He asked, what Business we had out of our own Islands, unless upon the Score of Trade or Treaty, or to defend the Coasts with our Fleet. Above all, he was amazed to hear me talk of a mercenary standing Army in the Midst of Peace, and among a free People.

It will hardly be denied that at this point Swift's own senti-ments are well expressed in the King's words. The King, indeed, has very little to do with the words in his own person; only enough to hold them together and to introduce them at that moment. These are Swift's sentiments, in the first instance, and directly continuous with his attack upon standing armies in the *Examiner* essays and elsewhere; continuous, too, with his charges against Marlborough. It may be argued that Swift is taking the risk of stepping outside the frame of fiction for a moment to share a joke with his Tory readers, but it is more reasonable to think that he takes very lightly indeed the restrictions implied in that reference to the frame of fiction. He is not seriously concerned to attach these thoughts either to the King of Brobdingnag or to Gulliver; or he is willing to let them attach themselves to those personages without fuss. His first interest is to have the reader meet these sentiments at this moment: there are obvious advantages in having them issue from the King, but these are by the way. The book is an object, ostensibly independent of its author: there is a corresponding sense in which the marks on the page may be cut adrift from their ostensible speaker. In an oral culture, this monster of dissociation would be impossible: in a visual or print culture, it is a constant resource, absent only if the writer disowns it. In *A Tale of a Tub* Swift played the wilful game for all it was worth: no book, not even *Tristram Shandy*, takes more advantage of the gargoyle-life effected by print. In *A Vindication of Isaac Bickerstaffe* and *Predictions for the Year 1708* Swift gives comic versions of the life of a book as separate from the life of its author; where Partridge the almanac-maker is declared to have died on 29 March although his almanacs keep appearing.

There is a manic element, it would appear, in Swift's procedures, but the same element is often found in the Gutenberg era. Father Walter Ong has argued in *The Presence of the Word* that by the eighteenth century books had already begun to irritate people, touching their nerves. Print culture released many demons of its own invention, their only home the book. Some of them were tricksy sprites, innocent enough, but others were melancholy, contorted devils. Swift's *Tale* provides a roof for all. So we cannot encompass the book by referring everything to the poor Hack. *Gulliver's Travels* is an easier book, because it takes its plural form more genially. The main facility offered to Swift in the *Travels* is that he can introduce anything he wants, when he wants it; taking his material from any convenient source, Bolingbroke, Ormonde, Oxford, Temple, Sheridan, travellers, alchemists. If there are traces of Temple in Lord Munodi and of Bolingbroke in the Houyhn- hnms, the reason is that in plural form virtually anything is allowed, for the good reason that it cannot be forbidden. Plural form allows Swift to be 'loose' and to make a virtue of looseness: print leads us by the eyes, not by the ears. The nearest equivalent in modern fiction, anonymity apart, is where a character offers us elaborate evidence as if it were true, only to deny it later. The lying narrator is a fictional device to represent the universal loss of innocence, the continuous Fall of Man: in Beckett's later fiction, for instance, we are given nothing but words, ostensibly declaring, ostensibly denying. In *Comment c'est* declarations and denials are equally virtual.

I have described Swift's tradition as sustaining plural form, but it may be asked in what sense procedures as loose as these are called 'form' at all. There is no simple answer: *Gulliver's Travels* gives an impression of artistic order largely because of its symmetry, but *A Tale of a Tub* might easily have been different. It is useless to invoke the criterion of proper words in proper places; we have no means of verifying either the words or the places. Indeed, it must be conceded that the characteristic instruments of modern criticism are of little use when we approach a tradition as wayward as Swift's in the *Tale*. Only a bold reader would undertake to show that the *Tale* is as it is because it could not have been otherwise. To speak of the relation between one part of the work and another is to assume the operation of artistic unity and then to find some evidence, however tenuous, on the page. It is extremely difficult to define a principle of order or unity which is em- bodied in the *Tale*: or anything resembling 'un réseau de convergences', in Jean Rousset's phrase. We may be driven to describe plural form very obliquely, by naming certain modes of the mind which seem to endorse it. The obvious mode is paradox. A mind possessed by paradox is not necessarily brought to a halt, but it is unlikely to proceed smartly from point A to point B. Linear movements of thought will seem too easy, a distortion in the cause of simplicity. Like paradox, plural form is never single-minded: it takes wry pleasure in defeating single-minded readers, since defeat is its own fate. The words of the page lead the reader in a dozen directions, lest he settle comfortably for one. So the movement from first word to last is likely to be devious, elliptical, walking with a limp in circles drawn awry. The surprise is that the end is ever reached; sometimes it is not reached, the book merely breaks off with yet another and final hiatus in manuscript. In *Paradoxia Epidemica* Rosalie Colie has described a paradoxical tradition and a correspondingly paradoxical mode of perception. It is enough to say now that what I call plural form is propelled, however obliquely, by a paradoxical sense of life: the writers differ only in the tone with which inescapable paradox is entertained. The masters of plural form are Democritus, Lucian, More, Erasmus, Rabelais, Burton, Montaigne and Swift; the masters, those who showed the potentialities of the medium.

It may be remarked, incidentally, with Swift in mind, that this tradition is more vigorously pursued in the seventeenth than the eighteenth century. There are marks of its force in Sterne, but even with Sterne in mind it is better to think of Swift in association with certain sixteenth- and seventeenth-century writers than with any of his contemporaries. We speak of him as an Augustan writer, and in some respects this is valid, but the category does not hold him if it is strictly enforced. He has some Augustan traits, but increasingly he strikes me as a man of an earlier time, kin to Marvell rather than to Pope. His imagination works in terms which invite association with Marvell in one way, as the connexion with *The Rehearsal Transpros'd* nicely shows, and with Burton in another, for the *Anatomy of Melancholy* is the best gloss upon *A Tale of a Tub*. Indeed, in many respects it is easier to read

Swift in the context of Raleigh, Donne, Jonson, Marvell, Clarendon, the Butler of *Hudibras*, Milton, and Dryden than in that of Pope, Gay, and Johnson: he is closer to the historians and pamphleteers of an earlier day than to the poets and novelists of his own, even when we reckon his traffic with the 'paper warriors' of his time, Oldmixon, Mainwaring, Steele, and the rest.

One of the immediate results of plural form in Swift is that Gulliver is not, strictly speaking, a character at all. If we say that he is someone to whom things happen, we go some distance to meet the case; but we have still to say that what happens is far more important in its own right than the fact that it happens to Gulliver. If the distinction is denied, the proof is that words on a page are an event, but they may or may not be identified with the feelings of a particular speaker; they may have no personal life at all. 'Character' is a personal sign which applies to some fictional occasions but not to all. In the *Voyage to Lilliput* Gulliver has more to do with contemporary English politics than with fiction. The fall of the Oxford–Bolingbroke ministry, the defeat of good Tories, the events leading up to 1714: these are the materials of the Voyage, so far as cause and effect are concerned. The events are translated, transformed into fictional equivalents. They do not cease to be events, historical facts; rather, their historical force becomes moral force when its meaning is realised as form. In this sense the *Voyage to Lilliput* comes from the same context of feeling as *The Conduct of the Allies* and *The History of the Four Last Years of the Queen*, marking the continuity of propaganda and fiction in Swift's imagination. So the question of Gulliver's character hardly arises; events are important because the moral pattern they disclose is true and therefore permanent. The interest is accomplished in the pattern, not in the character. Tom Jones is a character, because the fiction implies a very high degree of unity in his experience, and he gives the impression of having traits of character beyond official requirement:

he seems capable of living beyond the covers of the book. Gulliver begins at the beginning of his book and ends at the end. We speak of impressions. Gulliver has no traits of character beyond the few implied in his experience; he has no experience beyond what is implied in the rhetorical force of the book as a whole. This applies also to the Houyhnhnms. The critical perspective which they impose upon Gulliver is real and it cannot be set aside. But they are merely the sum of their experiences. They are just as rigidly determined by their history as Gulliver by his; the figure of their development is an arithmetical not a geometrical progression. The only difference is that, by comparison with Gulliver, they are the sum of better experiences. They are not characters. Like the Struldbrugs, they are figures in a landscape. Gulliver is not a character in any sense worth proposing. This is not to impute to Swift a failure of imagination; it is to mark, yet again, the nature and the direction of that faculty. Writing *Gulliver's Travels*, Swift performed a moral and political act, an exercise of pressure. The words begin with history and are completed in history; they are resolved, in a sense, beyond the book itself, in the world at large. The book aspires to the condition of art, but indirectly and as a secondary merit; its first object is to change the world. This is why Swift's characters, if they can be said to exist at all, are never offered as 'profound'; they are not meant to be profound. Gulliver is not a tragic hero, he is not a hero, he is not tragic, he is the vehicle of certain occasions, the sum of certain events. Profundity is irrelevant, because it lives in depth, underground. Remarking the conceptual force in Voltaire, Roland Barthes argues that it has no need of depth. 'Le résultat de cette conceptualisation, c'est que le voyage voltairien n'a aucune épaisseur; l'espace que Voltaire parcourt d'une marche forcenée...n'est pas un espace d'explorateur, c'est un espace d'arpenteur.' The first consequence is in the nature of the voyage itself: 'il n'est même pas une opération de connaissance, mais seulement d'affirmation;

c'est l'élément d'une logique, le chiffre d'une équation'. So in Voltaire, the Oriental countries of his mind are 'des sortes de cases vides, des signes mobiles sans contenu propre, des degrés zéros de l'humanité dont on se saisit prestement pour se signifier soi-même'.[1] This is also the situation in Swift, where everything returns to plague the reader. There is perhaps only one moment in *Gulliver's Travels* when depth is implied, in the fifth chapter of *Brobdingnag*: 'I likewise broke my right Shin against the Shell of a Snail, which I happened to stumble over, as I was walking alone, and thinking on poor England.' This is astounding, in its literal context: it has something of the effect of Johnson's stumble into profundity in conversation with Boswell. At one point Boswell mentions a young man who was last seen running about the town shooting cats. 'And then in a sort of kindly reverie', Boswell recalls of Johnson, 'he bethought himself of his own favourite cat, and said, "But Hodge shant be shot; no, no, Hodge shall not be shot".' The thought of poor England is just as moving as this because just as unexpected in depth. Otherwise, the idiom of the book is political; politics is above ground, historical, rhetorical, directed toward a future in which the reader will act as persuaded. Indeed, the chief characteristic of Swift's style is that it has little use for the recesses of language. It is not concerned with tentacular roots or the reverberation of words; only with the flow of energy from one word to another. One word, calling little or no attention to itself, reaches toward another, for relation and thence for a specific effect. This is what the simplicity of his style comes to; attention to the local occasion. The intended force of the style consists in the vigour with which it implicates forms of energy akin to its own but distinguishable from its own; the style is always pleased to serve. Indeed, Swift has very little interest in the literary use of words, if we distinguish that use from the political use. A great writer, he is not deeply committed to literature, except as a form of politics;

[1] Roland Barthes, *Essais critiques* (Éditions du Seuil, Paris, 1964), pp. 98–9.

and he has very little interest in language except as an index to the state of a nation. He is like Dryden in one respect. William Empson has made the point that Dryden 'is not interested in the echoes and recesses of words'; on the other hand, 'he is interested in the echoes and recesses of human judgment'. This goes along with the common understanding that Dryden is 'interested in rhetoric but not in character'.[1] When Dryden uses words flatly, knowing their flatness; when he puts one word beside another with no particular fuss; he tests the sentiment to see how well it stands up to the strain of flatness. If it survives, so much the better. His interest in the recesses of judgment is usually given in the rhetoric, as if to imply his own direct responsibility. The characters live, in their fashion, while more important things are going on. Dryden does not let the characters take over his job; he sees no cause to trust their judgment in preference to his own. For similar reasons, Swift never tries to surround a character with an aura of suggestion or atmosphere. The force of his rhetoric is invariably the force of critique; the critique is going on, line by line, in the crevices of the fiction, and it is reluctant to be distracted by fictional requirements. In Dryden the recesses of judgment are explored, as it were, 'above' the characters; in Swift, 'below': but in both, the requirements of fiction as such are not tended until other, more important ends have been secured.

This implies a certain kind of style, the kind in which you make sure, when you have to count ten, that you count it right. Swift has no interest in the sounding effect, or in anything that smacks of theatre; reverberation, Shakespeare, the Marlowe of *Tamburlane*. Such effects reach all too evidently for the sublime. The heroic note is not to be heard in Swift's prose. The English tradition, since the sixteenth century, has been based largely upon the exigencies of the theatre and it encourages sounding

[1] William Empson, *Seven Types of Ambiguity* (Chatto and Windus, London, 1953 edition), p. 199.

effects. Johnson's reception of Swift may be explained in these terms: he did not admire Swift's style, because he could not hear it. The words did not seize his imagination as sounds; mainly, I think, because Swift did not conceive them as sounds. But it may be urged that Swift's style reaches back beyond the theatre of Shakespeare, Marlowe, and Kyd to certain effects which hardly survived the deaths of Chaucer and Langland: specific effects, daylight effects, words used for lucidity at any cost to reverberation. There is something of this lucidity, this refusal of aura, in the Elizabethan satirists, and especially in the poems of Skelton, Raleigh, Greville, and Jonson. This is the note of Swift's English; a recognition of other kinds of excellence than its own, but, at the same time, first things first: the first things being directness, lucidity, the exertion of force upon the matter in hand.

A problem arises at once. Swift is normally considered a supreme ironist; he claimed as much in the 'Verses on the Death of Dr. Swift', and we have ignored the fact that his concept of irony is not the same as ours. In fact, very few of his writings are ironic at all. *A Tale of a Tub, Gulliver's Travels, A Modest Proposal* and *An Examination of Certain Abuses* represent one mode of his genius, but only one mode: modern discussion which implies that Swift's work is all of this kind ignores the fact that most of his writings are like *Contests and Dissensions,* direct and straightforward. We read Swift in our own terms; that is to say, we insinuate into his work our own tensions, ambiguities, ironies, so that we may possess him. We resent the fact that, in most of the work, he is not 'one of us' at all. I have spoken of Swift and paradox; but Swift did not cultivate paradox for any of our modern reasons. He deployed paradox to deflate the pretensions of others.

But the onus is on me to show that there is, indeed, continuity of feeling throughout Swift's work. The clue is in its object. Swift wrote *Gulliver's Travels* to vex the world. The same object determined the whole course of his work. He did not

23

write to please, or, as Fielding wrote *Tom Jones*, 'to laugh mankind out of their favourite follies and vices'. He wrote to provoke. The range of his writing is the range of his provocative powers. Sometimes he vexes the world, as in the *Tale*, to render its possessions null; sometimes, as in the pamphlets, to inhibit the facility of its opinions; sometimes, as in the *Drapier's Letters*, to shame the world into action; and sometimes, as in the poems, to exert certain amateur powers. The Earl of Orrery was right, therefore, when he said of Swift: 'he tries to make us uneasy with ourselves, and unhappy in our present existence'. This is the force of Swift's 'dry mock'. Coleridge's formula in *Table Talk* is relevant: '*anima Rabelaisii in sicco*,—the soul of Rabelais dwelling in a dry place'. But the place was dry because Swift scorned to connive with the world or to put up with its absurdity. So his rhetoric is invariably forensic or deliberative. If we keep this object in mind, we find that difficulties persist, but at least we can imply the unity of the work in demonstrable terms. The *Tale*, for instance, is a young man's book, brilliant of course; its object, to drive its readers from the commonplaces of their banality. But even in the *Tale*, as I have urged, Swift was often more direct than we have allowed. Indeed, this is probably the major obstacle which stands between us and Swift; we are scandalised by his directness, because it reflects his commitment to a fixed order in life. If we read Swift and then compare our experience of his work with our experience of Conrad, James, Dostoevsky, Kafka, or Lawrence, we are scandalised by the persistence with which he disavowed all those values for which modern writers strive; the sense of self, the autonomous imagination, the risks of freedom, the multiple demands upon life which always come to mind when we recall such works as *The Trial*, *Sons and Lovers*, *Portrait of a Lady*, *The Brothers Karamazov*, *The Death of Ivan Ilych*, *Heart of Darkness*. If one or two moments in modern literature may stand for many; think of that sentence in Tolstoi's story:

Ivan Ilych's life had been most simple and most ordinary and therefore most terrible.

There, at one stroke, we have separated ourselves from Swift; not merely because he would use 'simple' and 'ordinary' as terms of definitive praise, or even because he did not conceive the sense in which such a life is 'most terrible'. He knew precisely what that phrase meant, but he suppressed the knowledge. He denied, for himself and for everyone else, the demand upon life, which is reflected in the phrase. He would think such a claim monstrous. If the modern demand gets short measure in his work, the reason is not that he did not understand it, but that he repudiated it. We can fancy his rejecting it as a gross pretension of Pride. We have not forgiven him.

'Try to be one of the people on whom nothing is lost', Henry James advised the young novelist; providing that novice also with a corresponding emblem. In 'The Art of Fiction' he says:

Experience is never limited, and it is never complete; it is an immense sensibility, a kind of huge spider-web of the finest silken threads suspended in the chamber of consciousness, and catching every air-borne particle in its tissue.[1]

It is a nice problem to consider whether Swift was one of the people on whom nothing is lost. But James implies a scale of value which Swift would have found contemptible. James is sufficiently a Romantic artist to be thrilled by the possibility of finding a new image, an impression, a sensation. Swift thought most of the world well lost, if it had to be found in those terms. Anything that came to him, in any form, was tested; if it justified itself in common or public terms, it was allowed; if not, suppressed. In the image of the spider's web James defines experience as a personal value, miraculously fine, delicate, and strong. Every particle is precious. To Swift, only some particles were precious, and it was hard to specify them, except by the implication that all other particles were

[1] Henry James, *The Future of the Novel*, edited by Leon Edel (Vintage Books, New York, 1956), p. 12.

rubbish. The further difference is that, to James, the measure of every impression is its generative value in terms of consciousness, the inner vibration. To Swift, the measure had little or nothing to do with consciousness except as a critical test imposed upon the impression in the light of public order. Vibrations were irrelevant. So we are scandalised again.

II

The fifth Parliament of William III was prorogued on 24 June 1701. The Tory majority in the House of Commons had tried and failed to impeach the Whig ministers of the preceding administration. Within a few weeks Swift was at work upon the *Contests and Dissensions*:

This encourages me to hope, that during this lucid Interval, the Members retired to their Homes, may suspend a while their acquired Complexions, and taught by the Calmness of the Scene and the Season, reassume the native sedateness of their Temper. If this should be so, it would be wise in them, as individual and private Mortals, to look back a little upon the Storms they have raised, as well as those they have escaped: To reflect, that they have been Authors of a new and wonderful Thing in England, which is, for a House of Commons to lose the universal Favour of the Numbers they represent; To observe, how those whom they thought fit to persecute for Righteousness sake, have been openly caress'd by the People; and to remember how themselves sat in fear of their Persons from popular Rage.[1]

It is a fair example of Swift's average style. We receive it rather with a general sense of its force than with a specific sense of any particular moments in which the force is concentrated. The chief characteristic of the style is that it does not invite attention to itself, apart from the continuous attention to be given to the matter in hand. The impression of force arises from certain qualities in the structure of the sentences, the deployment of large-scale resources rather than local effects. Style, in these

[1] *A Discourse of the Contests and Dissensions between the Nobles and the Commons in Athens and Rome*, edited by Frank H. Ellis (Clarendon Press, Oxford, 1967), p. 124.

sentences, has very little to do with felicities of diction, and nearly everything to do with the prescriptive force of grammar and syntax. In the first sentence the rhetorical pressure which relates the author's 'hope' to 'this lucid Interval' goes on to define the interval in terms of rural intelligence. The members, 'retired to their Homes', will now be affected by the 'Calmness of the Scene and the Season'. Sanity is 'native sedateness'; the phrase resumes a set of implications which have just been insinuated, that it is natural to live at home and there to be calm, and so forth. When the Members leave their homes for the House they become perverse, acquire unnatural 'Complexions', run to faction. Nature is the good teacher, whose lesson is the quiet life. The political equivalent is peace, harmony. In the second sentence the 'lucid Interval' is translated into the idiom of place; it allows reflexions as in a garden. The connexion with Temple's *Upon the Gardens of Epicurus* is clear enough. The Members are to look back; to reflect, to observe, and then to remember. The rhetoric enforces a full-scale examination of conscience to register 'the Storms they have raised, as well as those they have escaped'. It may be said that the verbs (to reflect; to observe; to remember) do a lot of work and must be paid accordingly; but some of the work is done by their sequence and the rest is a matter of supporting the weight of specification placed upon each. They are not detachable felicities. What the verbs support is a structure of feeling and attitude for which the word 'Horatian' is available shorthand. In fact, the whole passage is a version of pastoral, in Empson's sense, where the complex is tamed by being put into a simple container. Swift is appealing to 'native' excellence, to a kind of virtue which finds itself at home in a quiet garden, in daylight and lucidity. In Nature the disposition of things is happily contrived: a mountain does not usurp the place of a river; complexions are natural, not acquired. The Party equivalent is an appeal to the landed class, rather than to the moneyed men, the City.

It is unnecessary to labour the point, beyond remarking the degree of continuity between these average occasions and the most intense moments in Swift's satire. Vagaries of feeling meet the resistance of an attitude, a stance, a gesture, and are brought up short. Swift adopts the same stance to confront the world outside and to curb the world within. His favourite gesture is rigorous, military: he stands on guard, stands to attention, before the ingenuities of feeling. The first requirement is to separate the mind, as a form of energy, from its own contents; to separate the mind from the casualty of its experience, the objects of its habit; and then to separate these objects, one from another. When we advert to the structure of a sentence, as in the passage quoted from *Contests and Dissensions*, we mark the executive nature of Swift's mind, its expression in lucid arrangements. Swift's consciousness is a mode of defence, and thereafter, in the major satires, a mode of attack involving the same gestures. In these procedures the first requirement is to dispose the world as a relevant substance, or an available structure, but not to admit it as a presence. Swift's satire is a method of keeping the world in its place, preferably at a safe distance. In this sense it is the logical extension of his characteristic gesture. The sensibility engaged in the passage from *Contests and Dissensions* is assuaged by distance, silence, and fixity: it fears incrimination, detests complicity. It is the sensibility of an administrator, dealing with things by separating them from the consciousness of their perceiver. The world must be opaque so that the perceiver may preserve his own opacity. There must be no transparence, because to be transparent is to be exposed.

There is a passage in Yeats which bears upon our theme, the cast of Swift's mind. Near the end of *A Vision* Yeats is pondering Roman decay; or rather, the characteristically Roman gesture which features power bending towards its death. He thinks of ancient sculpture, and remarks: 'The Greeks painted the eyes of marble statues and made out of enamel or glass or precious stones those of their bronze statues, but the Roman was the first to drill a round hole to represent the pupil, and because, as I think, of a preoccupation with the glance characteristic of a civilisation in its final phase.' Yeats distinguishes between the glance, the stare, and the gaze. The glance represents that sense of life characteristic of 'the administrative mind', where 'rhythm, exaltation of the body, uncommitted energy' have been driven out and replaced by 'alert attention'. This is the sign of 'measurement', where the dancing-master has outlived the dance. Of Greek sculpture, on the other hand, Yeats says: 'Those riders upon the Parthenon had all the world's power in their moving bodies, and in a movement that seemed, so were the hearts of man and beast set upon it, that of a dance.[1]' This is the gaze, the sign of that 'unity of being' in which the barrier between subject and object is dissolved and subjective unity is all in all. In the poem 'In Memory of Major Robert Gregory' the 'secret discipline' is the method by which 'the gazing heart doubles her might'; the gaze, the demanding vision by which the seer finds himself everywhere. To Yeats at that point the Roman qualities seem timid and puny; set off against 'vague Grecian eyes gazing at nothing, Byzantine eyes of drilled ivory staring upon a vision, and those eyelids of China and of India, those veiled or half-veiled eyes weary of world and visions alike'.

'Power bending towards its death': Yeats's phrase may be construed to remind us that Swift, choosing the 'glance', choosing to look at experience as if it could still be held at a safe distance, knew that this was a desperate choice. He decided that, among the limited possibilities currently available, this way was the best of a doubtful lot. It was the best, but that is not to say that, to Swift, it was good. If he had been content with it, he would have become the bland Modern he persistently attacked. When Swift chooses, it is always on this basis, that no choice is adequate. The power which choice makes available

---

[1] W. B. Yeats, *A Vision* (Macmillan, London, 1962), pp. 276-7.

to the one who chooses is bending towards its death: its death is the decline and fall of that empire. There is reason to believe that Swift knew this fall and, in despair, thought that it could not be avoided. Nihilism is the position he never went to the extremity of defining, but something close to it is implicit in his characteristic work: 'a mind for which experience has been too much', in R. P. Blackmur's phrase applied also, with whatever justice, to Sterne, and D. H. Lawrence.

Perhaps Yeats's paragraph is a little fanciful. But it marks, when we think of Swift, a certain force which for good cause may be called Roman; with the further implication that force is not enough. The glance tries to subdue experience by imposing administrative pressure upon it, while the going is good. In Swift we find a mind committing itself to a set of terms remarkable for local effect, and certainly good enough in the short run. The tragedy of his mind is that its experience included occasions of violence for which the official terms were inadequate; chaos, passion, the unconscious. We must try to consider these matters in a larger context.

III

To begin with, we would propose Swift as a master of the Negative, the great principle of negation which, if Kenneth Burke is right, may well be the distinctively human invention. The device is purely linguistic in the sense that there are no negatives in Nature, there are only 'positives': what man 'adds' to Nature is the negative; in ethical terms, 'Thou shalt not'. If Swift were God, he would declare himself through the Decalogue, the series of Thou-Shalt-Nots; and persist thereafter in silence. As it is, he builds his great work from the resources of negation, featuring as his characteristic gestures the imagery of veto, voiding, riddance, cleansing, deletion, and the like. Far from wishing to enrich the world by adding his own mite to its possessions, he wants to make it poor but honest. Hence the energy he expends to rid the world of its false riches. Hence also the directness of his style, the verbal equivalent of moral rigour, antiseptic, penitential. 'I'll deny all', Burton says in the *Anatomy of Melancholy*, '(my last refuge), recant all, renounce all I have said...' Gertrude Stein wrote of Juan Gris: 'He has black thoughts, but he is not sad.' Swift scourges the world to scourge himself, finding in himself worldly motives which he hates, and, still more, fears. This will be difficult, perhaps impossible, to show. There is always a sense in which a satirist scourges others for vices he discovers in himself. But among the great satirists there are those who exhibit a quality of hatred or disgust in which the satirist himself is peculiarly implicated. Pope and Swift may be distinguished in this way. We do not feel that Pope is dangerously involved in the satire he visits upon the world: he does not cry of the world, 'The horror, the horror', when his eye falls upon his own image. In Swift we feel that the first cause of disgust is himself, and that the evil and stupidity of the world are the results of contagion. But much of this will have to be taken for granted and felt in the detail of his writing. A provisional motto is the famous passage in 'Little Gidding' in which the 'familiar compound ghost' offers cold advice to his pupil. Eliot told Maurice Johnson that the ghost was Swift, whom he then associated, appropriately enough, with Yeats.[1] Among the gifts reserved for age, the ghost says, there is first 'the cold friction of expiring sense/Without enchantment'; second, 'the conscious impotence of rage/At human folly'; and last:

> the rending pain of re-enactment
> Of all that you have done, and been; the shame
> Of motives late revealed, and the awareness
> Of things ill done and done to others' harm
> Which once you took for exercise of virtue.[2]

[1] Maurice Johnson, *The Sin of Wit* (Syracuse University Press, Syracuse, 1950), p. 131.
[2] T. S. Eliot, *Four Quartets* (Faber and Faber, London, 1959 edition), p. 54.

So our first term of reference is this poor ghost; Swift, here linked with Yeats and both perhaps with the Old Man in Yeats's *Purgatory*. In that play the Old Man who has killed his father now kills his son to break the chain of consequence: 'Twice a murderer and all for nothing', he says, as he hears the hoof-beats returning. In our frame of reference the two murders are essays in negation.

If this account is at all just, it may help to qualify the common view that Swift's work is 'merely' negative. We have been admonished to think of his work, in the last reckoning, as negative in a sense in which that of Blake is positive.[1] It is true that there is nothing in Swift to place beside such terms as Energy and Vision in Blake: the few positive values to which Swift commits himself are held and defined in much more limiting contexts; even terms like Nature and Reason are, as we shall remark, tentative by such comparison. Blake's terms glow and radiate: Swift's are offered in another key, for what they may be worth in force. But we do not need Freud to tell us, as he did, that negation is a complex phenomenon. In his essay on Negation Freud says that 'the subject-matter of a repressed image or thought can make its way into consciousness on condition that it is *denied*'. In this sense negation is a method of entertaining what is repressed: as Freud says, 'it is actually a removal of the repression, though not, of course, an acceptance of what is repressed'. The aim is to make room in the consciousness for matter which must be banned from the realm of action. 'The result is a kind of intellectual acceptance of what is repressed, though in all essentials the repression persists.'[2] The mind is therefore enriched and amplified, in an oblique way, by the very subject-matter which it banishes from the field of action. Unofficially, then, Swift could admit into his consciousness anything and everything that insisted on

[1] F. R. Leavis, *The Common Pursuit* (Chatto and Windus, London, 1952), p. 86.
[2] Sigmund Freud, *Collected Papers*, edited by James Strachey (Hogarth Press, London, 1950), vol. v, p. 182. See also Norman O. Brown, *Life against Death* (Vintage Books, New York, 1959), p. 160.

coming his way; while officially he would rid himself of it, or of some of it, as the Yahoos employed their excrement, by discharging it on his enemies. As long as this magic worked, he could live, if not happily at least productively. The horror of his last years is that his mind was unable totally to rid itself of excremental experience. In those last years he thought of himself, 'my blood soured, my spirits sunk, fighting with Beasts like St. Paul, not at Ephesus, but in Ireland.'[1]

Meanwhile, the officers of his mind were God, Nature, and Reason, an amiable if conventional federation, as valid on earth as in Houyhnhnmland. Reason meant the power of understanding or correct judgment, not as a process but as an intuition; ideally, it went into action at once, like Taste, or like Instinct in animals, without proceeding through argument or opinion. The description given in the *Voyage to the Houyhnhnms*, already quoted, is entirely in keeping with the cast of Swift's mind. If, under ideal conditions, reason strikes with immediate conviction, it must be a force like conscience, or taste, or—in some theologies—faith. In these circumstances, as the verbs imply, reason is simple (in the chemical sense), bright (as in optics), and primary (as in discriminations of colour). The most important analogy is that of light: reason should strike one with immediate conviction, as light reaches us from the sun.[2] If Interest and Passion interrupt the natural flow of light, we must repress them. To Swift, reason was light; but he also allowed, however reluctantly, for dark places which reason could not penetrate. These were the areas of faith. Locke spoke of 'the proper matter of faith' as those things which are 'beyond the discovery of our natural faculties, and above reason'.[3] Swift echoes this part of the *Essay* in his

---

[1] *Correspondence*, edited by Harold Williams (Clarendon Press, Oxford, 1965), vol. IV, p. 79.
[2] 'Memoirs of Martinus Scriblerus', in *Satires and Personal Writings by Jonathan Swift*, edited by W. A. Eddy (Oxford University Press, London, 1932), p. 136.
[3] John Locke, *An Essay concerning Human Understanding* (Tegg, London, 1846 edition), p. 529 (IV.xviii.7).

sermon 'On the Trinity' and elsewhere; 'It is an old and true Distinction, that Things may be above our Reason without being contrary to it.' Besides, 'Reason itself is true and just, but the Reason of every particular Man is weak and wavering, perpetually swayed and turned by his Interests, his Passions and his Vices.'[1] The gap between the universal and its concrete manifestation was the source of despair. Reason is true, but Swift is part of that Augustinian tradition which emphasises that, in each man, reason is pathetically vulnerable. Nearer home, in a famous passage of *The Advancement of Learning* Bacon writes:

For the mind of man is far from the nature of a clear and equal glass, wherein the beams of things should reflect according to their true incidence; nay, it is rather like an enchanted glass, full of superstition and imposture, if it be not delivered and reduced.[2]

Fulke Greville in *Mustapha* and again in the *Letter to an Honourable Lady* speaks of the mind's propensity to delusion; the 'rebellious senses, as apt to flatter as to be flattered'. The King of Brobdingnag is convinced 'that instead of reason, we were only possessed of some Quality fitted to increase our natural Vices; as the Reflection from a troubled Stream returns the Image of an ill-shapen Body, not only larger, but more distorted'. Gulliver has no answer to this; nor can Swift testify in defence of the mind. We must eventually be defeated by experience, since the primary instrument for dealing with it is itself defective. The only hope is to go as far as possible in keeping the enchanted glass 'delivered and reduced'; to deliver is, indeed, to reduce; the process is critical. Reason is delivered and reduced by common sense, subjecting the productions of the mind to the critique of common sense, the testimony of time, history, and Christian belief. If we do not commit ourselves to God, we are lost.

[1] *Irish Tracts, 1720–1723, and Sermons*, edited by Herbert Davis (Basil Blackwell, Oxford, 1963), pp. 164, 166.
[2] Bacon, *Philosophical Works*, edited by R. L. Ellis and James Spedding (Routledge, London, 1905), p. 118.

In the ideal condition, apart from the two exceptions described in *Thoughts on Religion*, the mind wins the fight against passion: the best hope resides in maintaining a direct relation, if possible, between Nature and mind. This implies, in turn, the validity of reflexion; Locke's term is crucial, the King of Brobdingnag is Locke's pupil. Allen Tate has argued that in the Age of Johnson 'men assumed a static relation between the mind and its object';[1] in other words, a stable relation between Locke's primary and secondary qualities. But in Swift this assumption is a matter of grim faith. A static relation between the mind and its object is devoutly to be wished, so he must insist upon it. The happiest relation is a fixed relation, since freedom is chaos.

The standard by which vagaries of passion are to be judged and corrected is Nature; a standard, as A. O. Lovejoy has described it, 'universal, static, uncomplicated, uniform for every rational being'.[2] Gulliver's master in Houyhnhnmland speaks of Nature as teacher of the great lesson, universal benevolence, and again as the force that 'worketh all things to Perfection'. In the *Tale of a Tub* Nature is anatomised; but she knows that the outside of things is a better bet than the inside and she acts accordingly. So she puts 'her best Furniture forward'; the disclosure of her alleged flaws is the work of mischievous science. Swift's Supreme Fiction is the discreet harmony of God, Nature, and Reason. Indeed, he often gives the law of God and the law of Nature as one and the same, as if in keeping with Spinoza's equation, *Deus sive natura*. It is an ancient axiom. Seneca writes:

All this, says Epicurus, we are to ascribe to Nature. And, why not to God, I beseech ye! As if they were not both of them one and the same Power, working in the whole, and in every part of it. Or, if you call him the Almighty Jupiter; the Thunderer, the Creatour, and Preserver of us all; it comes to the same Issue: Some will

[1] Allen Tate, *Collected Essays* (Alan Swallow, Denver, 1959), p. 500.
[2] James L. Clifford (editor), *Eighteenth Century English Literature. Modern Essays in Criticism* (Oxford University Press, New York, 1959), p. 337.

35

express him under the Notion of Fate; which is only a Connexion of Causes, and himself the Uppermost and Original, upon which all the rest depend.[1]

This marks the official side of Swift, assent to a triple law. Officially, the unity to which his mind refers is, in theological terms, the image of the Christian God; in political terms, the notion of a harmonious balance of the three Estates; in moral terms, the assumption of a sustaining order available to man in society. To Swift, there are no other terms. The idiom of feeling and sensibility was alien to him; Diderot's idiom, later, incited by Shaftesbury and others. Swift is closer to 'the ingenious Mr. Locke'. But the strain which we feel in his work is the result of his fear that the image of God is dark, the political balance precarious, and the moral order merely figurative. These fears were dramatically justified in the events which constituted, in miniature, a new Fall of Man; the breach between Oxford and Bolingbroke, the death of the Queen, the rise of the new and alien ministry.

Meanwhile, he protects himself, partly by negation and partly by constructing a working model of life which enables him to hold the essential forts. The model must be a simple affair, strong rather than subtle: its chief characteristic a habit of reducing complex phenomena to extremely simple terms; everything thrown away is deemed inessential or offensive. The best model is not the most capacious or the most liberal; it takes possession of a certain area of experience and fends off rival forces. Its terms are quantitative, geometrical, terms of position, size, and shape. The ideal analogue is the self-enclosed diagram in geometry, the triangle or the square, anything that exhibits a blocked-off unity of apprehension, no loose edges.[2] There is a passage in Locke's *Essay* to the effect that Self depends on Consciousness:

[1] *Seneca's Morals, abstracted by Sir Roger L'Estrange* (London, 1688), p. 53.
[2] Walter J. Ong, 'Swift on the Mind', *Modern Language Quarterly* (September 1954).

Self is that conscious thinking thing,—whatever substance made up of (whether spiritual or material, simple or compounded, it matters not)—which is sensible or conscious of pleasure and pain, capable of happiness or misery, and so is concerned for itself, as far as that consciousness extends.[1]

This is very much in Swift's spirit: the mind defends its own integrity, and God permits it to do so. In the sermon on *Doing Good* Swift argues that *Love thy Neighbour as Thyself* means 'Love other people in the same way in which you love yourself and according to the same pattern; but not, of course, to the same degree, because a copy is not the same as the original.'[2] Swift constantly justifies his relation to the world by these expedients. God allows every man to secure himself, and puts the necessary means at his disposal. In Swift's case the necessary means were negation and reduction: difficulties were either repressed or melted down. In *The Conduct of the Allies* he insists that the primary responsibility for the security of a state rests upon that state itself. If a country is in danger of being over-run by an enemy and if this is likely to undermine one's own trade or liberty, it is only prudent to help the victim 'to win a strong secure Frontier'. But even then the victim must bear the heaviest burden. Swift's proof of this is again a domestic analogy:

If a House be on fire, it behoves all in the Neighbourhood to run with Buckets to quench it; but the Owner is sure to be undone first; and it is not impossible that those at next Door may escape, by a Shower from Heaven, or the stillness of the Weather, or some other favorable Accident.[3]

I do not claim, of course, that Swift was unique in these stratagems of self-defence. Much of Augustan literature is a series of strategic withdrawals, retreats in good order from positions

---

[1] Locke, *Essay*, p. 226 (II.xxvii.17).
[2] *Irish Tracts, 1720–1723, and Sermons*, p. 232.
[3] *Political Tracts 1711–1713*, edited by Herbert Davis (Basil Blackwell, Oxford, 1964), pp. 8–9.

deemed too metaphysical or Faustian to be held. A common tone is represented by Pope in the *Essay on Man*: or in the 'Note on the Design of the Essay', where he follows Dryden, Swift, and common policy in saying:

The science of Human Nature is, like all other sciences, reduced to a few clear points: There are not many certain truths in this world. It is therefore in the Anatomy of the Mind as in that of the Body; more good will accrue to mankind by attending to the large, open, and perceptible parts, than by studying too much such finer nerves and vessels, the conformations and uses of which will for ever escape our observation.[1]

But there are differences. Pope speaks of himself as 'steering between extremes', like a good navigator. Swift draws in his lines of defence, standing fast at that position against the pressure of vanity and pride. Reduction was a congenial mode of the mind. Indeed, many of Swift's effects are attained not by adding some unusual character to his sentences (heightened rhetorical force, for instance) but by deleting an expected quality; sympathy in *A Modest Proposal*, a sense of outrage in *A Tale of a Tub*, Christian fervour in the *Argument*, shock in *Gulliver's Travels*. He makes gargoyles by suppressing one or more characteristics normally regarded as essential; the result is that we are driven to note what is missing as well as what is present. The reader's vexation is often his outraged sense of those assumptions which, in the work itself, have been denied.

In *The Structure of Complex Words* Empson considers how radically writers in the eighteenth century pruned their emotional lives without actually killing the tree. Clearly there was a danger of killing it, he says, because 'the more you respect reason the more you fear the irrational'. The 'complex word' he is examining is 'dog', and he argues that in much of Augustan literature the dog stood for the unconscious, 'for the source of the impulse that keeps us sane, and may

[1] Pope, *An Essay on Man*, edited by Maynard Mack (Methuen, London, 1950), p. 7.

mysteriously fail as in drought'. The dog's processes of 'thought' are mysterious, 'but the results are homely and intelligible'. The dog 'makes what we do not know about the roots of our minds seem cheerful and not alarming'. Swift 'kept himself sane for as long as he did on secret doses of this feeling'.[1] There is a good deal more to be said about it. You could comfort yourself with this feeling only by thinking of the unconscious as a domestic animal. In *The Seasons*, Thomson took comfort from the fact that birds know when a storm is coming. They are like us. But if you equated the unconscious with the orang-utang, you would have to be Lord Monboddo before you could extract much comfort from that assumption. Anyway, it was a delicate matter, as the machinations of *Gulliver's Travels* make clear. The choice was stark enough: you had to decide whether what you did not know about the mind was terrifying or amiable. The silence of the infinite spaces terrified Pascal: Swift hoped that what he did not know would not hurt him, but he could not be sure. He could save himself distress by cultivating prudence; insisting upon the limits of human knowledge, and making grim fun of anyone who pretended otherwise. Unofficially the terrors would keep breaking in.

All we can say at this stage is that he would not willingly delude himself. While he comforted himself with the notion that God intended man to have reason as He intended animals to have instinct, he could not escape the conclusion that, in practice, the reason of individual men is seriously corrupt. One should try to preserve one's intelligence and live accordingly. This explains his distrust of classical rhetoric, although indeed he used its instruments. In one of his sermons he preached upon the passage in the *Acts* in which the young man Eutychus falls asleep during one of St Paul's longer orations. On the question of rhetoric in the sermon, the art of 'moving Men's

[1] William Empson, *The Structure of Complex Words* (Chatto and Windus, London, 1951), p. 169.

Passions, so common among the Orators of Greece and Rome', Swift says that it is not the business of the Christian orator to do anything of the kind; his only business is 'to work upon Faith and Reason'. All other eloquence, he continues, 'hath been a perfect Cheat, to stir up Men's Passions against Truth and Justice, for the Service of a Faction, to put false colours upon Things, and by an Amusement of agreeable Words, make the worse Reason appear to be the better'. He continues:

This is certainly not to be allowed in Christian Eloquence, and therefore, St. Paul took quite the other Course; he came not with Excellency of Words, or enticing Speeches of Men's Wisdom, but in plain Evidence of the Spirit, and Power: And, perhaps, it was for that Reason the young Man Eutychus, used to the Grecian Eloquence, grew tired, and fell so fast asleep.[1]

So here again he prunes back the tree: he will not even allow himself to unpack his heart with words.

Swift often tries to convince himself that, like Locke's 'clear and distinct ideas', every relevant consideration is straightforward enough if we will only 'let be'. He constantly implies that he is bored by anything extreme, metaphysical, or speculative. Burke and the later Augustans follow him in this. But in Burke, at least, the boredom is genuine. Swift is not bored by these things; he is terrified of them. So much so, that he is driven to seek them out in others and to destroy them. The critical work is begun in *A Tale of a Tub*.

IV

There is, for instance, the spectacularly appropriate form of the book itself; even though Swift seems to have borrowed the figure from L'Estrange's *Dissenter's Sayings*. 'Sea-men have a Custom', Swift says, 'when they meet a Whale, to fling him out an empty Tub by way of Amusement, to divert him from laying violent Hands upon the Ship'.[2] There could be no more

[1] *Irish Tracts, 1720–1723, and Sermons*, pp. 213, 214.
[2] *A Tale of a Tub*, p. 40.

beguiling figure of negation and riddance. Swift rids himself of dangerous luggage under the guise of keeping his enemies flustered. He prepares himself for this full-scale riddance by many minor acts of the same kind: as in the 'Apology' he says that the author, 'by the assistance of some Thinking, and much Conversation', had 'endeavour'd to Strip himself of as many real Prejudices as he could'.[1] So we should look out for other occasions on which seemingly positive acts and experiences are employed for purposes of negation. Later, Swift says that 'one of the greatest, and best of human Actions' is 'to remove Prejudices, and place Things in their truest and fairest Light'.[2] In the 'Digression Concerning Madness' when he has considered many of the more offensive varieties of madness, he says:

That even, I my self, the Author of these momentous Truths, am a Person, whose Imaginations are hard-mouthed, and exceedingly disposed to run away with his Reason, which I have observed from long Experience, to be a very light Rider, and easily shook off; upon which Account, my friends will never trust me alone, without a solemn Promise, to vent my Speculations in this, or the like manner, for the universal Benefit of Human Kind. . . . [3]

Parody does not conceal the fact that these are Swift's own idioms. Stripping, venting, casting, and so forth are not merely good things to do; they are essential for health and equilibrium. Evil is always something added to what is tolerably good already; it is never, as in Scholastic terminology, a lack, a privation. This is a conventional emphasis; particularly the implication that man's contribution to the world is specious complexity. Jeremy Taylor writes, in the Preface to *Ductor Dubitantium*, 'What God has made plain, men have intricated.'[4]

[1] *Ibid.* p. 4.
[2] *Ibid.* p. 161.
[3] *Ibid.* pp. 179–80.
[4] Jeremy Taylor, *Whole Works*, edited by Reginald Heber, revised by Charles P. Eden (London, 1852), vol. IX, p. xii. See also George L. Mosse, *The Holy Pretence: A Study in Christianity and Reason of State from William Perkins to John Winthrop* (Basil Blackwell, Oxford, 1957).

41

In the *Tale* Swift writes, taking a hint from Temple:

For, as Health is but one Thing, and has been always the same, whereas Diseases are by thousands, besides new and daily Additions; So, all the Virtues that have ever been in Mankind are to be counted upon a few Fingers, but his Follies and Vices are innumerable, and Time adds hourly to the Heap.[1]

In the allegory of the *Tale* Swift attacks the Catholics for adding to the primitive structure of Christian belief; such things as Purgatory, the cult of oral Tradition, the inclusion of the Apocrypha, images of Saints, Papal Infallibility, Indulgences, clerical celibacy, and Transubstantiation. He attacks the Dissenters for imposing absurd extremes of interpretation on a Bible which is, to start with, 'plain' and 'easy'; for quoting sacred texts upon all occasions; and for inventing Predestination. Generally, what was there to begin with was satisfactory and might have been improved by judicious abbreviation. If you add anything, it is bound to be wrong and you reveal your corruption by this gesture. In the 'Digression Concerning Critics' he ascribes to Pausanias the following description of the breed:

They were a Race of Men, who delighted to nibble at the Superfluities, and Excrescencies of Books; which the Learned at length observing, took Warning of their own Accord, to lop the Luxuriant, the Rotten, the Dead, the Sapless, and the Overgrown Branches from their Works.[2]

In the same spirit the past is invariably to be preferred to the present, on the grounds that the original is innocent and the later additions are likely to be sophistries. Indeed, while it is possible to argue that Swift's part in the quarrel between the Ancients and the Moderns was merely a gesture of loyalty to his master Temple, at the same time it is clear that, temperamentally, he fought on the only possible side. In that section

[1] *A Tale of a Tub*, p. 50.
[2] *Ibid.* p. 98.

of the *Tale* where Martin's patience has enraged Jack, Swift says that what most afflicted Jack was 'to observe his Brother's Coat so well reduced into the State of Innocence'. Reduction is good. Innocence is either the original state or the splendid state to which we come if we are intelligent enough to reduce ourselves, cutting off the sophisticated additions. For the same reasons, Swift argues (and we have no reason to discount the case), memory is to be preferred to invention. Memory is the acknowledgment we give to the validity of the past; invention is the arrogance with which we repudiate it. It is one of the more painful facts of life that truth is constantly left behind by fiction, as it must be, since the imagination is unlimited and irresponsible. Swift argues that Fate, alas, is on the side of the big battalions of invention; the only reasonable reply, he suggests, is to reduce the structures of imagination and, if necessary, delete them altogether.

The best way to do this while remaining an artist is to deflate alien pretensions. The ideal means is parody. From our point of view, parody is the very principle of negation, and it has all the Freudian advantages. Parody enabled Swift to entertain in his consciousness the features he would repress in action; by this means he would rid himself of their potency. In parody you eat your cake and evacuate it: alternatively, you neutralise the venom of your sins.

As an Ancient, for instance, Swift might have been expected to endorse some of the simpler analogies; the idea of the Body Politic, as a case in point, or the relation of the microcosm to the macrocosm. Certainly when there was a choice between two rival analogies, he chose the modest version. But there are signs, evident throughout his work, that he distrusted the assumptions of analogy and would have preferred to live without them. He does this by ridiculing these assumptions in Bacon, Boyle, the Cabbalists, anyone. The question of metaphor was complicated in the same way; sometimes he accepted it on its own terms, only to repudiate it later. So it is typical of him to make hilarious play in the *Tale of a Tub* with the body politic and microcosm. Marjorie Hope Nicolson has pointed out[1] that centuries of loose analogy were swept aside when Swift wrote in the *Tale*:

The Worshippers of this Deity had also a System of their Belief, which seemed to turn upon the following Fundamental. They held the Universe to be a large Suit of Cloaths, which invests every Thing: That the Earth is invested by the Air; The Air is invested by the Stars; and the Stars are invested by the Primum Mobile. Look on this Globe of Earth, you will find it to be a very compleat and fashionable Dress. What is that which some call Land, but a fine Coat faced with Green? . . . To conclude from all, what is Man himself but a Micro-Coat or rather a compleat Suit of Cloaths with all its Trimmings?[2]

He returns, later in the *Tale*, to make fun of 'Man's little world'. Indeed, he brings the two notions together as the first platitude to be teased in *A Tritical Essay upon the Faculties of the Mind*:

Philosophers say, that Man is a Microcosm or little World, resembling in Miniature every Part of the great: And, in my opinion, the Body Natural may be compared to the Body Politick.[3]

It begins to appear that Swift thought himself contaminated by practically everything in the public domain, especially if he had lived with it for some time; and then he had to get rid of it or perish.

Get rid of these 'disquisitions vain'—Dryden's phrase—or at least reduce them to manageable proportions. No writer in English literature is less exhilarated by the possibilities of growth, expansion, enlargement or range: to think of a phrase like Henry James's 'heightened sensitivity to the promises of

---

[1] Marjorie Hope Nicolson, *The Breaking of the Circle* (Northwestern University Press, Evanston, 1950), p. 53. See also Hélène Tuzet, *Le Cosmos et L'Imagination* (Librairie José Corti, Paris, 1965).

[2] *A Tale of a Tub*, pp. 77–8.

[3] *A Tale of a Tub, with Other Early Works 1696–1707*, edited by Herbert Davis (Basil Blackwell, Oxford, 1957), pp. 246–7.

life' is to see dimensions of possibility which Swift was prepared to disown. Dryden adverts to 'the sad variety of Hell'. Swift's characteristic rhythm of mind is the reduction of the case in hand to a state in which he is willing to tolerate its presence. The *Tale of a Tub* is an anthology of such gestures, clear enough even when Parody is at work. 'Is not Religion a Cloak', he asks, 'Honesty a Pair of Shoes, worn out in the Dirt, Self-love a Surtout, Vanity a Shirt, and Conscience a Pair of Breeches, which, tho' a Cover for Lewdness as well as Nastiness, is easily slipt down for the Service of both.'[1] It is said that here Swift is parodying Hobbes; but he is using a characteristic figure congenial to his own mind. Both Hobbes and Swift are devoted to the possibilities of simplification. The difference is that Swift simplified as a way of dealing with difficult material, difficult because intangible; Hobbes implies that the enforced simplicity is the real Truth of things. The difference is certainly important enough to allow Swift to make fun of Hobbes; but the parody should not be taken as breaking the demonstrable correspondence of the two minds. Swift is ridiculing in Hobbes an intellectual procedure highly congenial to his own mind but in many parts of *Leviathan* carried to pretentious extremes. The object of attack is the pretension. In his own behalf, he delights to take several words, loosely related, draw them all together, and supply a synonym that effects their reduction. Later in the *Tale* he considers several words for the 'informing form' of Man, words like *spiritus*, *animus*, *afflatus*, and *anima*; but only to say, 'What are all these but several Appellations for Wind? which is the ruling Element in every Compound, and into which they all resolve upon their Corruption.'[2] He offers the same violence to all forms of speculation and subtlety. In *The Battle of the Books* he makes fun of the Moderns for being 'light-headed', conceiving 'nothing too high for them to mount'; while 'in reducing to Practice', he says, they 'discover a mighty Pressure about their

[1] *A Tale of a Tub* (Guthkelch and Nichol Smith), p. 78.   [2] *Ibid.* p. 151.

45

Posteriors and their Heels'.[1] He hunts the Cabbalists without mercy for their bogus ingenuity.

So the fundamental technique of the *Tale* is to scale everything down. If you offer a metaphysical equation making something small 'really' equal to something large, Swift denies your claim and answers it in kind; taking the small thing and reducing it further still. If you say that man is a little world made cunningly, Swift answers that he is not a world at all, he is only a suit of clothes, and even these are not made cunningly:

'Tis true indeed, that these Animals, which are vulgarly called Suits of Cloaths, or Dresses, do according to certain Compositions receive different Appellations. If one of them be trimm'd up with a Gold Chain, and a red Gown, and a white Rod, and a great Horse, it is called a Lord-Mayor; If certain Ermins and Furs be placed in a certain Position, we stile them a Judge, and so, an apt Conjunction of Lawn and black Sattin, we intitle a Bishop.[2]

Critics are equated with asses and the equation pursued. Religious inspiration is wind; zealous priests carry it from the fountain head in bladders and displode it over their flock. If you are foolish enough to discriminate between the different winds or breaths, Swift answers:

Mists arise from the Earth, Steams from Dunghills, Exhalations from the Sea, and Smoak from Fire; yet all Clouds are the same in Composition, as well as Consequences: and the Fumes issuing from a Jakes, will furnish as comely and useful a Vapor, as Incense from an Altar.[3]

It is useless to say that here the Hack is making a fool of himself: mud is flung and it sticks; this time, the Hack is not soiled. Again, Swift rarely offers a discrimination between things which, he thinks, have been confounded; he is much more likely to say that things which have been carefully separated are in blunt fact identical. He says in the *Tale*: 'The very same Principle that influences a Bully to break the

[1] *A Tale of a Tub*, p. 225.   [2] *Ibid.* p. 79.   [3] *Ibid.* p. 163.

Windows of a Whore, who has jilted him, naturally stirs up a Great Prince to raise mighty Armies, and dream of nothing but Sieges, Battles, and Victories.'[1] It matters little whether we ascribe these words to Jonathan Swift or to the official Author of the *Tale*.

As we might expect, Swift is never happy to adjudicate between rival qualities: he is uneasy in the presence of any value that cannot be given in quantitative terms. In the *Tale*, when he sneers at the Moderns for their sexual lore, he immediately measures their accomplishment; the Moderns are like the Indian Pygmies, 'whose Stature did not exceed above two Foot'; *sed quorum pudenda crassa, et ad talos usque pertingentia*.[2] When he makes fun of the Catholic Church for its alleged inventions, he represents Peter going mad because of the mental strain involved: 'But, alas, he had kept his Brain so long, so violently upon the Rack, that at last it shook itself, and began to turn round for a little Ease.'[3] Later he speaks of the brain 'in its natural Position and State of Serenity',[4] and on several occasions he refers to madness not as a deterioration of the brain, or a loss of its power, a failure of its quality, but as a convulsion, the brain shaken loose from its natural place. When it is a question of relating one faculty to another, Swift agrees to do this only when he has given each a local habitation as well as a name. This is normally the function of the verbs:

But when a Man's Fancy gets astride on his Reason, when Imagination is at cuffs with the Senses, and common Understanding, as well as common Sense, is Kickt out of doors; the first Proselyte he makes, is Himself... [5]

Here an imbalance among man's faculties is given as a Brueghel or a Hogarth painting, a Hell's Kitchen; this is possible when the faculties are fixed in visual relation and then, with a roar,

---

[1] *Ibid.* pp. 165–6. [2] *Ibid.* p. 147. [3] *Ibid.* p. 114.
[4] *Ibid.* p. 171. [5] *Ibid.* p. 171.

loosed for battle. But it would not work at all if qualities were to resist translation, as here, into quantities.

I have argued that the ideal form for an artist committed to negation is parody. This applies in the configuration of the work as a whole. When we think of the same motives carried down into the detail of the writing, line by line, word by word, it becomes clear that the classic form, in this miniature, is the pun. The pun has many advantages. For one thing, it has the same effect in the detail as the famous Digressions have in the large; it throws another tub into the mouth of the whale, thwarts the conventional hopes of departure and arrival, turns things upside-down, and rids words of their agreed meaning. Finally, a language committed to the pun pushes the discourse adrift from 'meaning' and, like *Finnegans Wake*, sets it spinning in purely verbal water. Once there, the language develops resources of its own, without responsibility to the 'things' from which it has parted or to the speaker who finds himself abandoned. In the 'Digression in Praise of Digressions' Swift writes:

The most accomplisht Way of using Books at Present, is twofold: Either first, to serve them as some Men do Lords, learn their Titles exactly, and then brag of their acquaintance. Or secondly, which is indeed the choicer, the profounder, and politer Method, to get a thorough Insight into the Index, by which the whole Book is governed and turned, like Fishes by the Tail. For, to enter the Palace of Learning at the great Gate, requires an Expence of Time and Forms; therefore Men of much Haste and little Cere- mony, are content to get in by the Back-Door. For, the Arts are all in a flying March, and therefore more easily subdued by attack- ing them in the Rear. Thus Physicians discover the State of the whole Body, by consulting only what comes from Behind. Thus Men catch Knowledge by throwing their Wit on the Posteriors of a Book, as Boys do Sparrows with flinging Salt upon their Tails. Thus Human Life is best understood by the wise man's Rule of *Regarding the End*. Thus are old Sciences unravelled like old Stock- ings, by beginning at the Foot.[1]

[1] *A Tale of a Tub*, p. 145.

This is like a parody of Browne's *Vulgar Errors*, its parade of useless analogies held together by the whim of their master. In detail, it works by turning upside-down a principle which we have seen in Swift's polemic; the technique by which he throws a rope around several cognate terms and pulls them down with a low synonym. Here he does precisely the opposite: he takes the word 'end', thinks of several synonyms, including rear, behind, tail, back, posterior, foot. For each of these he supplies an appropriate situation; the army being attacked in its rear, and so forth. The fact that the words are synonyms sets loose their variants, wherever one word is used, and it allows Swift to plead innocent when indecencies are disclosed. When the rope is thrown around these situations, it is for a different purpose, to laugh at the absurd resources of analogy, now that Swift has yielded to our prompting and taken the analogies at their word. 'Thus Human Life is best understood by the wise man's Rule of *Regarding the End*.' This is not merely a laugh at the sober preacher, or even a warning that now he quotes Solon at his peril: it warns the reader that the genius of Language itself is on Swift's side, offering ironies within irony, and that the only way to avoid being punctured is by not being inflated. This passage, and other passages in the same spirit, are counterparts to Swift's direct reductions and negations; there, he cuts away the absurd or offensive matter at one blow; here, he shows what happens when you fail to do so. The most spectacular example of this procedure in the *Tale* is where he shows the reader what happens when you live by words. Jack soils himself because he cannot think of a phrase from Scripture appropriate to the occasion. He does not clean himself because he recalls a passage in *Revelation* which seems to forbid it: 'He which is filthy, let him be filthy still.'

To bring these notions into order I choose a passage from the 'Digression Concerning Madness'. Swift has been treating of delusion and insanity, finding their marks in virtually every part of the world's culture. Then he says, in one of the most celebrated formulations:

For, if we take an Examination of what is generally understood by Happiness, as it has Respect, either to the Understanding or the Senses, we shall find all its Properties and Adjuncts will herd under this short Definition: That, it is a perpetual Possession of being well Deceived. And first, with Relation to the Mind or Understanding; 'tis manifest, what mighty Advantages Fiction has over Truth; and the Reason is just at our Elbow; because Imagination can build nobler Scenes, and produce more wonderful Revolutions than Fortune or Nature will be at Expence to furnish. Nor is Mankind so much to blame in his Choice, thus determining him, if we consider that the Debate meerly lies between Things past, and Things conceived; and so the Question is only this; Whether Things that have Place in the Imagination, may not as properly be said to Exist, as those that are seated in the Memory; which may be justly held in the Affirmative, and very much to the Advantage of the former, since This is acknowledged to be the Womb of Things, and the other allowed to be no more than the Grave.[1]

This is the Hack, but it is also Jonathan Swift. The passage begins with a characteristic figure; all the properties and adjuncts herd under one, the lasso deftly thrown. The thought itself is not new. Swift probably found it in Temple. Bacon gives it at least twice. In the essay 'Of Truth', discussing the pleasures of deception, he asks: 'Doth any man doubt, that if there were taken out of men's minds vain opinions, flattering hopes, false valuations, imaginations as one would, and the like, but it would leave the minds of a number of men poor shrunken things, full of melancholy and indisposition, and unpleasing to themselves?'[2] Bacon allows that some men would escape this fate, presumably because their minds are not utterly dependent upon consolatory illusion; but Swift admits no exception. In the second Book of the *Advancement of Learning* Bacon returns to the thought in considering Poesy as 'feigned history'. 'The

---

[1] *A Tale of a Tub*, pp. 171–2.
[2] Bacon, *Essays*, edited by F. Storr and C. H. Gibson (Longmans, Green, London, 1891), p. 2. See also *A Tale of a Tub*, p. 172 n.

use of this feigned history', he says, 'hath been to give some shadow of satisfaction to the mind of man in those points wherein the nature of things doth deny it, the world being in proportion inferior to the soul; by reason whereof there is, agreeable to the spirit of man, a more ample greatness, a more exact goodness, and a more absolute variety, than can be found in the nature of things... And therefore [poesy] was ever thought to have some participation of divineness, because it doth raise and erect the mind, by submitting the shows of things to the desires of the mind; whereas reason doth buckle and bow the mind unto the nature of things.'[1] Bacon is primarily concerned to do full justice to the occasion; he is not scoring points or throwing down gauntlets. So he acknowledges that what imagination gives is merely 'some shadow of satisfaction'. Swift gives over the human mind completely to illusion, the possession of which, to be of any use, must be 'perpetual'. Similarly in measuring the advantages of imagination over memory; Swift lines up his qualities and faculties in position until he is ready to use them; things *have place* in the imagination and other things *are seated* in the Memory. When Locke deals with the same theme he is much more judicious, content to lose in vigour what he gains in justice. 'And in this sense it is', he says, 'that our ideas are said to be in our memories, when indeed they are actually nowhere, but only there is an ability in the mind when it will revive them again ...' Discussing the fact that our recollection can fade, he says—in a remarkable passage—

Thus the ideas, as well as children, of our youth often die before us; and our minds represent to us those tombs to which we are approaching; where though the brass and marble remain, yet the inscriptions are effaced by time, and the imagery moulders away.[2]

Swift, going over the same material, cuts away Locke's philosophic gravity. Officially, he prefers memory to imagination;

[1] Bacon, *The Advancement of Learning*, edited by William Aldis Wright (Clarendon Press, Oxford, 1900), pp. 101, 102.
[2] Locke, *Essay*, pp. 87, 88 (II.x.2, 5).

so much so, that to think of the odds in favour of imagination is enough to induce a rueful note. The only way to deal with the obscurity of this position is by giving the shadowy devil his due between the eyes. So he takes the symbols of his official defeat and brandishes them in his own face. He takes the harm out of the defeat by the air of patient explication with which he registers it, as if every grace were willingly sacrificed to precision. All the vague lines are sharpened, dark corners illuminated, qualifications which he might advance in his own official favour are refused. The last magnificent gesture acknowledges an alien cliché; imagination is the womb of things, and memory the grave. So let it be.

But there is more than this in Swift's rhetoric. One of the most bewildering marks of his style is the intensity which it generates on occasions when intensity is not, in the nature of the case, a declared aim. Often this is done by sudden acts of violence performed upon the equable body of the prose; the more equable, the more violent. In the first sentence of the passage from the 'Digression on Madness' the tone implies the patience of reasonable enquiry: if we examine a set of circumstances we shall find a certain principle at work which can then be embodied in a definition, that happiness, either of the understanding or the senses, is 'a perpetual possession of being well deceived'. The violence of 'deceived' is committed upon the urbane cadence which precedes it, the sequence of benign terms, 'perpetual', 'possession', 'well'. We do not register the shock merely by remarking the unexpected word at the end of the sentence. The point is that at the last moment, when our critical sense of the argument has been lulled, Swift suddenly swings from one idiom to another. Bentham is peculiarly gifted in the analysis of this procedure. In the *Table of the Springs of Action* and again in the *Handbook of Political Fallacies* he distinguishes between neutral and censorious terms. Terms are neutral which are, so far as possible, disinterested, words of description which take care to avoid every implication of bias. Censorious terms insinuate an attitude, for or against; as one man might speak of hunger, another might call it voraciousness and a third might invoke 'love of the social bowl': the first is neutral, the second dyslogistic, the third eulogistic. Bentham proposed to induce a peaceable note in society by translating all censorious terms into the corresponding neutral terms. He implied that, at first, all our words were neutral, descriptive, pacific; but gradually as we voiced our militant attitudes, for or against, we altered the language accordingly. It was time to go back, for the sake of peace and lucidity. This prompts us to see that Swift's procedure would eliminate the neutral terms and bewilder us by jumping from eulogy to dyslogy and *vice versa*. Often the only way to resist his rhetoric (if that is in question) is to translate the subversive term either into a neutral equivalent or into its eulogistic opposite; as the eulogistic version of 'deceived' would be 'charmed', or 'beguiled'. 'It beguiled attention, charmed the sight', Shakespeare writes in *Lucrece* of Nestor's rhetoric.

The procedure is active through the 'Digression on Madness'. The official argument is that the nature of things is irrelevant; what matters is the collision of their forces. These collisions, it is implied, are casual, circumstantial: the same vapours, going one way, lead to a certain result; turning in another direction, they make a different result. The difference is contingency. A quality which is bad in Bedlam, such as fury, is good at Flanders. One man leaps into a gulf and comes out a hero; another leaps and is forever deemed a lunatic. The case is unanswerable if its terms are accepted. But Swift enforces the argument by enforcing the terminology. He defeats us in the major case by defeating us in a hundred minor cases; verbal details like 'deception'. Violence of argument is administered through the detailed violence of the language as one idiom ousts another. Sometimes the first part of a sentence implies one stance, the next part another, entirely different:

Yesterday I ordered the Carcass of a Beau to be stript in my

Presence; when we were all amazed to find so many unsuspected Faults under one Suit of Cloaths: Then I laid open his Brain, his Heart, and his Spleen; But, I plainly perceived . . .

If we give these words to a personal source, the speaker is an anatomist, the rationalist already invoked; a Modern, a virtuoso, surrounded by his slavish pupils. But the sentence ends:

. . . I justly formed this Conclusion to my self; That whatever Philosopher or Projector can find out an Art to sodder and patch up the Flaws and Imperfections of Nature, will deserve much better of Mankind, and teach us a more useful Science, than that so much in present Esteem, of widening and exposing them (like him who held Anatomy to be the ultimate end of Physick).

The irony here turns upon the point that the alleged flaws and imperfections of Nature are the destructive interventions of Man: the 'conclusion' is banal only because it is wrongly applied; Nature would be excellent if left alone. The only answer to one project is another project. But at the end of the sentence the speaker can hardly be identified any longer with the professional anatomist, the mad scientist of fiction; he is moving toward the Augustan norm of prudence. The paragraph ends:

And he, whose Fortunes and Dispositions have placed him in a convenient Station to enjoy the Fruits of this noble Art; He that can with Epicurus content his Ideas with the Films and Images that fly off upon his Senses from the Superficies of Things; Such a Man truly wise, creams off Nature, leaving the Sower and the Dregs, for Philosophy and Reason to lap up. This is the sublime and refined Point of Felicity, called, the Possession of being well deceived; The Serene Peaceful State of being a Fool among Knaves.

'What is left?', F. R. Leavis asks in his analysis of this passage, implying that at this stage 'the positives', such as they were, have disappeared; we are at a blank wall. But perhaps our conclusion may not yet be desperate. The reference to 'a Fool among Knaves' may be, as Dr Leavis reads it, a trap; but I am

not certain that it is. It is sometimes urged that the hint is
given in 'superficies', that Swift is using the word as a wink to
the wise. But in fact the word was regularly used as a geometrical term without any hint of modern 'superficiality': its
first meaning is surface, visible form, in geometry a magnitude
of two dimensions, length and breadth. My own reading
suggests that Swift means specifically, a garden, and that the
whole paragraph is a description of Sir William Temple.
Swift usually took the conventional view of Epicurus, that his
philosophy was an invitation to sensuality: this is his view, for
instance, in the *Tritical Essay, On the Death of Stella, Thoughts on
Various Subjects,* and the Sermon *On the Excellence of Christianity.*
Earlier in the *Tale* Epicurus was one of several mad philosophers, including 'Des Cartes, and others'. But Swift was well
aware of Temple's *Upon the Gardens of Epicurus* as one of several
essays, like Charleton's *Epicurus's Morals,* in which the
philosopher is vigorously defended. In any event, 'he, whose
Fortunes and Dispositions have placed him in a convenient
Station to enjoy the Fruits of this noble Art' is, I think, Temple
the Epicurean Gardener, and 'He that can with Epicurus
content his Ideas with the Films and Images that fly off upon
his Senses from the Superficies of Things' is Temple writing
in praise of the quiet, unmeddling life; also Temple when he
writes in the *Epicurus* that 'the best Figure of a Garden is
either a Square or an Oblong'.[1] Such a man, 'truly wise',
creams off Nature, 'leaving the Sower and the Dregs, for
Philosophy and Reason to lap up': this man is Temple who
ridiculed the pretensions of natural science and was no friend
to rationalists. So: is Temple a fool? Yes, but only in a specially
defined sense. 'Fool' is a 'complex word' in William Empson's
sense, and we ought to recall not only his account of the rami-
fications of folly in *King Lear* but also the tradition of Stultitia
which culminates in Erasmus. But we can bring the matter
nearer home. There is a rather odd passage in Temple's

[1] Temple, *Works* (London, 1750), vol. I, p. 185.

Epicurus, when he acknowledges himself a fool of a particular kind; as it includes a defence of 'deception', it is worth quoting at some length:

For my own Part, as the Country Life, and this Part of it more particularly, were the Inclination of my Youth itself, so they are the Pleasure of my Age; and I can truly say, that, among many great Employments that have fallen to my Share, I have never asked or fought for any one of them, but often endeavoured to escape from them, into the Ease and Freedom of a private Scene, where a Man may go his own Way, and his own Pace, in the common Paths or Circles of Life.

> Inter cuncta leges et percunctabere doctos
> Qua ratione queas traducere leniter aevum,
> Quid curas minuat, quid te tibi reddat amicum,
> Quid pure tranquillet, honos an dulce lucellum,
> An secretum iter, et fallentis semita vitae.

> But above all, the Learned read and ask
> By what Means you may gently pass your Age,
> What lessens Care, what makes thee thine own Friend,
> What truly calms the Mind, Honour, or Wealth,
> Or else a private Path of stealing Life?

There are Questions that a Man ought at least to ask himself, whether he asks others or no, and to choose his Course of Life rather by his own Humour and Temper, than by common Accidents, or Advice of Friends; at least if the Spanish Proverb be true, That a Fool knows more in his own House, than a Wise Man in another's.

The Measure of choosing well is, Whether a Man likes what he has chosen, which I thank God has befallen me; and though, among the Follies of my Life, Building and Planting have not been the least, and have cost me more than I have the Confidence to own; yet they have been fully recompensed by the Sweetness and Satisfaction of this Retreat, where, since my Resolution taken of never entering again into any publick Employments, I have passed five Years without ever going once to Town, though I am almost in Sight of it, and have a House there always ready to receive me.[1]

To be a fool among knaves is consciously and conscientiously to seek the life of the garden, rejecting the life of the world

[1] Temple, *Works*, vol. I, pp. 188–9.

which, in this Epicurean setting, is the work of knaves. It is
Temple's choice, one kind of folly rather than another, Moor
Park rather than the Court. So the sentence is not a trap.
But it drives the reader from one idiom to another without
warning; the energy at work is critical, sceptical, and subversive. The object is good riddance. Kenneth Burke has
spoken of 'the ingredient of twisted tragedy behind Swift's
satire', where the object is 'not to lift himself up, but to pull all
mankind down (the author himself being caught in the general
deflation)'.[1]

Yeats said of Edmund Burke that he is tolerable only in his
impassioned moments, but Swift is continuously splendid
because of his animation and clarity, no matter what the
occasion.[2] This is true, but much of the animation and the
clarity is graveyard humour. *A Tale of a Tub* is a *tour de force*,
its energy to an unparalleled degree engendered from need.
The idea of negation is again relevant; so far from being
'merely negative' Swift works up tremendous energy to get
rid of his burdens. The first piece of excess baggage is pride:
he attacks it in others to neutralise its working in himself.
Lovejoy has observed that 'the eighteenth-century denuncia-
tions of pride are often, at bottom, expressions of a certain
disillusionment of man about himself—a phase of that long
and deepening disillusionment which is the tragedy of a great
part of modern thought'. He also makes the point that Swift's
Yahoos are an extreme example of this: the Yahoo 'crowns
his fatuity by imagining himself the aim and climax of the
whole creation', while in fact he is lower than the animals.[3]
Swift was not the first to think this or to say it. His splendid
and special quality is that while other writers were merely rueful
about man's pride, he cleared away the rue in riddance. The

[1] Kenneth Burke, *Attitudes toward History* (Hermes Publications, Los Altos,
1959), p. 313.
[2] W. B. Yeats, *Explorations* (Macmillan, London, 1962), p. 293.
[3] A. O. Lovejoy, *Essays in the History of Ideas* (Johns Hopkins University Press,
Baltimore, 1948), p. 65.

cause is evident enough: he turned violently against the blithe spirits from Thomas Vaughan and Traherne to Edward Young and the other traders in the Sublime who, in a second wind, convinced themselves that man was now greater than ever before. Swift could not bring himself to this consolation.

CHAPTER 2

PERSPECTIVE

On 24 March 1775, Boswell noted of Johnson: 'I wondered to hear him say of *Gulliver's Travels*, "When once you have thought of big men and little men, it is very easy to do all the rest". '[1] Boswell's answer is not recorded. He might have reminded Johnson that several writers, including Cyrano de Bergerac, Rabelais, Fontenelle, and Algarotti, had thought of big men and little men without turning the thought into a masterpiece.

When Gulliver is captured in Lilliput and ordered to turn over his possessions, he gives up his handkerchief, snuff-box, money, sword, razor, pistols, knife, watch, and comb; but he does not disclose a private pocket in which he keeps a pair of spectacles, a 'pocket perspective', and, as he reports, 'several other little conveniences'.[2] Later, he uses the perspective glass to spy upon the fleet anchored in the harbour at Blefuscu. Later still, in the *Voyage to Laputa*, when he is set adrift in a canoe, he uses it to see the islands southeast of the pirate ship. The pocket perspective, like the modern opera-glass, gives from one end a magnified image and, from the other, far sight. Looking through one end, Gulliver saw the Brobdingnagians; through the other, the Lilliputians. He studied the Lilliputians, Marjorie Nicolson says, 'as the virtuoso studied ant-hills, bee-hives, "Eels in Vinegar", blades of grass swarming with life'.[3] This is particularly relevant to Marjorie Nicolson's purposes, because her theme is the effect of the

---

[1] Boswell, *Life of Johnson*, edited by G. Birkbeck Hill, revised by L. F. Powell (Clarendon Press, Oxford, 1934–50), vol. II, p. 319.

[2] *Gulliver's Travels*, p. 37.

[3] Marjorie Hope Nicolson, *Science and Imagination* (Cornell University Press, Ithaca, 1956), p. 197.

microscope and the telescope upon the English literary imagination. Donne, Milton and Swift are her exemplary figures. I hope to turn the theme in another direction. I should remark at once that considerations of perspective are a congenial mode of Swift's mind, even on mild occasions. In one of his 'Intelligencer' essays, for instance, on the vices of modern education:

By these Methods, the young Gentleman is in every Article as fully accomplished at eight Years old, as at eight and twenty; Age adding only to the Growth of his Person and his Vices; so that if you should look at him in his Boyhood through the magnifying End of a Perspective, and in his Manhood through the other, it would be impossible to spy any Difference; the same Airs, the same Strut, the same Cock of his Hat, and Posture of his Sword (as far as the Change of Fashions will allow) the same Understanding, the same Compass of Knowledge, with the very same Absurdity, Impudence, and Impertinence of Tongue.[1]

Things which seem the same but are not; things which seem different but are, in fact, identical; perspective, comparison, proportion: these are the characteristic modes of Swift's satire. Gulliver has poor eyesight, he needs glasses, sees strange sights and dubious relations between the things he sees. Swift's work is developed from contemporary resources in politics, religion and science: he is a poet of local occasion. Indeed, he did not need to go far to be stimulated by exercises in the nature of perspective. There are hints in the *De Origine Mali* of Archbishop King. Molyneux's *Dioptrica Nova* is a detailed account of telescopes and microscopes: his *Sciothericum Telescopicum* is 'a new contrivance of adapting a telescope to an horizontal dial for observing the moment of Time by day or night'. Berkeley's *Essay toward a New Theory of Vision* takes up a famous conundrum, posed first by Molyneux and then by Locke, which depends upon obliquities of vision. A little further afield, in similar meditations, one encounters Kepler,

[1] *Irish Tracts 1728–1733*, edited by Herbert Davis (Basil Blackwell, Oxford, 1955), p. 50.

Descartes, Fontenelle, Pascal, Pope, Wotton, Malebranche's *Recherche de la vérité*, Voltaire's *Micromégas*.

The context of these enquiries was the Renaissance concern with the 'truth' of perspective. Wylie Sypher has argued that the painters who now appear as representative figures of Renaissance art are Leon Battista Alberti, Piero della Francesca, Sebastiano Serlio, 'those austere scientists devoted to proportion and perspective'. 'The final problem of all Renaissance artists', he says, 'is not to represent objects naturalistically but instead to *dispose* objects within a rationalized composition, to reconstruct about the figure of man a cosmos whose proportions are determined from a fixed point of view.'[1] We will consider later the implications of the fixed point of view. But now we remark that while the Renaissance sculptor, as Sypher argues, 'situated the image of man, confidently, within a new world-order, within a new coherent space and perspective', Swift accepted the object but lacked the confidence. He used the same means to a modest version of the end, but he did not share the Renaissance confidence that all would then be well. 'Measurement began our might', Yeats said in a rueful moment. Swift trusted measurement as much as he trusted anything, but only because there was little enough to trust. We are all afflicted, like Gulliver, with bad eyes.

Meanwhile the Renaissance interest in perspective sponsored experiment in the relation between the figure and the scene.[2] Certain ambiguities in the language of vision sent students to considerations of optical illusion, false perspectives, magic, witchcraft and demonology. There is a famous passage in Bacon's *New Atlantis* which describes Salomon's House, where the wonders of experimental science keep the inhabitants even busier than Swift's scientists in Lagado:

Wee have also Perspective-Houses, wher wee make Demonstrations of all Lights, and Radiations: And of all Colours: And out of Things

[1] Wylie Sypher, *Four Stages of Renaissance Style* (Doubleday, New York, 1955), pp. 60–1.
[2] *Ibid.* p. 28.

uncoloured and Transparent, wee can represent unto you all severall Colours; Not in Raine-Bowes (as it is in Gemms, and Prismes,) but of themselves Single. Wee represent also all Multiplications of Light, which wee carry to great Distance, and make so Sharp, as to discerne small Points and Lines. Also all Colourations of Light; All Delusions and Deceits of the Sight, in Figures, Magnitudes, Motions, Colours, All Demonstrations of Shadowes ... Wee procure meanes of Seeing Objects afarr off; As in the Heaven, and Remote Places. And represent Things Neare as afarr off; and Things afarr off as Neare; Making Faigned Distances ... Wee have also Glasses and Meanes, to see Small and Minute Bodies, perfectly distinctly ... Wee represent also all manner of Reflexions, Refractions, and Multiplications of Visuall Beames of Objects.[1]

Reginald Scot lists virtually the same optical wonders in his *Discoverie of Witchcraft*, when he discusses 'strange conclusions in glasses, of the art perspective'.[2] Walter Charleton recurs to them in *The Immortality of the Human Soul, Demonstrated by the Light of Nature*. The object of Scot's book was to deal with the most oppressive ambiguities, 'that we be not deceived'; but, like Charleton, he was fascinated by the deceptions. The most spectacular illusion was the anamorphosis, where a portrait seen from the front is weirdly distorted, but seen from an oblique point of view presents the standard image.[3] These and other vagaries of perspective, physical conceits, were pondered for their own sake, and they were often invoked in considerations of epistemology and ontology. More to our purpose, they were regularly translated into psychological terms. In the second Act of *Richard II* the Queen complains that she feels a nameless dread, a disturbing 'nothing' which at the same time is 'some thing'. Bushy, cheering her up, answers:

> Each substance of a grief hath twenty shadows,
> Which shows like grief itself, but is not so;

[1] Bacon, *New Atlantis*, edited by G. C. Moore Smith (Cambridge University Press, Cambridge, 1900), p. 41.

[2] Reginald Scot, *The Discoverie of Witchcraft* (London, 1584), p. 315.

[3] E. H. Gombrich, *Art and Illusion* (Phaidon Press, London, 1960), p. 252 reproduces an anonymous sixteenth-century portrait of Edward VI showing both the distorted and the standard images.

For sorrow's eye, glazed with blinding tears
Divides one thing entire to many objects,
Like perspectives which, rightly gaz'd upon,
Show nothing but confusion—ey'd awry,
Distinguish form.

Sorrow's eye is therefore 'false'. The mind which flashes from
paradoxical conceits in nature to paradoxical conditions in
human feeling, and back again, is largely what we find in
Elizabethan and Jacobean poetry. What distinguishes one
poet from another in this respect is the tone in which the
transitions are made. The most conceited moments in that
poetry are like gargoyles and depend upon the kind of imagination by which gargoyles are made. The chief characteristic
of metaphysical poetry is the speed with which transitions are
made. This is part of Swift's inheritance. Many of his choice
ironic effects are achieved not by repudiating the metaphysical
transitions but by retarding them, holding them back to his
own speed so that they are compelled to obey him. The metaphysical conceit depends upon the speed with which it is
delivered and the élan which jumps the absurdity. Swift points
up the absurdity by giving the transition in slow motion.
Slowed down, the procedure allows him to set one perspective
against another. This is one of the typical patterns of his
imagination.

Rosalie Colie has argued that Swift used these paradoxes and
false perspectives to insist upon the relativity of our moral
judgments. 'His relativities plead as eloquently for other
relativities, those of common sense, or ordinary social life'.[1]
This goes a little too far. There were some values on which Swift
was not prepared to yield: as we have seen, he tended to
reduce everything else to these. There operates throughout
his work a Law of Parsimony comparable to Occam's; *Non*

---

[1] R. L. Colie, 'Some Paradoxes in the Language of Things, in J. A. Mazzeo
(editor), *Reason and the Imagination* (Columbia University Press, New York, 1962),
pp. 93–128. See also her *Paradoxia Epidemica* (Princeton University Press, Princeton, 1966).

est ponenda pluralitas sine necessitate. Enforcing the law, Swift insists upon his few fundamental terms, God, Nature, Commonsense, and defends them by discouraging everything else. The only hope of making a tolerable life, he thought, was by shifting people from the complacency of their rationalism. He must rebuke the Faustian pride which identifies Truth with the contents of one's own mind. A few things, verified by common sense, were, he hoped and prayed, immune to the vagaries of perspective. His chosen point of view was the point from which these few verities were constantly visible. Fixed there, he could exert the strongest pressure, by irony, parody, and the deployment of rival perspectives. Like the seventeenth-century metaphysical poets, he brings his conceits to the end of the line.

La Rochefoucauld says in one of the *Maxims* that some things should be seen closely and others at a distance; a maxim verified in Poe's story, *The Sphinx*, where a monster in the distance turns out to be an insect seen very close. Swift took his master's common sense literally. Vico says in the *New Science* that 'when men are ignorant of the natural causes producing things, and cannot even explain them by analogy with similar things, they attribute their own nature to them. The vulgar, for example, say the magnet loves the iron.'[1] Recently, E. H. Gombrich echoed this remark in discussing the embarrassments of perspective. 'In our perceptions', he said, 'we are completely self-centred, and for good reason: we constantly scan the world for things which may concern us directly; we will assume that an eye looks at us, or a gun points at us, unless we have good evidence to the contrary.'[2] Hopkins writes in his *Notebooks*: 'What you look hard at seems to look hard at you.' Bringing our several idioms together, I would offer this gloss. Benevolists like Shaftesbury and

[1] Vico, *The New Science*, translated from the 1744 edition by T. S. Bergin and M. H. Fisch (Cornell University Press, Ithaca, 1948), p. 63.
[2] Gombrich, *Art and Illusion*, p. 276.

Hutcheson thought that man was naturally good and encouraged him to find this assumption endorsed by Nature. Swift thought that this assumption had the effect of turning life into a peepshow designed by a flattering impresario for sentimental gulls, each peeping lovingly at his own image. Swift's work is a circus with a difference. The best answer to a sentimental peepshow is a hundred rival peepshows in which the proffered visions are sufficiently recognisable to be compelling and at the same time, beyond that, a horror. The reader is driven from his own complacency by seeing himself among freaks. Without this pressure of perspective we are all like the tiny Emperor of Lilliput who looked into his own peepshow and reported the vision as follows:

...most Mighty Emperor of Lilliput, Delight and Terror of the Universe, whose Dominions extend five Thousand Blustrugs, (about twelve Miles in Circumference) to the Extremity of the Globe: Monarch of all Monarchs: Taller than the Sons of Men; whose Feet press down to the Center, and whose Head strikes against the Sun ... [1]

So the sin of Pride, a spiritual delusion, is treated as if it were a gross optical delusion, and the Emperor appears like Mr Magoo. This is in keeping with Swift's general procedure; to translate spiritual conditions into physical terms, a state of soul into a state of matter. At the beginning of the third Book of his *Ethics* Spinoza proposes to consider human passions as if they were lines, planes, and solids; a strategic simplification which permits a certain latitude. The problem is to compel the intangible, making it receive tangible terms. Satire is a secular Jeremiad, treating evil as a monstrous absurdity; Swift gets rid of sin and evil by treating them as excrement.

To shift from one perspective to another demands a certain mobility. In *The Gutenberg Galaxy* Marshall McLuhan argues that until late in the seventeenth century a 'point of view' in

[1] *Gulliver's Travels*, p. 43.

prose was impossible. A point of view implies that the mind is heavily committed to one sense, the sense of sight; as the perceiver confronts the available scene, his eyes hold it, keeping it at a distance. The prose which for centuries after the invention of printing remained oral in its character sponsored a certain heterogeneity of tone; the result is that Elizabethan prose is like an improvisation in jazz, a solo by Louis Armstrong, but Augustan prose is like a camera, fixing its object in a moment of arrest.[1] The composer John Cage has remarked that 'nothing needs to be connected to anything else since they are not separated irrevocably to begin with'.[2] Right or wrong, this prompts us to see that to Swift things always needed to be connected, since they showed every sign of flying apart. In perception, the only way to hold things together, short of an enabling Act of God, was to place yourself in front of them, staring hard. McLuhan argues that until Addison the available forms of prose prevented a writer from taking this position. The problem is: how could the perceiver be sure that he was not merely staring into the peepshow? Committed to the 'point of view', he seems to be trapped, like a seaside photographer. Of course the telescope is helpful, but it does not guarantee the disclosure of truth. In 'The Elephant in the Moon' Butler laughs at astronomers who are so keen to discover life on the moon that they mistake a mouse in their telescope for a lunar elephant. In *Hudibras* Sidrophel the Rosicrucian sees a boy's kite through the telescope and thinks it a comet.

McLuhan's problem is implicit in Molyneux's study of optics. To what extent is sensation determined, Molyneux asked, by the sense which receives it; by the sense of sight, for instance? Much of eighteenth-century epistemology is an attempt to answer this question. Earlier, Cudworth tried to

[1] H. M. McLuhan, *The Gutenberg Galaxy* (Routledge and Kegan Paul, London, 1962), p. 136.
[2] John Cage, *Silence* (Wesleyan University Press, Middletown, 1961), pp. 228–9.

dispose of the problem by accepting the limitations of sense while insisting upon the capacity of mind. In his *Treatise concerning Eternal and Immutable Morality* he compared the relation between sense and mind to that between a narrow perspective and the full truth. Sense is like a narrow telescope, giving only piecemeal and successive views; mind gives 'one comprehensive idea of the whole', which he identified with truth. There is no evidence that the question, as long as it could be presented in these terms, really disturbed Swift. As long as it could be contained as a matter for scholars, he was happy to leave it to Newton, Molyneux, Locke, and Berkeley. Locke's position was clear enough: he would favour better vision, if it could be achieved at a reasonable price, but he thought the price exorbitant. He writes in the *Essay*:

Nay, if that most instructive of our Senses, Seeing, were in any Man 1000 or 100,000 times more acute than it is now by the best Microscope, things several Millions of times less than the smallest Object of his Sight now, would then be visible to his naked Eyes ... But then he would be in a quite different World from other People: Nothing would appear the same to him, and others; the visible Ideas of every thing would be different.[1]

So God, the 'infinite wise Contriver', is again proved right, pragmatically right. This was a congenial result to Swift, who faced the problem in other terms; the degree to which moral and political judgments depend upon primary acts of perception. His answer to the problem of the 'point of view' was, as usual, prudential; a man could train himself to move with proper caution from one position of strength to another. Just as Swift slowed down the metaphysical rush so as to control the transitions, so he could place himself in position for as long as he wanted to hold that perspective and then, with due care, move to another 'post of observation'. This did not solve the difficulty of perception as such, the ambiguities and defects of that sense, but it made life tolerable. The move could be a

---

[1] Locke, *Works* (London, 1727), vol. I, p. 129. (II. xxiii. 12).

strategic advance, not a metaphysical leap. This is where his appeal to common sense comes in; to sanction the fixed point of view, where the issues were fundamental, and elsewhere to facilitate safe transitions.

There is clearly some relation between this prudence and the fixity of the printed word. Movable type is itself a perspective, an assertion in space. If words are given as conventional marks on a page, they can be locked in their positions; or, without loss, they can be moved from one position to another. This is the 'character' of print. McLuhan argues that the relation between print and a 'corresponding' mode of perception is that of cause to effect. The case is not proven; but it is hard to discount at least a lively correspondence between the modes of perception which attend upon print, the sense of sight as a method of dealing with experience, and (to be specific) the position of embattled possession and 'distance' which I would ascribe to Swift. It was essential to Swift's equilibrium to maintain a safe distance between subject and object. To many people the gap between subject and object is a terrifying abyss; to Swift it was the only hope of security. In his world, things are compatible while they remain fixed and separate. The problem, never satisfactorily resolved, is to reconcile 'Truth' with 'that which is seen'. The only recourse was to say: I believe some few things to be true, many things are probable but their truth is beyond man's reason, and everything else depends upon the eye of the beholder. When Gulliver is obtuse, the reason is that he is bogged in errors of perspective. The implication is that things which are true are given to us in that state and require from us only that minimum of intervention which constitutes the application of common sense.

This implies a certain wariness in Swift. Wylie Sypher has argued that 'the humanist concept of "nature" is really an assertion of a will to reconstruct man's environment from a certain angle of vision, which is, in effect, not only a technique— a style—but also a perception of how things "happen" and "appear".[1] But what we find in Swift is not a desire to re-construct man's environment, but rather a need to do so on a more restricted basis. The 'certain angle of vision' holds, by and large, since the movements I have posited are strategic changes subject to one's choice and control. If style is a percep-tion of the way things happen and appear, it is delivered with a prayer against delusion. The perceiver prays that what he sees as form is indeed form, not another anamorphosis. It might be argued that Pope wrote his Imitation of Horace's 'Nil Admirari' Epistle as a prayer of this kind. Among the senses, the eye is liable to be dazzled by surfaces and appearances; so it must be controlled by evidence from the inner eye, the philosophic eye which sees things truly. The only safeguards against the dazzle of appearance are this inner eye of faith and that *consensus gentium* which is at least a shadow of the divine perspective. Swift's procedure is to move from one perspective to another: whatever in human experience sur-vives the strain of several perspectives is likely to be true. It is a modest truth, of course, and it is available only in the cool of the evening.

The Renaissance artist treats the world as a 'realised' place for man's action, but Swift takes care to ensure that the place is not pretentiously grand or cluttered with furniture. His motto is: keep things small, clear a space, make the diagram simple. His favourite technique is to construct a distorted picture on the basis of a curiosity in perspective and then to exploit the absurdities of identity and difference. The dis-proportion between Gulliver and the Lilliputians, for instance, would be merely a curiosity, an anamorphosis, if the difference were total; but Swift, having forced Europe and Lilliput thus far apart, shows that the constant factor, the place where both worlds meet, is folly. The shock is the discovery that European vanity and Lilliputian vanity are identical. When Gulliver refuses to enslave the people of Blefuscu, a faction breaks out

[1] Sypher, *Four Stages of Renaissance Style*, p. 60.

against him at Court. Gulliver concludes, as if he were Jonathan Swift surveying the vanity of princely wishes and the tragedy of 1714: 'Of so little weight are the greatest Services to Princes, when put into the Balance with a Refusal to gratify their Passions.'[1] In Lagado the mathematicians are stupid and pretentious in exactly the same spirit as their European colleagues. Once the disproportion is established, any instance of proportion becomes comic. Swift ensures a comic effect merely by showing that something there is the same as something here. Describing the Lilliputian ladies, he remarks:

I shall say but little at present of their Learning, which for many Ages hath flourished in all its Branches among them: But their Manner of Writing is very peculiar; being neither from the Left to the Right, like the Europeans; nor from the Right to the Left, like the Arabians; nor from up to down, like the Chinese; nor from down to up, like the Cascagians; but aslant from one Corner of the Paper to the other, like Ladies in England.[2]

Normally the comedy comes from similarity; the satire, from difference. Gulliver thinks a breach of trust a light enough matter, but the Emperor of Lilliput thinks it monstrous. In Lilliput only men of good morals are appointed to public office; we order such things differently at home. In Brobdingnag Gulliver finds that the Maids of Honour have a foul smell; the men make the same complaint of Gulliver. In that country there is no respect for rank or merit; none in England, either. In the Flying Island women long for the metropolis, and when they go there cannot be persuaded to return; like women in England. As Gulliver says:

This may perhaps pass with the Reader rather for an European or English Story, than for one of a Country so remote. But he may please to consider, that the Caprices of Womankind are not limited by any Climate or Nation; and that they are much more uniform than can be easily imagined.[3]

Johnson thought Swift's style too heavily dependent upon facts, too little concerned with the thought between the facts. But he

[1] *Gulliver's Travels*, p. 54.   [2] *Ibid.* p. 57.   [3] *Ibid.* p. 166.

did not appreciate that Swift did his thinking, silently, passing from one fact to another. His characteristic thought issues not in a concept, but in the juxtaposition of facts which, thus deployed, require no gloss. This explains why his mind exhibits its peculiar strength in comparison, contrast, similarity, difference, the habit of making things significant by giving them crucial roles in dramas of conjunction. He deals with the requirement of significance by putting one fact where it must be seen in the light of another.

The theory is given, by implication, in the *Voyage to Brobding-nag*, when Gulliver says:

In this terrible Agitation of Mind I could not forbear thinking of Lilliput, whose Inhabitants Looked upon me as the greatest Prodigy that ever appeared in the World; where I was able to draw an Imperial Fleet in my Hand, and perform those other Actions which will be recorded for ever in the Chronicles of that Empire, while Posterity shall hardly believe them, although attested by Millions. I reflected what a Mortification it must prove to me to appear as inconsiderable in this Nation, as one single Lilliputian would be among us. But, this I conceived was to be the least of my Misfortunes: For, as human Creatures are observed to be more Savage and cruel in Proportion to their Bulk; what could I expect but to be a Morsel in the Mouth of the first among these enormous Barbarians who should happen to seize me? Undoubtedly Philosophers are in the Right when they tell us, that nothing is great or little otherwise than by Comparison. It might have pleased Fortune to let the Lilliputians find some Nation, where the people were as diminutive with respect to them as they were to me. And who knows but that even this prodigious Race of Mortals might be equally overmatched in some distant Part of the World, whereof we have yet no discovery?[1]

So the Brobdingnagians are to Gulliver in their country as Gulliver is to a weasel in England; he is lifted with the same caution. When the farmer's wife sees him, she screams, Gulliver says, 'as Women in England do at the Sight of a Toad or a Spider'. Contemporary speculation on the plurality of worlds

[1] *Ibid.* pp. 86–7.

71

was tedious to Swift as long as it persisted in its planetary way. But it gratified his mind to ponder the plurality of little worlds on earth, and the errors we commit in perspective.

In Gulliver's moral universe the first error is to treat the accident of a thing as if it were its essence. In Lilliput Gulliver quenches the fire in Her Majesty's palace by urinating upon it. Later, the Lilliputians plan to impeach him for doing so, treating the urine as essence and the quenching of the fire as accident. Another error is the failure to allow for relative considerations. When Gulliver is disgusted by the nurse's huge nipples, he says:

This made me reflect upon the fair Skins of our English Ladies, who appear so beautiful to us, only because they are of our own Size, and their Defects not to be seen but through a magnifying Glass, where we find by Experiment that the smoothest and whitest Skins look rough and coarse, and ill coloured.[1]

Forgetting this truth, the King's dwarf in Brobdingnag swaggers before Gulliver because Gulliver is smaller still. Gulliver himself, as he says, 'winked at my own Littleness, as People do at their own Faults': when he comes back to England, after Brobdingnag, he thinks he is in Lilliput. The King of Brobdingnag makes fun of 'human Grandeur', which 'could be mimicked by such diminutive Insects' as Gulliver. Another error is the assumption that the common notion of a scale of being, in which man is placed somewhere between animals and angels, has any absolute validity. When the Houyhnhnms first see Gulliver they think he is some kind of Yahoo. He thinks the Yahoos detestable creatures, inferior to himself in every respect. The Master Houyhnhnm thinks that Gulliver differs from the Yahoos only for the worse. After a while Gulliver begins to speak of Englishmen as Yahoos, but horribly human. In Houyhnhnmland the country is governed by the Houyhnhnms and the Yahoos are servants: in England, the reverse is the case. When Gulliver meets the Portuguese sailors he

[1] *Gulliver's Travels*, pp. 91-2.

thinks they are Yahoos and Captain Pedro de Mendez a slightly superior Yahoo, like Gulliver himself in Houyhnhnmland. Returned to England, he can tolerate only horses: he cannot bear the presence of his wife and children until, several months later, the effect wears off and truth becomes English again. Another error in perspective brings us back to the peepshow. When Gulliver's master in Houyhnhnmland is comparing the situation there with Gulliver's report of England, he offers an explanation of the 'gross Defects' from which England suffers. Gulliver reports:

He was the more confirmed in this Opinion because he observed, that as I agreed in every Feature of my Body with other Yahoos, except where it was to my real Disadvantage in point of Strength, Speed and Activity, the Shortness of my Claws, and some other Particulars where Nature had no Part; so, from the Representation I had given him of our Lives, our Manners, and our Actions, he found as near a Resemblance in the Disposition of our Minds. He said, the Yahoos were known to hate one another more than they did any different Species of Animals; and the Reason usually assigned, was, the Odiousness of their own Shapes, which all could see in the rest, but not in themselves.[1]

This is related to the last page of the *Travels*, where Gulliver says he could tolerate the European Yahoos if they would confine themselves to the vices natural to them, lies, obscenity, theft, and the rest; but, he says, 'When I behold a Lump of Deformity, and Diseases both in Body and Mind, smitten with Pride, it immediately breaks all the Measures of my Patience.'[2] It is also related, of course, to Swift's reflexion that general satire is useless because everyone applies it to his neighbour.

To be human is to err. To see is to misconstrue. We return to the question of the fixed point of view: since Berkeley there have been many attempts to evade its restrictions. I have mentioned one of Swift's stratagems; to move with proper caution from one achieved position to another, using the

[1] *Ibid.* p. 260.   [2] *Ibid.* p. 296.

occasion to recite a moral lesson on human pride. There are other possibilities. Yeats hoped to evade the trap of perception, the ambiguity of perceiver and the thing perceived, by invoking the analogy of drama. Hence his quest for images of unity, to transcend the dualism, as Attis's image hangs between 'that staring fury and the blind lush leaf'. There is a passage in *A Vision*, where he writes:

My instructors identify consciousness with conflict, not with knowledge, substitute for subject and object and their attendant logic a struggle towards harmony, towards Unity of Being. Logical and emotional conflict alike lead towards a reality which is concrete, sensuous, bodily.[1]

If you identify consciousness with conflict, you make struggle a 'good' word in a new idiom of action. Its highest form eliminates the dichotomy of subject and object in the concrete, sensuous, and bodily condition of drama. This is one reason why, in 'Lapis Lazuli' and other poems, Yeats's tragic hero laughs into the face of death. The idiom of action is one way out of the trap of knowledge. Another way, more devious, is to accept the situation of subject and object while endowing the subject with powers which transcend his predicament. The common name of these powers is Imagination: hence the remarkable promotion of this word at the end of the eighteenth century from the lowly position it held in early Augustan thought. In Romantic thought the imagination is creative because our need is great. If the imagination is not creative, man cannot evade the absurdity of his station. If the imagination is sufficiently inventive, the perceiver's little world becomes 'an everywhere'. Coleridge's poems and Wordsworth's *Prelude* are testaments to this hope; Blake's prophetic poems insist upon it. From Blake to Stevens the imagination is heard demanding that its powers shall be transcendent. When Stevens says, 'God and the imagination are one', he means, 'I demand that this be so.'

[1] W. B. Yeats, *A Vision* (Macmillan, London, 1962), p. 214.

74

Another way brings us back to Swift. Even if you do not claim for your imagination any divine powers, you may posit a mode of knowledge beyond the human range within which human experience may be tolerably understood. That is: you retain the idiom of knowledge, but you posit a mode of knowledge raised to the *n*th degree. More briefly; you say, if human perspectives are fallible, there is always God. If human perspectives are inevitably limited, God is what is not limited. If our confidence cannot range beyond Nature and common sense, perhaps these are glimmers, fragments of the divine light. Some fragments are larger and brighter than others. The distinction between Reason and Religion in the opening lines of Dryden's *Religio Laici* is a difference of perspective: Reason is to Religion as 'the borrow'd beams of Moon and Stars' to 'Day's bright Lord'. This is what a believer believes; as in *Four Quartets* Eliot appends an epigraph from Heraclitus which reads: 'Although the Word (Logos) is common to all, most men live as if each of them had a private intelligence of his own.' Eliot's rhetoric of discipline, thought, and prayer acknowledges a divine truth, the Logos, toward which the only appropriate stance is humility: 'Humility is endless.' A trial version of this divine perspective is the figure of Tiresias in *The Waste Land*, as Eliot's footnote to the poem makes clear:

Tiresias, although a mere spectator and not indeed a 'character', is yet the most important personage in the poem, uniting all the rest. Just as the one-eyed merchant, seller of currants, melts into the Phoenician Sailor, and the latter is not wholly distinct from Ferdinand Prince of Naples, so all the women are one woman, and the two sexes meet in Tiresias. What Tiresias sees, in fact, is the substance of the poem.[1]

Indeed, many of the difficulties of *The Waste Land* are eased if we take the footnote seriously and think of Tiresias not as a

[1] T. S. Eliot, *Collected Poems, 1909–1935* (Faber and Faber, London, 1958), p. 80.

man or a woman but as an artificial consciousness, an adumbration of divine knowledge which, knowing all, has fore-suffered all; the Truth, we find ourselves saying, of which human knowledge is a shadow or, more frequently, a false face. Eliot's method on this occasion is remarkably like Swift's, the application of pressure by which one perspective dislodges another. In his *Lectures on the English Poets* Hazlitt said that Swift took a new view of human nature, 'such as a being of a higher sphere might take of it'. Perspectivism is another name for this view. The reader is moving to a safe place when he has given up all pretensions to his own private truth. In Rilke's *Elegies*, to cite another version, the role of Tiresias is played by the angel, to whom Rilke ascribes 'infinite consciousness'. He writes to his Polish translator:

The angel of the *Elegies* is that creature in whom the transformation of the visible into the invisible, which we are accomplishing, appears already consummated. For the angel of the *Elegies* all past towers and palaces are existent, *because* long invisible, and the still standing towers and bridges of our existence *already* invisible, although (for us) still persisting physically... All the worlds of the universe are plunging into the invisible as into their next deepest reality; a few stars immediately intensify and pass away in the infinite consciousness of the angels... others are dependent upon beings who slowly and laboriously transform them, in whose terrors and ecstasies they attain their next invisible realization.[1]

For Rilke, these 'transformers of the earth' are the poets themselves, mediators between man and the angels of infinite consciousness. What these several texts have in common is the idea of an absolute perspective within which all the fallible human perspectives are held in suspense. The idea is perhaps definitely given in three fragments of Heraclitus which come together in the section on paradox and relativity:

104: The handsomest ape is ugly compared with humankind; the wisest man appears as an ape when compared with a god—in wisdom, in beauty, and in all other ways.

[1] R. M. Rilke, *Letters*, translated by Jane Bannard Greene and M. D. Herter Norton (Norton, New York, 1945–48), vol. II, p. 376.

105: A man is regarded as childish by a spirit, just as a boy is by a man.

106: To God all things are beautiful, good, and right; men, on the other hand, deem some things right and others wrong.

This last fragment sounds odd, but a recent editor, Philip Wheelwright, explains that the reference is not 'to just any supernatural power, as in fragments 104 and 105, but to the perspective that is universal and all-comprehensive'.[1] But if this example is forbidding in its starkness, we may recall a more urbane version in Ortega's *Meditations on Quixote*, the chapter called 'The Forest'. The forest is distinct from the trees. The forest is depth, 'and depth is fatally condemned to become a surface if it wants to be visible'. The forest is invisible, composed of the trees we do not see; it is the realm of depth and possibility, invisible nature, always 'a little beyond where we are'.[2] The trees we see are where we are, the forest is always beyond, 'hidden and aloof'. This invisibility 'transforms the thing it hides'. Ortega's terms are similar to Rilke's, though his tone is different. Rilke does not say, as Ortega does, that 'God is perspective and hierarchy; Satan's sin was an error of perspective'; nor does Rilke write a chapter on the Doctrine of the Point of View or call his philosophy 'perspectivism', as Ortega does in *The Modern Theme*. Indeed, in that book Ortega elaborates the idea that whereas each of us has a perspective, a point of view, and perhaps the poets encompass more than one, God 'enjoys the use of every point of view, resuming and harmonising in his own unlimited vitality all our horizons'.[3] Of course this is a perennial motif, as Pope in the second Epistle of the *Essay on Man* says:

> 'Tis but by parts we follow good or ill,
> For, Vice or Virtue, Self directs it still;

[1] Philip Wheelwright, *Heraclitus* (Atheneum Press, New York, 1964), p. 151.

[2] Ortega y Gasset, *Meditations on Quixote*, translated by Evelyn Rugg and Diego Marin (Norton, New York, 1961), p. 61.

[3] Ortega y Gasset, *The Modern Theme*, translated by James Cleugh (Harper, New York, 1961), p. 95.

Each individual seeks a sev'ral goal;
But Heav'n's great view is One, and that the Whole:

It is for this reason, incidentally, that dramatic irony makes a choice appeal: as long as it lasts, we have the advantage of two perspectives, our own and the narrower perspective projected on the stage. As long as it lasts, we are little gods. Swift gains the same effect when he wilfully blocks off one perspective, normally the obvious and natural one, so as to confine his victim to obliquity. The modern science of symbolism, we are told, tries 'to utilize all past frames of thought, regardless of their apparent divergencies from us'.[1]

To bring these speculations toward the conventions of fiction and the traditions available to Swift: Leo Spitzer has shown, in a study of *Don Quixote*, that Cervantes tends 'to stand above, and sometimes aloof from, the misconceptions of his characters'. The *Quixote* applies the strongest pressure to literature itself, the world of words, where words are shown to be the sources of hesitation, 'error, deception—dreams'.[2] Cervantes postulates the realm of God, the Absolute, in the terms enunciated by Spanish Catholicism: God is what is beyond the human perspective. It is within these terms and subject to this limitation that Cervantes enjoys his powers, 'a freedom beneath the dome of that religion which affirms the freedom of the will'. We think of it somewhat along these lines. The sky of all things is God, the Absolute, the Logos, at once Truth and its speaker. Beneath this there is the artist, the imagination, Cervantes, a demigod in his own realm but loyal to God. Beneath this, in turn, there is the little world of his creation, the world of imaginative forms and gestures to which he gives his name. Beneath that still, there are all the remaining worlds, created by the characters of the novel. These remaining worlds are sometimes 'true', often not true at all but fictions,

---

[1] Kenneth Burke, *Permanence and Change* (Hermes, Los Altos, 1954), p. 118.
[2] Leo Spitzer, *Linguistics and Literary History* (Princeton University Press, Princeton, 1948), pp. 41 ff.

sometimes dreams, illusions. It is precisely because Cervantes
sees all the worlds in relation to 'the dome' that he enjoys such
freedom. He plays 'as if' he were God, but he does not think
he is God. To think of Swift in this tradition is to appreciate
that he does not enjoy this Spanish freedom. He lives, rather,
by precaution and stratagem. To him, the pressure of perspective is a choice in despair. At the top there is, indeed, God,
the God enunciated by the Anglican religion and sustained by
Tory politics. This God is related to man as a universal concept
is related to its partial embodiment. Beneath this Supreme
Fiction there is the writer, Swift; but it would not be true to say
Swift viewed everything in relation to 'the dome'. There is a
chasm which separates the two realms. The most that can be
said, in this setting, is that he did what he could, given his
terms of reference. There was no rich freedom to be enjoyed.
Swift made up for constraint by training himself to live with it;
as he would deal with misery by reducing his desires. But the
world of his creation, even in *Gulliver's Travels* and the *Tale of
a Tub*, has little of Cervantes's freedom and abundance. The
figures which inhabit that world have as much life as their
creator gives them, enough life for his purposes; but this life
is a mode of constraint, because it is forced to serve the
occasions of argument and critique. Santayana speaks of
Dickens's 'vast sympathetic participation in the daily life of
mankind', and at once we sense again Swift's constraint.
Henry James said of Flaubert that 'his case was a doom because
he felt of his vocation almost nothing but the difficulty'. This
comes close to Swift, who felt of his vocation almost nothing
but the constraint. Nothing human was alien to Cervantes, free
beneath the dome. To Swift, many human things were alien.
Indeed, Swift concerned himself with man only in his social,
moral, and political aspects. Man in his other moments,
religious, metaphysical, speculative, Swift thought better
left alone. So we think of Swift as an administrator who con-
fined himself to what immediately concerned him and

admonished man to do the same. The administrative rationale was the pressure of perspective; where an imperious order took the place of freedom. The aim was a reasonable, tolerable order, founded on the few things a true-born Englishman ought to believe. Everything else would have to be buried somewhere, deep in the dreadful unconscious, if it could not be contained by Swift's common terms.

The result is that Swift can deal with his subject only from an embattled point of vantage. He clings to surface, suspicious of depth. He makes no journey into the interior, for he is terrified of that unknown place. He does not wish to secrete himself within the object or the experience: it is safer to stand, as a surveyor, in front of them. Merleau-Ponty says of vision that it is a dissecting sense, it delights in anatomy and fraction. Swift's vision is consoled by the presence of a demanding object, an object which cannot be denied as long as common sense is acknowledged. The object of vision is an obstacle, valued because it 'proves' that there is something solid between the self and the void. I have remarked that Swift's characters are not 'profound'; because the word implies not only the risk of depth but the will to risk that depth. Racine's heroes and heroines are profound, it may be said, because behind the surface of their actions there are shadows and, behind these shadows, more shadows, until what remains is everything or nothing. Jean Starobinski has remarked that when Racine's characters confront each other, look at each other, the visions are so incriminating that we have to speak of 'un *contact* par le regard'. 'Dès lors, la distance qui sépare les personnages rend possible, en contrepartie, l'exercice d'une cruauté qui se fait tout regard et qui atteint les âmes à travers leurs reflets dans les yeux de l'amour ou de la haine. Car il y a—malgré la distance et aussi grâce à elle—un *contact* par le regard'.[1] There is nothing of this incrimination in Swift's visionary world; vision has done everything it is allowed to do when it

[1] Jean Starobinski, *L'Oeil vivant* (Gallimard, Paris, 1961), p. 75.

has asserted the separation of one thing from another. Rilke's poem 'Wendung' is a meditation on the quality of vision; here, sight is loving attention to the world, so that the objects of sight 'come' to the seer. The poem says that this is not enough; the work of the eye must be fulfilled in the work of the heart, completed in love. This is vision in one idiom, but it is alien to Swift. He does not look at the world the better to love it; rather, the more imperiously to vex it. In Rilke's poem vision leads to love, and love to further possibilities of feeling; as by committing ourselves to one idiom, going beyond our contract, we transcend its limitations. But the character of Swift's language is to limit the reception of meaning; not to mean as much as possible but to mean one thing at a time and that decisively.

Terrified of depth, he cannot presume upon the dome. What remains is a constricted world, 'the common forms', Monday followed by Tuesday, often what Stevens, translating Laforgue, called 'the malady of the quotidian'. What is remarkable in Swift is the intensity of feeling developed from constriction; as if he felt with greatest intensity when he had elected not to feel at all. He is the classic example of a man who chooses the values by which he will live, knowing they are likely to fail; knowing at the same time that no other values are, to him, relevant. The effort to live is, for such men, a constant battle, defensive in the first instance and aggressive thereafter. Victory is impossible, the times being what they are; but one tries to defend the fort and to rout the enemy. What Swift achieved in these conditions is remarkable, nothing less than an Anatomy of the World.

We see something of his powers in the *Argument to Prove that the Abolishing of Christianity in England may be Attended with Some Inconveniences*. It is a masterpiece of irony. Instead of persuading his readers to take their religion more seriously, Swift pretends to assume that real Christianity is outmoded and that the next question is the abolition of nominal Christianity. So he silences

the Freethinkers by ostensibly conceding victory. This is the
ironic pattern of the essay: when he confronts a common
irreligious argument, he concedes the victory and asks, 'why
then do we need to change anything?' A paraphrase would
run something like this. It is argued that it is a waste of time
to observe the Sabbath. But no one observes the Sabbath.
Why propose a change? It is argued that the mischief of
justice, piety, patriotism and the like must be blamed upon our
education. But this cannot be the case, for we have already
degraded our education so that it produces nothing but evil.
Why, then, is there any need to alter its principles by abolishing
the Christianity on which it is based? It is argued that Christianity was invented by politicians to keep the mob in check.
Not so; for the vulgar no longer believe in Christianity, they
recite its dogmas for fun. It is argued that ministers should not
be employed to preach against sin. But sinners love their sins
and are delighted to hear that they are sinners. So why should
we talk of change? Indeed, it would be excellent if we could
discover a few new sins, because sinners are becoming bored
with their current stock. So the ironic pattern is unfolded.
If we glance at a straightforward defence of Christianity which
does not use the resources of perspective, we see more vividly
how Swift wins the game by changing the Book of Rules in
his own favour. Archbishop King's *Discourse concerning the
Inventions of Men in the Worship of God* is an attack upon the
Dissenters, based upon *Mark* vii. 7: 'In vain do they Worship
me, teaching for Doctrines the Commandments of Men.'
King's argument is congenial to Swift: it sets out what the
Scriptures prescribe concerning prayer, communion, praise,
and so forth. Then it compares the procedures of the Anglican
Church in each respect. Finally, it describes the procedures of
the Dissenters. The conclusion, in each case, is that the Dissen-
ters are fonder of their own inventions than of God's commandments. 'And there is an obvious natural reason for it, since what
Man invents must needs have a nearer agreement to the

Carnal and Corrupt Inclinations of our depraved Nature, than what God prescribes: which is the very Reason that induces Men to change the Institutions of God, and substitute their own Inventions instead of them.'[1] The case is virtually identical with Swift's *Argument*. But King's difficulty is that he is confronting the Dissenters on their own ground: his only resources are those of logic and conviction. Swift's approach is much more devious:

For the rest, it may perhaps admit a Controversy, whether the Banishing all Notions of Religion whatsoever, would be convenient for the Vulgar. Not that I am in the least of Opinion with those, who hold Religion to have been the Invention of Politicians, to keep the lower Part of the World in Awe, by the Fear of invisible Powers; unless Mankind were then very different from what it is now; For I look upon the Mass, or Body of our People here in England, to be as Free-Thinkers, that is to say, as staunch Unbelievers, as any of the highest Rank. But I conceive some scattered Notions about a superior Power to be of singular Use for the common People, as furnishing excellent Materials to keep Children quiet, when they grow peevish; and providing Topicks of Amusement in a tedious Winter Night.[2]

This is like a debate conducted on the principle that only irrelevant arguments may be entertained. The result is an anamorphosis, a conceit. Swift will not discuss the truth of religion; only its convenience for purposes other than those for which it was declared. Opinions are received by turning every common notion of relevance upside-down. Swift touches his opponents only when he equates Freethinkers with staunch unbelievers, as if they were 'upright in standing for nothing'. Again, the faithlessness of those in 'the highest Rank' is not matter for dispute. Not only is it taken for granted; it is deemed to be the standard of comparison, an absolute. Throughout the passage Swift applies pressure only where it is ostensibly

[1] King, *A Discourse concerning the Inventions of Men in the Worship of God* (London, 1694), p. 190.
[2] *Bickerstaff Papers*, edited by Herbert Davis (Basil Blackwell, Oxford, 1957), p. 34.

redundant; on the official body of the dispute he applies no pressure at all. The method is to win by refusing to fight. The implication is that everything must be scaled down to meet his enemies on their own trivial level; like an adult talking to a peevish child. Swift reduces the argument until he meets his enemies in the possession of 'scattered notions'. The main pressure of perspective is designed to make fun of the opponent by using his terms. It is like the argument that Sunday is a waste of one day in seven. Swift answers:

Are not the Taverns and Coffee-Houses open? Can there be a more convenient Season for taking a Dose of Physick? Are fewer Claps got upon Sundays than other days? Is not that the chief Day for Traders to sum up the Accounts of the Week; and for Lawyers to prepare their Briefs? But I would fain know how it can be pretended, that the Churches are misapplied. Where are more Appointments and Rendezvouzes of Gallantry? Where more Care to appear in the foremost Box with greater Advantage of Dress? Where more Meetings for Business? Where more Bargains driven of all Sorts? And where so many Conveniences, or Incitements to sleep?[1]

Swift is defending religion by enforcing a secular 'point of view', held until the blow hits target. He shows the world what happens when it is taken at its own word. If churches are used like theatres, do not protest; use the theatrical idiom and show how well it fits. God's servant then moves to another vantage point and shoots again. Ortega says in *The Modern Theme* that the provincial man is defined by the possession of a single perspective which he mistakes for the whole divine truth. Swift is writing as a Christian, a minister, a servant of God; so he possesses, with whatever degree of limitation or constraint, the perspectives of his Church, his City of God, and he looks upon the provincialism of his enemies with that metropolitan advantage. The speaker, as a nominal Christian, is provincial; his ostensible opponents are provincial only in greater degree. Difference of degree; similarity of kind. The

---

[1] *Bickerstaff Papers*, p. 31.

irony is to show that there is no discrepancy between the two idioms.

I am arguing that these are the terms in which Swift's work may be understood: perspective, pressure, irony, discontinuity, parody, comparison, contrast; one thing, and then (obliquely) another. In the polemical writings he saw himself larger than his enemies. In failure, he was Gulliver among the Brobdingnagians. But even in defeat he committed himself to the same terms. In December 1736 he wrote to Lord Castle-Durrow:

Your last Letter hath layn by me about a fortnight unacknowledged, partly by the want of health and lowness of Spirits, but chiefly by want of Time, not taken up in busyness, but lost in the Teazings of insignificant people who worry me with Trifles. I often reflect on my present life as the exact Burlesque of my middle age, which passed among Ministers, in those days that you and your Party since call *the worst of Times*. I am now acting the same things in Miniature, but in a higher Station, as a first Minister, nay sometimes as a Prince; in which last quality, My House-Keeper, a grave elderly woman, is called at home and in the Neighborhood Sr. Robert. My Butler is Secretary, and has no other defect for that office but that he can not write yet that is not singular; for I have known three Secretaryes of State upon the same level, and who were too old to mend, which mine is not. My Realm extends to 120 Houses, whose Inhabitants constitute the Bulk of my Subjects; my Grand Jury is my House of Commons, and my Chapter the House of Lords: I must proceed no further because my Arts of Governing are Secrets of State.[1]

Here Swift is bringing to bear upon himself, at last, the pressure of perspective. Playing with small things by giving them large names, he gains a certain distance, a measure of disinterestedness, otherwise impossible. The saving genre is burlesque, an old favourite, in which we deal with high things by taking them in low terms. The effect is to bring everything, great and small, into a middle ground, before death the only safe place.

---

[1] *Correspondence*, edited by Harold Williams (Clarendon Press, Oxford, 1965), vol. IV, p. 555.

CHAPTER 3

BODY, SOUL, SPIRIT

When Gulliver reaches Balnibarbi he is graciously received by
Lord Munodi, one of the great exemplars of alienation in a
continent given over entirely to music, mathematics and
abstract thought. Munodi complains that 'about Forty Years
ago, certain Persons went up to Laputa, either upon Business
or Diverson; and after five months Continuance, came back
with a very little Smattering in Mathematics, but full of
Volatile Spirits acquired in that Airy Region'.[1] As a result, he
says, these people determined to change the state of things in
Lagado, beginning by setting up an Academy of Projectors.
When Gulliver visits the Academy he finds there strange
methods of scholarship: in the School of Mathematics, the
Master teaches his Pupils, Gulliver observes, 'after a Method
scarce imaginable to us in Europe'. 'The Proposition and
Demonstration were fairly written on a thin Wafer, with Ink
composed of a Cephalick Tincture. This the Student was to
swallow upon a fasting Stomach, and for three Days following
eat nothing but Bread and Water. As the Wafer digested, the
Tincture mounted to his Brain, bearing the Proposition along
with it.'[2] But the prescription generally failed, Gulliver finds,
because the 'bolus' was vomited before it could work, and in
any event the pupils could not be persuaded to abstain from
food for the required period. This is one of Swift's favourite
sequences: men commit themselves to some perverse scheme
and are protected from their vanity by the stubborn common
sense of their bodies. Trust the body; never trust the spirit. I
shall argue that much of Swift's energy is directed against the

---

[1] *Gulliver's Travels*, p. 176.   [2] *Ibid.* p. 186.

86

pretence of spirit which is endemic in the Western tradition.

We often say that Swift loathed the body. Aldous Huxley argues that 'Swift could not forgive men and women for being vertebrate mammals as well as immortal souls'.[1] But in fact Swift found this offence a venial sin. What he loathed was man's arrogance in denying the primacy of the body. The tradition which he attacked with greatest persistence was that which affected to despise the body and to find value only in extremities of spirit. G. R. S. Mead has observed that the idea of man's body as 'the exteriorization of an invisible subtle embodiment of the life of the mind' is a very ancient belief.[2] It is found in the Cabbalistic texts and in neo-Platonic writings; through Platonic sources it makes its way into many of the Christian Fathers. The basic feeling is that, as Plato says in the *Phaedrus*, we are imprisoned in the body like an oyster in its shell. This assumes that we are identified with something more subtle than our bodies, and that, however we describe this essence, it certifies and defines us. Therefore value resides in an invisible realm of essences or forms, the Realm of Spirit, as Santayana calls it. Body, like matter itself or the sensory object, is at best a poor relation, and normally—in Yeats's phrase—a dying animal. In Christian belief the body is justified and ennobled by the Incarnation: the Word, which may be thought of in one sense as soul, is made Flesh in the body of Christ, the meeting of the timeless with time. But the promise of the Resurrection of the Body is ambiguous, and early Church Fathers wrestled over its meaning; Tertullian arguing for the resurrection of the body in its full material sense, Origen interpreting the promise in more rarefied and symbolic terms. The neo-Platonic ghost continued to haunt the imagination. In the early eighteenth century the ghost was often engaged in arguments about the nature of men and animals. If the

[1] Aldous Huxley, *Do What You Will* (Chatto and Windus, London, 1949), p. 100.

[2] G. R. S. Mead, *The Doctrine of the Subtle Body in Western Tradition* (Watkins, London, 1919), p. 1 and *passim*.

chief difference was the power of speech, this was a sufficient glory to some, but to others it was not enough to cancel man's inordinate vanity. Swift was not the first to suggest that in most respects the comparison between men and animals was an insult at least to higher animals, like horses. No writer harried man's spiritual pretensions with greater persistence or more critical intent.

The Mechanical Operation of the Spirit can be approached from many directions. Basically, it is a parody of any neo-Platonic writing that is pretentious and volatile, up in the air, like the Flying Island. More narrowly it parodies books like Ralph Cudworth's *The True Intellectual System of the Universe* (1678), in which the tone is, by Swift's measure, offensively high. The parody also challenges the tradition of Christian Platonism, especially that part of the tradition which offers the contemplative man as its highest image, Milton's Platonist scholar in his lonely tower. As Swift says near the end of the fragment: 'Too intense a Contemplation is not the Business of Flesh and Blood; it must by the necessary Course of Things, in a little Time, let go its hold, and fall into Matter.'[1] The *Mechanical Operation* is also an attack upon the saturnine aspirations of man; on all those claims by which man is identified with Saturn in his contemplative image. Swift's god is Jupiter, who is concerned with man in society; the argument is just as pointed as in Yeats when, in one of the 'Conjunctions', Yeats says:

> If Jupiter and Saturn meet,
> What a crop of mummy wheat![2]

In the *Mechanical Operation* the saturnine assumptions of men are rebuked by Jupiter's social light; value resides in time and place, in the social world, if it resides anywhere.

To keep the symmetry exact one would expect Swift to carry his parody of Christian Platonism into the texture of his

---

[1] *A Tale of a Tub*, edited by A. C. Guthkelch and David Nichol Smith (Clarendon Press, Oxford, 1920), p. 291.

[2] W. B. Yeats, *Collected Poems* (Macmillan, London, 1952), p. 333.

essay. But he needed an even more obvious target since he proposed to make fun of all the pretensions of Enthusiasm, in religion, scholarship, and philosophy. He wanted to show that these and other forms of arrogance are artificial procedures designed to work up a vast head of spiritual steam. So he chose as the formal diagram of his parody the rhetorical manual, the handbook of ways and means to reach the heights of eloquence. *Longinus on the Sublime* stands for many insidious aids to rapture; their final object is to achieve the Sublime, Enthusiasm, or Inspiration. The basis of Swift's attack is simple. The object of the rhetorical manual is to achieve the height of eloquence. The ostensible aim of all such artifices in religion is to scale the heights of spirit. But their real aim, Swift implies, is to achieve an orgasm.

The parody of the rhetorical manual is unmistakable.

Now, the Art of Canting consists in skilfully adapting the Voice, to whatever Words the Spirit delivers, that each may strike the Ears of the Audience, with its most significant Cadence. The Force, or Energy of this Eloquence, is not to be found, as among antient Orators, in the Disposition of Words to a Sentence, or the turning of long Periods; but agreeable to the Modern Refinements in Musick, is taken up wholly in dwelling, and dilating upon Syllables and Letters. Thus it is frequent for a single Vowel to draw Sighs from a Multitude; and for a whole Assembly of Saints to sob to the Musick of one solitary Liquid.[1]

So he shows what can be done with the letter *s* if you put half your mind to it. Swift goes on to deal with the traditional divisions of rhetoric, but always with an eye to their obscene variants. Among Platonic lovers, canting is related to whining and sighing and groaning; the corresponding gesture is called ogling; the style consists of 'insignificant Words, Incoherences and Repetition'. These are the Rules of Address to a mistress and they are performed with even greater dexterity by the Saints. 'Nay,' says Swift, 'to bring this Argument yet closer, I

---

[1] *A Tale of a Tub*, p. 281.

have been informed by certain Sanguine Brethren of the first Class, that in the Height and Orgasmus of their Spiritual exercise it has been frequent with them *******; immediately after which, they found the Spirit to relax and flag of a sudden with the Nerves, and they were forced to hasten to a Conclusion'.[1] Those who pretend to the heights of spirit have a set of allegiances which are at once elaborate and superficial. They always prefer the inside of things to the outside, because the inside is beyond the reach of the senses and its apprehension is proof of their superiority. Swift picked up this theme from Butler, and it became one of his own standard figures. There is a brilliant passage in the *Mechanical Operation* where he makes fun of the Enthusiasts for the incongruity between their outward form and their inward spirit. Then he says:

Upon these, and the like Reasons, certain Objectors pretend to put it beyond all Doubt, that there must be a sort of preternatural Spirit, possessing the Heads of the Modern Saints; And some will have it to be the Heat of Zeal, working upon the Dregs of Ignorance, as other Spirits are produced from Lees, by the Force of Fire. Some again think, that when our earthly Tabernacles are disordered and desolate, shaken and out of Repair; the Spirit delights to dwell within them, as Houses are said to be haunted, when they are forsaken and gone to Decay.[2]

There are endless possibilities of parody, given that 'spirit' can be construed to mean ghost, vapour, soul, breath, air, wind, distilled liquor, and many fugitive things. When Swift construes spirit as ghost, for instance, the body is inevitably a derelict house and the subversion is achieved.

Another kind of reduction is to take literally what is offered metaphorically. Swift implies that metaphor is a metalanguage used by those who claim that their thoughts are too profound for literal expression. His answer is to take the metaphors as if he were ignorant of their special nature. In *A Tale of a Tub* he laughs at Roman Catholicism by taking literally what its

[1] *A Tale of a Tub*, p. 290.   [2] *Ibid.* p. 285.

doctrines say 'substantially'; the doctrine of Transubstantiation is ridiculed when Peter serves up brown loaf as if it were mutton. When Gulliver gives his master in Houyhnhnmland an account of the chief causes of war, he refers to religious faction: 'Difference in Opinions hath cost many Millions of Lives: For instance, whether Flesh be Bread, or Bread be Flesh: Whether the Juice of a certain Berry be Blood or Wine.'[1] The same attack is renewed in the sermon *On the Trinity*.[2] The implication is that a literal language is good enough for any purposes sanctioned by common sense, and that purposes which aspire beyond that limit are suspect. In the *Tale* he makes fun of metaphor by showing that it is arbitrary and unlimited. He is speaking of wisdom:

Wisdom is a Fox, who after long hunting, will at last cost you the Pains to dig out: 'Tis a Cheese, which by how much the richer, has the thicker, the homelier, and the courser Coat; and whereof to a judicious Palate, the Maggots are the best. 'Tis a Sack-Posset, wherein the deeper you go, you will find it the sweeter. Wisdom is a Hen, whose Cackling we must value and consider, because it is attended with an Egg; But then, lastly, 'tis a Nut, which unless you chuse with Judgement, may cost you a Tooth, and pay you with nothing but a Worm.[3]

Or again, he begins a sentence as if he were using the crucial word metaphorically, only to mock this impression: 'To this End', he says in the *Tale*, 'I have some Time since, with a World of Pains and Art, dissected the Carcass of Humane Nature, and read many useful Lectures upon the several Parts, both Containing and Contained; till at last it smelt so strong, I could preserve it no longer'.[4] In the *Meditation upon a Broomstick* he sends the absurdity the other way; the broomstick ends by being 'worn to the Stumps in the Service of the Maids' and then either thrown away or used to make a fire. In the mock-analogy with man, Swift plays with the sexual meanings of

---

[1] *Gulliver's Travels*, p. 246.   [2] *Irish Tracts, 1720–1723, and Sermons*, edited by Herbert Davis (Basil Blackwell, Oxford, 1963), p. 163.
[3] *A Tale of a Tub*, p. 66.   [4] *Ibid.* p. 123.

flame and stump: 'His last Days are spent in Slavery to Women, and generally the least deserving; till worn to the Stumps, like his Brother Bezom, he is either kicked out of Doors, or made use of to kindle Flames for others to warm themselves by.'[1]

But Swift attacked directly the question of Body and Spirit. In the sermon *On the Trinity* he spoke of Soul and Body: 'The Manner whereby the Soul and Body are united, and how they are distinguished, is wholly unaccountable to us. We see but one Part, and yet we know we consist of two; and this is a Mystery we cannot comprehend, any more than that of the Trinity'.[2] He was prepared to concede such mysteries because his faith obliged him to do so; they were his last line of defence. But he was not inclined to go beyond the evidence of his senses very often or very willingly. Mead says that for some centuries in the Western Tradition 'the soul was believed to be air, and air breath, and breath spirit, and spirit and soul one— just simply air'. But for many of these writers spirit means 'subtle body, an embodiment of a finer order of matter than that known to physical sense'. Spirit came to be distinguished from soul; soul was thought of as 'utterly incorporeal'; spirit, not.[3] In the seventeenth century the Mortalist heresy was one of the most tendentious questions. It was easy enough to say, following Aristotle's *De Anima*, that the soul is the form of the body, since form cannot exist without its accordant material and yet form is not itself material. But if the soul is merely the form of the body, it must die with the body; so how can it be immortal? The question was often answered by declaring that the soul is essentially a spirit, a separate and independent substance; so it did not die with the body. Bacon distinguished between the animal soul, which he was ready to call 'spirit', common to man and animals; and the immortal soul, infused into man alone by God's favour. But this ran against the

[1] *A Tale of a Tub, with Other Early Works 1696–1707*, edited by Herbert Davis (Basil Blackwell, Oxford, 1957), p. 240.
[2] *Irish Tracts, 1720–1723, and Sermons*, p. 164.
[3] Mead, *The Doctrine of the Subtle Body...*, pp. 46 ff.

argument of Augustine and Aquinas that soul is unitary; there is only one soul. Hobbes wanted to repudiate the notion of incorporeal spirit; in *Of Human Nature* he wrote that spirit was 'a *body natural*, but of such subtility that it worketh not upon the senses'. Immaterial spirit seemed a contradiction in terms, for a spirit is a substance, and all substances have dimensions and corporeality. Of the soul, he wrote in *Leviathan* that 'the *Soule* in Scripture, signifieth alwaies, either the Life, or the Living Creature; and the Body and Soule jointly, the Body alive'. So Hobbes was certainly a Mortalist.[1] Swift seems to have acknowledged the Soul as an incorporeal quality, capacity, or value, the nature of which he was prepared to accept as mysterious. But he does not acknowledge spirit as anything more subtle than body: spirit is bodily fluid. This is the basis of his reductive procedures in the *Mechanical Operation*.

The first assertion is that spirit is merely a sublimation of body. In the seventeenth century it was commonly thought that spirit, as Burton said, 'is a most subtile vapour, which is expressed from the Bloud, & the instrument of the soule, to perform all his actions; a common tye or medium betwixt the body and the soul'. The same distinction is found in Donne's sermons, where the spirit is described as 'the thin and active part of the blood', designed to unite the faculties of the soul to the organs of the body. This spirit was thought to be of three kinds; Burton called them the natural, the vital, and the animal: they seem to correspond to the three powers of the Soul as defined by Aquinas, the *anima vegetativa*, *sensitiva*, and *rationalis*. (In the *Tale* Swift laughs at the Aeolists for adding a fourth, the *anima spiritualis*.)

But Swift would not take these attributions seriously. There is a remarkable passage in the *Mechanical Operation*:

[1] See Robert Hugh Kargon, *Atomism in England from Hariot to Newton* (Clarendon Press, Oxford, 1966) and George Williamson, 'Milton and the Mortalist Heresy', *Studies in Philology*, vol. xxxii, no. 4 (October 1935), pp. 553–79.

The Practitioners of this famous Art, proceed in general upon the following Fundamental; That, the Corruption of the Senses is the Generation of the Spirit: Because the Senses in Men are so many Avenues to the Fort of Reason, which in this Operation is wholly block'd up. All Endeavours must be therefore used, either to divert, bind up, stupify, fluster, and amuse the Senses, or else to justle them out of their Stations; and while they are either absent, or otherwise employ'd or engaged in a Civil War against each other, the Spirit enters and performs its Part.[1]

Norman O. Brown has interpreted 'corruption' to mean 'repression'; the repression of the senses issuing in the generation of the spirit, as Freud described the habit of sublimation. This would be in keeping with Swift's implication that spirit is merely the sublimation of body and can be accounted for in bodily terms. Since the body is unitary, the spirits which are its sublimation must be 'essentially' the same. It is necessary to make this point because it is crucial to Swift's parody: it is essential to the terms of his attack that all the manifestations which trade under the name of spirit should be seen as strictly 'one and the same'. It is not enough to say that the corruption of the senses is the generation of the spirit unless you rush in with the further assertion that what is generated in this way is 'all the same', the seeming differences being specious. Once you have done this, you can play fast and loose with those who claim the high possession of spirit. The *Mechanical Operation* is a merry dance in which Swift leads his victims by the nose; but the first rule of the dance is that all seeming forms or variations of spirit are one. In the *Tale of a Tub* he takes the Aeolists at their word: they say that 'the Original Cause of all things' is Wind; which they identify with the animating Breath, the Spirit, the *anima mundi*. Taking wind as the radical term, Swift demonstrates that things which are equal to the same thing are equal to one another. There is no difference between eloquence, belching, religious enthusiasm, breaking

---

[1] *A Tale of a Tub*, pp. 271–2.

wind, inspiration, they are all wind.[1] Since this is demonstrable, they are all equally absurd and probably evil. William Empson mentions that one of the meanings of spirit is 'devil', citing Marlowe's 'Thou art a spirit: God cannot pity thee.' So Swift has everything on his side. If Louis XIV's brain is animated by a certain spirit or vapour, the only question is, which way will it turn: if it goes up, he spends years in war and conquest; but when it goes down and sits in his backside, the world is at peace and he dies of a *fistula*.

Swift's strategy in these matters is clear enough; the only problem is, why he needed it so desperately. If we compare the *Tale* with Locke's observations on body and spirit, the nature of the soul, and the potentialities of matter, we find that Locke shares and anticipates many of Swift's leanings; but the difference is that Locke's integrity was not under the same stress, we do not feel that he needed to lay the ghosts as violently as Swift did. One result is that Locke, whose admiration of man's powers is no greater than Swift's, could think and wonder and argue with himself in a tone of greater disinterestedness. Locke divides and discriminates his themes, describes the situation when this is possible and pleads ignorance when ignorance is inescapable, but there is no venom in these gestures. Swift, terrified of what he cannot see, must cut back the will, and tie it down more firmly than Gulliver in Lilliput. In the *Tale* he praises 'the common Forms', and this is Augustan caution, but his dependence upon these forms is extreme. It is entirely characteristic, for instance, that he links the Body with common sense and Spirit with the perversities of fancy, invention, fiction, and imagination; so fancy drives out reason, imagination is at odds with the senses, fact is usurped by fiction, and invention threatens truth. Worst of all, God does little to thwart the big battalions.

Meanwhile a satirist does what he can to vex men into

---

[1] *Ibid.* p. 151.

sanity. He laughs, for instance, when men ascribe supernatural meaning to natural events. 'For, I think', he says in
the *Mechanical Operation*, 'it is in Life as in Tragedy, where,
it is held, a Conviction of great Defect, both in Order and
Invention, to interpose the Assistance of preternatural Power,
without an absolute and last Necessity'. He ridicules the
anthropomorphic lust: 'However, it is a Sketch of Human
Vanity, for every Individual, to imagine the whole Universe is
interess'd in his meanest Concern. If he hath got cleanly over a
Kennel, some Angel, unseen, descended on purpose to help him
by the Hand; if he hath knockt his Head against a Post, it was the
Devil, for his Sins, let loose from Hell, on purpose to buffet
him.'[1] Swift thought that the distinction between the physical
and the metaphysical was real and necessary; like the distinction between man and God. His motto in these reflexions was:
render to Caesar the things that are Caesar's and to God the
few things that are indisputably His.

A satirist can also, especially if he is Swift, relish every
occasion on which matter and the body are wise and the
spirit is foolish in its pride. Locke toyed with the possibility
that God might if he pleased 'superadd to matter a faculty of
thinking'. Swift does not follow up this notion in sober argument,
but he is delighted when the evidence points that way. When
silly people disown the body and fly away in spiritual pride, Swift
is the body's cheerleader, applauding when matter acts with
more intelligence than its ghostly fellow. In *The Battle of the
Books* the foolish Modern who undertakes to knock down two
Ancients from Parnassus is prevented from trying anything
so absurd by the weight of his fat body. I have already argued
that Swift is a master of riddance and negation: he is also a
devotee of prudent ignorance, delighted to find that there are
many things about which it is unnecessary to think, because
they act themselves. Much of this economy comes from the
body, which, as it were, 'knows its own mind'. Kenneth

[1] *A Tale of a Tub*, pp. 277–8.

Burke's hero in *Towards a Better Life* makes this discovery: 'We would not deny the mind', he says, 'but merely remember that as the corrective of wrong thinking is right thinking, the corrective of all thinking is the body.'[1] Wearied with thought, one takes, perhaps, exorbitant pleasure in this discovery. Yeats assumed that the answer to thought is action, but he conceived of action in superbly physical terms. There is a passage in *On the Boiler* where he ponders those modern plays which are all thought and talk and yet lack style; he is thinking also of those people who congratulated the Abbey Theatre Board 'upon its belated discovery that thought is more important than action'. But Yeats answers that thought is not more important than action: 'we are not coherent to ourselves through thought but because our visible image changes slowly'. Then, warming to his theme, he says: 'Our bodies are nearer to our coherence because nearer to the "unconscious" than our thought.' To support this he quotes a conversation with Sargent, who said: 'All people are exactly what they look. I have just painted a woman who thinks herself completely serious; here is her portrait, I show her as she looks and is, completely frivolous.'[2] Swift never publicly speculated along these lines, but he implied that we are coherent to ourselves only when we accept what we are given and make the best of it; and the first thing we are given, like it or not, is a body. Burke's fictional hero makes another discovery which is closely in touch with the first: 'But whereas', he says in a moment of notable misery, 'through fear of death, one may desire to die, and may find all his interests converging upon this single purpose, such notions are loath to permeate the tissues, and the wish never to have been born is unknown to our organs and our nerves.'[3] There is a passage in Yeats's *Autobiographies* in which he looks at a Strozzi portrait of a Venetian

---

[1] Kenneth Burke, *Towards a Better Life* (Harcourt, Brace, New York, 1932), p. 9.

[2] W. B. Yeats, *Explorations* (Macmillan, London, 1962), pp. 446–7.

[3] Kenneth Burke, *Towards a Better Life*, p. 41.

gentleman that hangs in the National Gallery in Dublin: 'Whatever thought broods in the dark eyes of that Venetian gentleman has drawn its life from his whole body; it feeds upon it as the flame feeds upon the candle—and should that thought be changed, his pose would change, his very cloak would rustle, for his whole body thinks.'[1] This is another version of that Unity of Being which Yeats pursued, his 'supreme fiction': something like it seems to me implicit in Swift, unacknowledged, indeed ostensibly rejected. It under-lies Swift's suspicion of words—a later theme—and his commit-ment to those things in life which defeat opinion and do not need proof. Something of this can be heard in his criticism of Thomson's *Seasons*: 'One Thomson, a Scots-man, has succeeded the best in that way' (he means blank verse) 'in four poems he has writ on the four Seasons: yet I am not over fond of them, because they are all description, and nothing is doing; whereas Milton engages me in actions of the highest importance.'[2] We are coherent to ourselves, it seems, when the body thinks; when thought is temporal and modest; when we acknowledge 'the sigh of what is'.

But we must avoid pushing Swift too far along this line. Eventually we would find him forming a party with Blake and Lawrence; their platform, the sacred wisdom of the body. This is clearly too much. It is enough to say that in any battle of words involving body and spirit he fought for body; but he did not propose a Yeatsian mystique by which the body, in splendid animation, encompasses spirit and certifies an un-dissociated unity of being. Enough is enough. Swift did not think the body a particularly remarkable thing, but it was demonstrable and could not be denied. This does not mean that he was a Materialist; he attacked Materialists, mainly I think because they identified Truth with their own rhetoric.

---

[1] W. B. Yeats, *Autobiographies* (Macmillan, London, 1961), p. 292.
[2] *Correspondence*, edited by Harold Williams (Clarendon Press, Oxford, 1965), vol. IV, p. 53.

Swift found it quite possible to deride the pretensions of the Materialists to the possession of Truth and, at the same time, to use the Materialism of common sense to burst the pretensions of Spirit. Equally he found no difficulty in using the machine to cut spiritual pretensions down to size; this does not make him a Mechanist.

So he vexes the pretentious world by disploding the afflatus: the best way to do this is to laugh at the bubble-blowers. The next best way—picking up an earlier theme—is to show that allegedly complex factors can usually be controlled by simple diagrams. In *Contests and Dissensions*, discussing the problem of radical changes in government, he says: 'Great Changes may, indeed, be made in a Government, yet the Form continue, and the Ballance be held; but large Intervals of Time must pass between every such Innovation, enough to melt down, and make it of a Piece with the Constitution.'[1] This might be Edmund Burke's sentence, but for the style. Burke offers the same acknowledgment of change, notably in the *Letter to Sir Hercules Langrishe*, and the difference of temper between the two writers becomes clear in the comparison.

We must all obey the great law of change [Burke says]. It is the most powerful law of nature, and the means perhaps of its conservation. All we can do, and that human wisdom can do, is to provide that the change shall proceed by insensible degrees. This has all the benefits which may be in change, without any of the inconveniences of mutation. Every thing is provided for as it arrives. This mode will, on the one hand, prevent the unfixing old interests at once: a thing which is apt to breed a black and sullen discontent in those who are at once dispossessed of all their influence and consideration. This gradual course, on the other side, will prevent men, long under depression, from being intoxicated with a large draught of new power, which they always abuse with a licentious insolence. But wishing, as I do, the change to be gradual and cautious, I would, in my first steps, lean rather to the side of enlargement than restriction.[2]

[1] *A Tale of a Tub, with Other Early Works 1696–1707*, p. 202.
[2] Edmund Burke, *Works* (Rivington, London, 1852), vol. IV, pp. 544-5.

Burke's sense of change is more delicately introduced: it is, in his view, a difficult question, to be approached warily and with the aid of moral terms. His sentences are moved by the force of terms like *obey, law, provide,* and *discontent.* He advances a careful discrimination; *on the one hand* and then *on the other.* The result is that every fact introduced proclaims its moral significance at once; people who get their independence too quickly are 'intoxicated' with 'a large draught of new power', new power being like new liquor, highly noxious. Burke tends to give all his meaning through the moral forms in which it obtrudes upon society, and he lets the reader deduce from those terms the political acts to which they refer. The word 'depression' is a case in point. The first meaning Johnson gives is the state of being pressed down; men long under depression are pressed down by the weight and authority of others. But Burke does nothing to dramatise this spatial meaning; he virtually suppresses it, or at most glances at it, he is so eager to get to its moral result, the wild intoxication caused when these men are suddenly lifted up. Unlike Swift, Burke does not persuade himself that there is a straightforward answer to the relevant question. Swift commits himself to spatial gestures, balancing one thing against another, putting one thing in one place, adjusting things on a field of action, boxing them off or fitting them together. As we have already seen, he tends to deal with a moral situation by translating it into spatial terms. He does not say, 'I would, in my first steps, lean rather to the side of enlargement than restriction'; he marches boldly into one position or the other and fights from base. In the sentence from *Contests and Dissensions,* having given away the possibility of 'great changes', he at once tries to take it back again; the 'form' of things is to continue, and because this is not precise enough, 'the Ballance' must be held. So he comes in on the conservative side, 'between every such Innovation, enough to melt down, and make it of a Piece with the Constitution'. This is government by simple chemistry, so that by the time the sentence is complete the innovations have disappeared in the original matter: matter has won again. Burke is constantly worrying about the people, acting and suffering through political events: Swift ignores this consideration, places his objects in position, deals with the new material by melting it down. The result is that his sentence has no moral terms at all; instead, mechanical terms designed to go about their business and fend off trespassing analogies.

The basis of this temper is the official Lockean view that mind works in much the same way as matter and can therefore be treated in material terms; especially since we have no special vocabulary for mental operations, we should be delighted to find that the material idiom works so well. It worked, of course, provided you separated the primary and the secondary qualities as Locke did. According to Locke, the primary qualities of matter are inseparable from the external body, in whatever state; they are not functions of the interaction of that body with other bodies, or with the human mind. These qualities are extension, solidity, figure, mobility and number. The secondary qualities are events of relation; they are the sensations produced in us by the primary qualities, sensations of colour, taste, sound and so forth. The primary qualities are objective; the secondary qualities are subjective, ideas in the mind of the perceiver. The sources of knowledge are sensations and reflexions. Sensations are the materials provided for us by God, *gratis*: we are passive in their reception. Reflexion is our mental craftsmanship, the faculty by which we work upon the given materials. Swift was somewhat disturbed by Locke's demolition of 'innate ideas', but otherwise he had no quarrel with him. Their minds were notably in tune. Indeed, Locke's 'primary qualities' are Swift's favourite materials. He was obviously relieved, for instance, to find a philosopher of modern cast justifying his reductive procedures; if it was a relief to treat spirit as the sublimation of matter, it was a prime necessity to know that the reduction could only go in one direction; he felt no need to derive matter from anything but the will of God. Once he had made his bow in the direction of God, he was free to defend, cut back, scale down and fend off as much as he needed for his own security. He was free because Locke and Hobbes gave him this freedom. His favourite moments were those in which he discovered that a complex *A* was 'nothing but' a simple *B*. In the *Mechanical Operation* the difference between Indians and Europeans is 'little more than this, That They are put oftener upon their Knees by their Fears, and We by our Desires'. The virtuoso thinks that rheums and colds are 'nothing else but an Epidemical Looseness...' The brain is 'only a Crowd of little Animals': invention is only the morsure of two or more of these brain-animals: the Dionysian ceremonies were 'nothing more than a Set of roaring, scouring Companions, overcharg'd with Wine': the spinal marrow is 'nothing else' but a continuation of the brain. Lovers, 'for the sake of Celestial Converse, are but another sort of Platonicks': the Philosopher's Stone, the Grand Elixir, the Planetary Worlds, the Squaring of the Circle, the Summum Bonum, and the Utopian Commonwealths 'serve for nothing else' but to employ the grain of Enthusiasm.[1] The immediate source of this gesture is Hobbes, especially in *Leviathan*: 'Imagination therefore', Hobbes says, 'is nothing but decaying sense.' Again: 'For Reason, in this sense, is nothing but reckoning, that is adding and subtracting, of the consequences of general names agreed upon for the marking and signifying of our thoughts.' This sentence is closer to Swift than we have been prepared to allow: implying the reduction of a difficult term to a very simple process of adding and subtracting, with the implication that in this process nothing essential is lost. Near the beginning of *Leviathan*, there is an even more Swiftian assertion:

[1] *A Tale of a Tub*, pp. 268, 276, 279, 281, 286, 289, 291.

For seeing Life is but a motion of limbs, the beginning whereof is in some principal part within: Why may we not say, that all automata (engines that move themselves by springs and wheels as doth a watch) have an artificial life? For what is the heart, but a spring; and the nerves, but so many strings; and the joints, but so many wheels, giving motion to the whole body, such as was intended by the artificer?[1]

Swift uses the same device to lead us like sheep through fields of bogus relation, mainly by comparisons that cheat as they illumine. In the *Mechanical Operation* he links the Art of Canting at one point with the Art of Musical Setting; because the Enthusiast takes words, makes nonsense of them, and turns them into Cant, as the composer takes words, makes nonsense of them, and turns them into song. For this reason, both arts are in greatest perfection 'when managed by Ignorance'. A few pages later he links women with flesh and flesh with beef, so that he can jeer at the lechery of the Fanatics: 'For, Human Life is a continual Navigation, and, if we expect our Vessels to pass with Safety, thro' the Waves and Tempests of this fluctuating World, it is necessary to make a good Provision of the Flesh, as Sea-men lay in store of Beef for a long Voyage.'[2] If we insist upon an analogical view of the world, we can hardly object when Swift runs our analogies into the ground. Hobbes and Locke are the nearest sources, but the reductive strategy is central in the main traditions of satire as far back as Lucian's *Dialogue of the Dead*. Ostensibly spiritual A is nothing but material B: if the assertion is denied, the critic is invited to demonstrate the error. The missing factor, being impalpable, cannot be offered in evidence.

But the malaise at the heart of Swift's work is not to be concealed by the brilliant surface, the athletic brio of his syntax; his energy is part fear, part despair, part vexation.

---

[1] Hobbes, *Leviathan*, edited by Michael Oakeshott (Basil Blackwell, Oxford, n.d.), pp. 5, 9, 25.
[2] *A Tale of a Tub*, pp. 288–9.

We think of this again in relation to Locke, though Swift's feeling was his own. Yeats saw the implication of Locke's philosophy with notable clarity and expressed it in an essay on Berkeley. He saw, for one thing, that Locke's separation of the primary and the secondary qualities was a mighty abstraction which could only be rejected with great labour. Indeed, he thought of it as the most insidious abstraction ever devised. 'And of all these (abstractions)', he said, 'the most comprehensive, the most useful, was invented by Locke when he separated the primary and secondary qualities; and from that day to this the conception of a physical world without colour, sound, taste, tangibility, though indicated by Berkeley...and proved mere abstract extension, a mere category of the mind, has remained the assumption of science, the groundwork of every text-book.'[1] Berkeley took up Locke's challenge: 'By Matter, therefore,' he said, paraphrasing Locke, 'we are to understand an inert, senseless substance, in which extension, figure, and motion do actually subsist.'[2] As Yeats said in his *Diary* of 1930: 'Descartes, Locke and Newton took away the world and gave us its excrement instead. Berkeley restored the world...Berkeley has brought back to us the world that only exists because it shines and sounds. A child, smothering its laughter because the elders are standing round, has opened once more the great box of toys.'[3] Where Locke urged that the mind works as matter works and therefore can be construed in the same terms, Berkeley liberated the mind by denying the existence of material substance independent of perception. In Berkeley's system the mind was the imagination, answerable in the first instance to its own integrity and, behind that, to the law of Nature which is the will of God. So Berkeley attacked Locke and Newton in behalf of religion; Yeats gratefully accepted his arguments and used

[1] W. B. Yeats, *Essays and Introductions* (Macmillan, London, 1961), pp. 400–1.
[2] Berkeley, *Works*, edited by George Sampson (Bell, London, 1897), vol. I, p. 183.
[3] Yeats, *Explorations*, p. 325.

them in favour of poetry. If the primary act was the act of imagination, and if the mind worked in accordance with its own powers and not at all by analogy with the operations of matter, then nothing more was needed for a complete poetry.

Nothing; provided you were not too distressed by the notion of a God absolutely separate from man. Yeats rejected Berkeley at this point, because the philosopher insisted upon the separation. Yeats wanted to go beyond Berkeley because Blake had already done so. The story is soon told. In the *Commonplace Book* Berkeley insisted upon the absolute separation of God and man, and of God and Nature. 'No sharing betwixt God & Nature or second Causes in my Doctrine', he says. Even more directly: 'We Imagine a great difference & distance in respect of Knowledge, power &c betwixt a Man & a worm. The like distance betwixt Man & God may be Imagin'd, or Infinitely greater.'[1] This assertion is fundamental in the *Essay of the Principles of Human Knowledge* and it is dramatised with remarkable resource in *Siris*. Even though the mind makes a chain of analogies stretching on all sides as far as the inner eye can see, nevertheless the separation of God and man is absolute. It was this insistence in Berkeley that Blake rejected. At one point, Berkeley argues that we must not assume in God anything comparable to our power of sensory knowledge:

There is no sense nor sensory, nor any thing like a sense or sensory, in God. Sense implies an impression from some other being, and denotes a dependence in the soul which hath it . . . God knoweth all things, as pure mind or intellect; but nothing by sense, nor in nor through a sensory. Therefore to suppose a sensory of any kind—whether space or any other—in God, would be very wrong, and lead us into false conceptions of His nature.[2]

Blake wrote in the margin: 'Imagination or the Human External Body in Every Man'.[3] In the next paragraph Berkeley

[1] Berkeley, *Works*, edited by A. A. Luce and T. E. Jessop (Nelson, London, 1948), vol. i, pp. 61, 78.
[2] *Ibid.* p. 89.
[3] Blake, *Poetry and Prose*, edited by Geoffrey Keynes (Nonesuch Library, London, 1961), p. 818.

distinguishes between God and man on the grounds that man is Body and Imperfect Spirit:

Body is opposite to spirit or mind. We have a notion of spirit from thought and action. We have a notion of body from resistance. . . . But in respect of a perfect spirit, there is nothing hard or impenetrable: there is no resistance to the Deity: nor hath he any body.

Again Blake interrupts in the margin: 'Imagination is the Divine Body in Every Man. . .'and then, 'Man is All Imagination. God is Man & exists in us & we in him.'

We can summarise this before thinking of Swift. Berkeley found in Locke a dead world. He restored to the poet his box of toys and the mind, the creative imagination, to play with them. Blake believed that this play, this imaginative vision of reality, is itself divine, and the power of play the only proof of divinity. So Blake would refute the absolute separateness of God and Man. Man was God to the extent of his imaginative vision.

The first point to make is obvious, that Blake's unity of mind and body was not available to Swift. Nor could he console himself, as Berkeley could, with the plenitude of man's perception. We have seen that Swift, like Locke and Hobbes, tended to reduce complex phenomena to simple terms, and especially to mechanistic and material terms: spirit was merely the sublimation of body. This would be tolerable if the body could be felt as animate and vital; as in Yeats's poem, where the dance and the dancer are marvellously one. But when Swift implied that all is body and matter, as a son of Locke he had to recognise that this 'all' did not amount to much, that it was inert, tasteless, colourless. Again as a son of Locke he was tied to the view that the human mind is a limited instrument, even if the limitation is, on most occasions and for most purposes, tolerable. So he was trapped in his own reduction. The only way of dealing with the situation was to make a virtue of necessity: if everything is limited, make limitation your 'good'. This is precisely what Swift did; hence his aesthetic of the reasonable minimum. Man should not go beyond 'reflexion'.

But it would be hard to relish this stratagem. What Louis Bredvold calls 'the gloom of the Tory satirists' is a political phenomenon, for which sound political reasons are available. In Swift's case the gloom culminated, as I have already argued, in the breach between Oxford and Bolingbroke. But the gloom was already implicit in his temper and the world-view which it sponsored. If you have to make limitation your chief good, you are only a step from the symptoms of withdrawal and neurosis. The only way to avoid this fate is to direct your wrath upon the world.

There are other aspects of this. One of Yeats's cryptic poems reads:

> Locke sank into a swoon;
> The Garden died;
> God took the spinning-jenny
> Out of his side.

Locke sank into the swoon of abstraction, as Yeats elsewhere says, 'more diagram than body'. Therefore the Garden died. In *The Gutenberg Galaxy* Marshall McLuhan glosses these lines: 'The Lockean swoon was the hypnotic trance induced by stepping up the visual component in experience until it filled the field of attention. At such a moment the garden (the interplay of all the senses in haptic harmony) dies.'[1] The justification of this gloss is an elaborate argument which says that the effect of the printing press upon our modes of apprehension was that it specialised them, reducing apprehension to one sense, the sense of sight, and neutralising the others. In support of this, there is again Blake, who spent a lot of energy castigating Bacon, Newton and Locke for their 'single vision', and 'Newton's sleep'. The single vision is the 'point of view'; we

[1] McLuhan, *The Gutenberg Galaxy* (Routledge and Kegan Paul, London, 1962), p. 17.

have already glanced at the observer fixed in position before the observed scene. On several occasions Yeats expressed his hatred of the literature which proceeds under these auspices; ultimately, the fixed point of view would become so congealed that it would be driven to the closed field of reference; experience would be limited to those items which the observer sees from his fixed position. At that stage the only recourse is the satisfaction of playing a strictly internal game according to one's own rules. Of this game the greatest masters are Lewis Carroll, whose style is debonair without being manic, and Samuel Beckett, whose style is manic without being debonair. Meanwhile, Swift is observing the scene from a fixed point of view, an observer without much hope, looking at a scene without much life; the mind, nothing but matter, matter itself nothing much. One could spend a lifetime doing this, but only by providing oneself with a ready set of gestures and stratagems which would go into action whenever they were needed; it would not do if one had to wonder and hope and fear and ponder when a new visitor turned up. If Swift were Swedenborg, he could extract all kinds of comfort even from the same circumstances: if he were Blake he could reject the dualism of soul and body, as in *The Marriage of Heaven and Hell*, and hold on to the body by keeping it tingling with its own life. As it was, he could not be 'Romantic' about the body, he could only be reasonable and sober. He could not feel, as Dante felt, as Blake felt, and as Yeats sometimes felt, that a 'perfectly proportioned human body' was the ideal human image. He could not transcend the dualism by appeal to a higher order of experience, as Yeats does in the Byzantium poems and Eliot in *Four Quartets*. All he could do was to bring together a set of procedures and keep them ready and armed, like the Marines. To prevent as much trouble as possible, he could get into the habit of modifying his desires. This is crucial. In the 'Prayer for Stella' he said: 'Give thy blessing to those endeavours used for her recovery; but take from her all violent desire, either of life or death, further than with resignation to thy holy will'.[1] Even his prayers were negations.

There is a passage in the *Mechanical Operation of the Spirit* which reveals perhaps more clearly than any other Swift's treatment of body and spirit:

For, it is the Opinion of Choice Virtuosi, that the Brain is only a Crowd of little Animals, but with Teeth and Claws extremely sharp, and therefore, cling together in the Contexture we behold, like the Picture of Hobbes's Leviathan, or like Bees in perpendicular swarm upon a Tree, or like a Carrion corrupted into Vermin, still preserving the Shape and Figure of the Mother Animal. That all Invention is formed by the Morsure of two or more of these Animals, upon certain capillary Nerves, which proceed from thence, whereof three Branches spread into the Tongue, and two into the right Hand. They hold also, that these animals are of a constitution extremely cold; that their Food is the Air we attract, their Excrement Phlegm; and that what we vulgarly call Rheums, and Colds, and Distillations, is nothing else but an Epidemical Looseness, to which that little Commonwealth is very subject, from the Climate it lyes under. Farther, that nothing less than a violent Heat, can disentangle these Creatures from their hamated Station of Life, or give them Vigor and Humor, to imprint the Marks of their little Teeth. That if the Morsure be Hexagonal, it produces Poetry; the Circular gives Eloquence; if the Bite hath been Conical, the Person, whose Nerve is so affected, shall be disposed to write upon the Politicks; and so of the rest.[2]

The 1651 edition of Hobbes's *Leviathan* carries a frontispiece which shows myriads of identical little figures contained within the body of the Great Ruler. In chapter xvii Hobbes considers Aristotle's question, how it comes about that certain living creatures such as bees and ants can 'live sociably one with another'. Hobbes offers several answers. Swift turns the little men into little animals by a transformation close to his temper: besides, he is capitalising upon the common pun of *animal* and *anima*. The word *animal* referred to 'any living being', its

---

[1] *Irish Tracts, 1720–1723, and Sermons*, p. 256.
[2] *A Tale of a Tub*, p. 279.

range was very wide: Cudworth, for instance, says, 'The Deity is generally supposed to be a Perfectly Happy Animal, Incorruptible and Immortal.' Swift had only to choose the common meaning and put all his little animals in Hobbes's commonwealth, to make the plot of his paragraph complete. Then to give them an appropriate 'character' he showed his animals living strictly according to their humours, since a sternly mechanical psychology is required by the reductive nature of his terms. The animals are 'of a constitution extremely cold', reasonably enough because of the dank climate in which they live. In the first Part of the *Anatomy of Melancholy* Burton says that one of the causes of melancholy is bad climate, bad air. The worst air, he says, is 'a thick, cloudy, misty, foggy air, or such as come from fens, moorish grounds, lakes, muckhills, draughts, sinks, where any carcasses or carrion lies, or from whence any stinking fulsome smell comes: Galen, Avicenna, Mercurialis, new and old physicians, hold that such air is unwholesome, and engenders melancholy, plagues, and what not?'[1] Swift's little animals not only live on bad air, but are thereafter the cause of it. The outer air is their food, which they transform to their own nature; phlegm is their excrement, colds their diarrhoea. Clearly, to make this paragraph work at all, he had to start his transformations at once; stretching the line of the first sentence, so that he can hang upon it more and more revolting analogies. He must send things sliding down a long scale of corruption; the little animals start out like the little men in Hobbes's frontispiece, then become bees swarming upon a tree, then carrion 'corrupted into Vermin', still preserving 'the Shape and Figure of the Mother Animal'. Once the slide begins, it can then be set off again in the next sentence: Invention has nothing to do with imagination or creative power, it is merely the biting of two or more of the little animals upon the capillary nerves. Two or more, presumably, because perception in the worlds of Locke and Hobbes is a matter of putting

[1] Burton, *Anatomy of Melancholy* (Tegg, London, n.d.), p. 156.

two or more impressions together. Hence our speech and action.

Swift begins with one pun, and ends with another. The brain is a crowd of little animals, hamated or hooked together until they are disentangled by heat. In the *Sylva* Bacon says: 'It is certain, that of all Powers in Nature, Heat is the chiefe.' Swift has only to make the heat sexual and he can agree. He can go further. He can say that all the pretensions of our minds, in eloquence, religion, poetry, and politics, are merely the result of sexual heat, which disentangles the little animals and gives them vigour to bite the nerves. The last implication is the most virulent; that without this heat there would be Nothing. So we come back to the Corruption of the Senses as the Generation of the Spirit. Each of its meanings is deployed at large in the essay; corruption as sublimation, as the principle by which bodies tend to the separation of their parts, as evil, as putrescence and sex; what is generated from these is pride, chaos, disease, and sin.

So the *Mechanical Operation of the Spirit* is the art of sinking in religion; its aim, to speed the sinking. Swift mockingly provides a mechanical or bodily explanation for the extravagances of feeling exhibited by Enthusiasts and Fanatics. If this explanation were not possible, he would have to concede that these men were indeed divinely inspired; or else, an equally distressing concession, that their movements of feeling were unconscious, the produce of that infernal region. His official stance is therefore to say: let us consider the symptoms of religious enthusiasm as closely as possible in our own natural terms, before interposing the assistance of preternatural power to explain them. So he treats the symptoms as if they were the marks of any other disease; in terms of the pathology of humours. Henry More moves in the same direction in the *Enthusiasmus Triumphatus*, treating the outward signs as symptoms of melancholy, quoting Burton and Sennertus for support. The difference is that More wants to clear the enthusiastic ground so as to make room for what he conceives to be genuine inspiration: his quarrel with Thomas Vaughan was on that crucial ground. Swift had no interest in this discrimination: it was all hot air to him. The parody begins with the first sentence:

It is now a good while since I have had in my Head something, not only very material, but absolutely necessary to my Health, that the World should be informed in. For, to tell you a Secret, I am able to contain it no longer.

Pope writes in the *Peri Bathous:* 'As I would not suddenly stop a cold in the head, or dry up my neighbour's Issue, I would as little hinder him from necessary writing.' Since the writer is a victim of the disease, he is in the best position to disclose its symptoms, the noxious vapours. In section XVII of the *Enthusiasmus* More discovers the mistake of heated Melancholy for holy Zeal and the Spirit of God:

The Spirit then that wings the Enthusiast in such a wonderful manner, is nothing else but that Flatulency which is in the Melancholy complexion, and rises out of the Hypochondriacal humour upon some occasional heat, as Winde out of an Aeolipila applied to the fire. Which fume mounting into the Head, being first actuated and spirited and somewhat refined by the warmth of the Heart, fills the Mind with variety of Imaginations, and so quickens and inlarges Invention, that it makes the Enthusiast to admiration fluent and eloquent, he being as it were drunk with new wine drawn from that Cellar of his own that lies in the lowest region of his Body, though he be not aware of it, but takes it to be pure Nectar, and those waters of life that spring from above.[1]

Most of Swift's ingredients are here, but they are differently combined, more diffuse, less pointed in their sequence. More uses the same idiom, terms of place, origin, and so forth, but he does not go as far as Swift in building, from these terms, an inviolable critique. It is typical of Swift, for instance, to speak of Good and Evil as territories, clearly defined in India but not

[1] Henry More, *Enthusiasmus Triumphatus* (London, 1662: Augustan Reprint Society, 1966), p. 12.

in England: he does not allow them to be considered as intangible qualities. The main difference between More's pamphlet and the *Mechanical Operation* is that Swift enforces a single critique, deployed at large; More tries one approach and then another. The demolition in Swift is therefore far more systematic. Inspiration is reduced to Possession, preaching to voice-production, the Inward Light is merely a large Memory full of inexplicable texts, Spirits are merely ghosts.

This requires, in Swift, the deployment of a middle term, to effect the reduction of one thing to another; or, more regularly, the translation of one quality into a demeaning quantity. Normally the middle term is also taken from the quantitative place, but unobtrusively:

Therefore, I am resolved immediately, to weed this Error out of Mankind, by making it clear, that this Mystery, of vending spiritual Gifts is nothing but a Trade, acquired by as much Instruction, and mastered by equal Practice and Application as others are.

The reduction of Mystery to Trade is begun with the trading verb 'vending', and the dubious nature of the Enthusiast's activity is implicit in the notion of selling gifts. He has got the stuff *gratis* and now he is to sell it. By now the cadence of reduction ('nothing but') is a cliché in Swift, but its work is already done. So to introduce the word 'Trade' merely names what is already implied. The point to make is that Swift is taking every advantage of the character of language itself. Kenneth Burke has observed, in his *Rhetoric of Religion* and elsewhere, that we have no language for the ineffable or the supernatural; the only language we have is derived from the natural, the empirical, by processes of analogy. There is really no justification for analogy, unless we admit our need. All the words for 'God', for instance, have to be taken analogically, Burke says, 'as we were to speak of God's "powerful arm" (a physical analogy), or of God as "lord" or "father" (a sociopolitical analogy), or of God as the "Word" (a linguistic analogy).[1] Burke does not remark, as far as I recall, that the process of analogy in language is always something of a strain and that the strain is greatest where a claim upon the ineffable is to be lodged. We have to use words in this way as if the use were natural, but knowing that it is not natural; analogy is an accredited fiction, but it depends upon the fervour with which it is acknowledged. There is always a force in language itself which must be overwhelmed if analogy is to be maintained or pursued. So it is easy, as Swift found, to defeat the pretensions of spirit: all you have to do is to withdraw the linguistic fervour which sustained them. Language itself is happy to do this at any time, since its allegiance is resolutely empirical, temporal, domestic: it is only waiting for an opportunity to turn spirits into ghosts, inspiration into wind, mysteries into trades. It is easy to turn high things into low things, simply by declining to raise them; language is on your side, a secularist by nature:

A Master Work-Man shall blow his Nose so powerfully, as to pierce the Hearts of his People, who are disposed to receive the Excrements of his Brain with the same Reverence, as the Issue of it. Hawking, Spitting, and Belching, the Defects of other Mens Rhetorick, are the Flowers, and Figures, and Ornaments of his. For, the Spirit being the same in all, it is of no Import through what Vehicle it is convey'd.

'Issue' is neutral, 'excrement' was already dyslogistic in Swift's day though not as far gone in that direction as it is now; in some usages of that day, however, the words were almost synonymous. So it required only a slight push to obscure the difference, degrading one in the company of the other. The effect is facilitated by treating the enterprise as a craft ('A Master Work-Man') and suppressing every consideration but its end, the finished product, the pierced hearts. The means are indifferent. To emphasise the ease with which this may be done, it is enough to say that effort is required only if the opposite

[1] Kenneth Burke, *The Rhetoric of Religion* (Beacon Press, Boston, 1961), p. 14.

effect is pursued; to distinguish between causes, natures, and motives. Language tends to flow downhill, back to its natural source.

We have to consider how seriously Swift conceived the *Mechanical Operation of the Spirit*. It is customary to read the fragment as if it were ironic from beginning to end. I have elected to read it differently, because many of its imaginative gestures and patterns are continuous with those invoked in other works where there is no question of irony. Some parts of the fragment are ironic, but some are not. The main object was to curb the pride of spirit. True, nearly everything I have said about the piece implies that Swift was, at least on this occasion, a Materialist; but we know that he often attacked that position. It is a nice question to decide how far Swift was driven by a natural desire to rebuke Pride, and how far by his conspiracy with certain qualities in language itself, urging him beyond his limited contract. It was not strictly a question of belief: rather, of the extent to which he was engaged by the possibility of vexing the world, regardless of his own belief. I have argued that this was Swift's dominant motive throughout his work; it is only necessary to add that a sense of the possibility of vexing the world often led him beyond the strict boundary of belief or disbelief. Two points are clear; that the idiom of reduction was congenial to his imagination; and that this idiom was implicit in the bias of language itself.

Think, for instance, how easy it would have been to imply a peaceful statement between body and soul. In *Tristram Shandy*, book IX, chapter 13, Sterne says that: 'the soul and body are joint-sharers in every thing they get'; the harmony of soul and body is certified by feeling, sentiment, sensibility. These terms mediate between soul and body; this is their significance. Much of Sterne's effort, in the last Books of *Tristram Shandy* as in the *Sentimental Journey*, the sermons and the letters, is to assimilate everything to that harmonising idiom. Shandeism is 'dear Sensibility', dear because it brings peace to the war

115

of soul and body. Sterne's own sensibility, faced with two
conflicting parties, delighted to embrace both. His imagination
says: *both/and*. Swift's imagination says: *either/or*. It was not
Swift's business, nor was it in the nature of his imagination, to
reconcile.

CHAPTER 4

WORDS

I

Swift's *via negativa*; a strategy adopted in response to certain temperamental needs and without any hope—which he might have received from Heraclitus—that the Way Down and the Way Up are the same. I have suggested that Swift's representative act is negation. Pushed to its logical conclusion, this results in the consecration of a state which we may call Nothing; the verbal equivalent is silence. But meanwhile Swift was, among other things, a writer, committed to words. Hence one of many ambiguous situations; a writer who puts little trust in words, speaking as if to advocate silence.

One of the richer curiosities of literature is that words, in a sense, outrun nature; the plenitude and freedom of language are Nature's envy. Nature lives in sober prose; words revel in shameless conjunctions, producing lights of language that never were on land or sea. Trees grow and live according to certain mysterious but prosaic laws: but the word 'tree' enters into an indefinite number of wild relationships, according to the imagination of the writer and the connivance of the language. Words are promiscuous by comparison with the legal things to which they refer. Many writers delight in this situation, conspiring with it to turn their real miseries into occasions of poetic pleasure. We may assume that Swift was often consoled by the power of his words, but this consolation was not enough. There is no evidence that he delighted in linguistic profusion, even in the *Tale*. If we think of words as Spirit and the things they name as Matter,[1] we mark Swift's scruple in terms which

[1] Kenneth Burke, *The Rhetoric of Religion* (Beacon Press, Boston, 1961), p. 16.

we have considered in another context. Just as he rejected the pretensions of spirit, reducing them as sublimations of matter, so he disavowed the pride of words. This partly accounts for his determination to ram words into the earth and mud, especially when he found planetary writers flying into the Sublime, urged aloft by their own pride. Just as there was much in religion which he was prepared to forgo, so there was much in language which he scrupled to enjoy. The two abnegations run together. When we doubt the plenitude of his religion, we think that his terms of reference left him too little to believe, too much to deny. It is a thin Christianity, after all. If we have any doubt about his language, it is not that he does less than mightily what he elected to do, but that his sense of possibility was restrictive, too compelling in its uniformity. His gifts are operative to an almost unparalleled degree; no writer in English is so commanding, where Swift is commanding. What he lacks, by the greatest comparisons, is variety; all those recognitions implied in such words as risk, exposure, nonchalance, gaiety.

We come to the relation between words and things. I shall argue that while Swift thought himself emancipated from the dreary argument, it touched some of the deepest issues in his work. *The Battle of the Books* is a celebrated encounter, even if we now share Macaulay's view of its origin as 'a most idle and contemptible controversy', but it is not as important as the Battle of the Words, the crisis of Logomachy, as Samuel Werenfels called it in a worried essay. The background to the war is the concern for the development of a language which would be useful, in the first instance, and thereafter eloquent to the degree of its utility; rather than the Elizabethan language, which sought eloquence in the first place and troubled itself little about the cost. Richard Foster Jones has documented this concern in an admirable book, *The Triumph of the English Language*, the triumph being largely the achievement of a single-minded language without losing all the flowers of splendour and *copie*. The story is well known. It is enough to emphasise here that after the Restoration the dominant rhetoric sponsored the ideal of a single, regular language in which—to cite the standard test—words would be brought closer than ever to things and judged in that intimacy. The words should match the things. This was the criterion which united the scientists, moral philosophers, Puritan reformers, moderate Whigs and moderate Tories, poets, journalists. Thomas Sprat writing of the Royal Society is only the most explicit of those who committed themselves to this standard; the deliverance of 'so many things, almost in an equal number of words' is the most famous programme of his *History*, and it depends upon another, only less celebrated, his vote for the language of artisans and craftsmen. These allegiances coincided, because at least in theory the language of the craftsman was sustained by the things of this craft. One purified the dialect of the tribe by ensuring that the dialect remained dependent upon tribal processes and daily things. By contrast, the language of poet or scholar was always in danger of eccentricity, because there were not enough things, palpable objects, to which it might be referred; by which its pretensions might be rebuked. The blacksmith had his anvil. The poet had every advantage of freedom, subject to the qualification that he had none of the advantages of necessity. So we hear again, especially in the first years of the eighteenth century, the old complaint against words; that controversies in philosophy and scholarship are merely verbal, referring to nothing beyond their self-engrossed occasions. The feeling behind these complaints is clear enough, the desire to sponsor a single-minded way of life, embodied in a single-minded language. The best safeguard in words was to hold them against the things to which they ostensibly referred. Elizabethan words are certified by their speaker; Augustan words are certified by the empirical order among the things they name and the demonstrable order in language itself. Restoration linguists imply that the best way of life is exemplified in the procedures of a disciplined language, the discipline enforced by a strict ratio between words and things. Language imitates Nature and, better still, Nature's order. The shortest way to achieve order in one's life is by consulting, under God, the double order of Nature and language. If Homer rhymes with Nature, it is because language is true. Linguists felt that language was constitutive, not merely instrumental; it marked an indefinitely large universe of thought, and its rules showed a man how to act in the daily world. This is not fanciful. A rational animal is a linguistic animal, as Descartes urged. So linguistic manners would foster the manners of good society, decorum, correctness. Perspicuity, the favourite literary virtue, was not merely a literary excellence. Ideally, a writer would take dictation from the structure of language itself, just as confidently as from Nature; when he writes, he transcribes a system already verified, as if written beneath the surface of the paper in invisible ink. The writer observes things, preferably things palpable in Nature; reaches for the words affixed to them; and writes these words down in the order sanctioned by grammar, syntax, and the lexicon. This may explain why Augustan writers were prepared to assert a connexion, which seems odd to us, between genius and rules; as if genius were merely a remarkably profound sense of those rules which Nature has already composed. The form of language was not deemed to be organic; rather, it was deemed to be fixed, hopefully, once for all, as the identity of human character was deemed to be fixed, hopefully, once for all. Language, one version of 'the good life', was reasonable rather than instinctive, since it was designed for men rather than for animals. Noam Chomsky has pointed out, especially in his *Cartesian Linguistics*,[1] that linguists were anxious to distinguish as human those features of language for which instinct could not possibly provide a sufficient explanation; since animals

[1] Noam Chomsky, *Cartesian Linguistics: A Chapter in the History of Rationalist Thought* (Harper and Row, New York, 1966), pp. 29 ff.

were invariably better equipped than men where the power of instinct was in question. It was necessary to distinguish men from animals, in one direction, and from automata, in another. Wise after the event, we think of Restoration linguistics as yet another grand conspiracy to produce a type of man amenable to official purpose, comfortably placed as 'rational animal' in the great chain of being as in official textbooks; but we forget that these forms of rhetoric are always at work. We cannot be sure that we are not their products. That, however, is another question. *The Triumph of the English Language* documents the achievement of a single language. To complete the account it is enough to emphasise that the motives at work were not, in the first instance, linguistic. The motives were social and scientific, as well as political; social, because they sponsored an image of society free at last from strife and faction, the record of the Civil War finally consigned to history; scientific, because they implied control over words on the analogy of the scientist's control over things, or the artisan's control over his material; and political, because they urged the sinking of Party difference and implied that the work could now be done.

To cite a case in point: Bolingbroke's *Dissertation on Parties* (1734) is Tory propaganda, but the basis of its rhetoric is the claim that Parties are now archaic, the remaining divisions merely nominal. Bolingbroke wanted to change the rules, because he saw better prospects in the vigour of a 'country' Party, opposed to the 'Court' Party. The Magna Carta was the Settlement of 1688, universally accepted; the new tabernacle was the British constitution, sponsored by Nature, endorsed by every true-born Englishman. Whig and Tory, 'the furious offspring of the inauspicious parents, roundhead and cavalier', were now free from real difference; let them put aside their nominal difference, that last figment. 'The spirit and principles of the constitution will prevail at last', Bolingbroke promised. Of course the general run of Tory propaganda was partisan, blunt, often savage; writers went the direct way to attack. But in its more subtle forms it tried to win by claiming the merit of superior values, implied in a superior idiom; as if intimations of unity were peculiarly dear to the Tory heart. There have been divisions and factions, the rhetoric says; let there now be one thing, peace. The pattern is the same in Bolingbroke as in Swift and Pope. In the *Dissertation* Bolingbroke presents himself as the apostle of unity. The language of Cavalier and Roundhead, Whig and Tory, was the rage of faction; now was the time for peace. The historical irony of the *Dissertation* is that it was addressed to Walpole, who had his own plan for the peace of the Augustans; he was hardly dazzled by Tory rhetoric, since he had already destroyed the Tory Party.

Hugh Kenner has offered another analogy, that of anatomy. In Sprat's view, reality is anatomised, divided into atoms, each of which is then given a verbal partner: the thing or the fact 'is the atom of knowledge as the word is the atom of language'. This depends upon the contemporary atomic theory, that atoms are qualitatively homogeneous, formed from a single universal substance or matter. The atom is to matter, then, as the word is to language, the entire 'body' of speech. This is the point where grammarians met the natural scientists; Sprat speaks the same language as Henry Baker. The scientific aim was to sort things out; the same object was applied to language. There were many things to be said in favour of the language used by Nashe and the Elizabethan translators, but it was not relevant, not timely, to say them: you could not hope to get things done, as long as you held to that way of words. Elizabethan language was too whimsical for social use. One of the most revealing aspects of the new linguistics was the conviction that meaning should not depend upon the nature of the individual speaker. Elizabethan prose is largely certified by the voice of the speaker; we attend to the voice and therefore we attend to what the speaker is saying. Literally, we go along with the voice. The oral character of speech does not impose any formal discipline upon speaker or listener. To entertain speech as voice is to accept a relation which is incorrigibly 'personal', since it does not allow a distinction between the speaker and 'what is being said'. The oral character of the relation makes such a distinction appear mechanical and superficial. When words lose their oral character; or rather, when a distinction arises between the speaker and 'what is being said', we move into a different world, with a different set of expectations. In this new world words lose their character as sounds and become, as I have remarked, black marks on a white page. The words aspire to the fixity of silence. We are in this world when Locke refers to words as 'marks for the ideas' within the speaker's mind. After the Restoration, literature tends less and less to depend upon the relation between speaker and listener: what is said does not now depend upon the nature of the speaker or the listener's sense of that nature. Increasingly, what is said becomes an object of scrutiny, and the speaker's voice becomes a secondary matter, a complication. The relation of subject to predicate, as Kenner remarks, is no longer 'something affirmed, by a speaker, but something verified, by an observer'.[1] Before the relation could be verified, of course, the words had to be fixed in place. What happens in a print-culture when words do not stay in place is shown in the *Voyage to Laputa*, the parody of the word-machine. In the Gutenberg era the more you prized the fixity of print and the corresponding fixity of grammar and syntax, the more you entertained the fantasy of words jumbled in wild configurations. The official purpose of the dictionary, in that age of dictionaries, was to make words stay until required.

It is useful to consider the assumptions of this programme. Men like Sprat thought that if you called a man a perceiving consciousness, you offered a designation good enough for any

---

[1] Hugh Kenner, 'The Man of Sense as Buster Keaton', *Virginia Quarterly Review*, vol. 41, no. 1 (Winter 1965), p. 87. A revised version appears in his *The Counterfeiters* (Indiana University Press, Bloomington, 1968).

purpose. The idea of a person was becoming archaic. Orthodoxy was no longer interested in the minute particulars of a personality. This marks the loss of what we may call the Shakespearean imagination. The official mind was now chiefly interested in the observation of a 'man of sense' on duty at his perceiving post. It was assumed, to begin with, that there are connexions between things, the benevolence of God being what it is. Man is usefully employed in perceiving these connexions; this is his best function. 'The infinite wise Contriver of us and all things about us', Locke writes in the second Book of the *Essay*, 'hath fitted our Senses, Faculties, and Organs, to the Conveniences of Life and the Business we have to do here.' The employment of those faculties is therefore a fundamental part of the good life, a continuous act of faith and devotion. Not until Hume was this position seriously challenged. When Hume maintained that the mind can never perceive any real connexion among distinct existences, the perceiving consciousness found itself unemployed. If personal identity is not verifiable by the congruence of its experience and the relation between the things perceived, the role of the man of sense is absurd. So he remained unemployed until Kant gave him a different job. If Hume is right; if the missing relation between things cannot be perceived; perhaps it may be prescribed, derived from the character of the mind itself. What the imagination has joined together may not be put asunder. 'The imagination is the will of things', Wallace Stevens said in our own time; meaning that the imagination is the will, engaged upon certain tasks congenial to its nature. The first task is the prescription of relation. Man and Nature are related because man's need is great. This is the chief cause of the critical preoccupation with the nature of the imagination; because in the Kantian universe the imagination is God. Or rather, the only meaning to be ascribed to 'God' is: the imagination. .

This is to look ahead in one direction. To look ahead in

another is to see that the assumptions of Sprat and, allowing for difference, of Swift himself are undone by Lewis Carroll and James Joyce. Capitalising upon the fact that the imagination delights in running beyond nature, Carroll and Joyce set words loose. In the dream-world of *Finnegans Wake*, Hugh Kenner observed on another occasion, 'the mind is detached from responsibility toward things, cut loose in the nowhere—the not quite trackless nowhere in which words remain'.[1] It is a long story, still incomplete. In *A Portrait of the Artist as a Young Man* Stephen reads the signatures of things, in this respect at least a Thomist, but in *Finnegans Wake* things have no signatures distinct from their verbal selves. Nature, which to Swift was still in some measure the word and proof of God, is now dissolved. Subject and object are one subject. In Lewis Carroll words mean whatever one pays them to mean; a condition possible because these words, liberated from Nature, move within a closed circle. In that circle, Elizabeth Sewell has observed, 'all the world is paper and all the seas are ink'. Carroll's aim is 'to make the mind create for itself a more orderly universe'; more like mathematics, or symbolic logic, that bachelor science. This achievement is possible as long as certain other achievements are deemed irrelevant. We are not to seek an available order in the world, for instance. There are intimations of this subversive game in *Tristram Shandy* and *A Tale of a Tub*, but neither Sterne nor Swift was prepared to give himself to Nonsense, Lewis Carroll's gay science. The odd attitude to mathematics, however, shows how deeply these writers felt that something weird was going on, and that strange things would happen if you detached words from their native responsibility. Words were responsible to things; or it was dangerous to think otherwise. The pun, I have argued, is a step in this subversive direction.

The attitude of Restoration linguists was not, indeed, new, but it was applied with new force. From Cicero to Bacon there

[1] Hugh Kenner, *Dublin's Joyce* (Chatto and Windus, London, 1955), p. 301.

were writers who deplored the *mardi gras* of words; the mind was sufficiently fallible without adding another snare. When Sprat hailed Bacon as the classic authority in language, he had in mind Bacon's attack in the *Advancement of Learning* upon the word-mongers, those who hunted more after words than matter, seeking *copie* rather than weight. Ascham and others had defended their linguistic procedures by appeal to the rights of humanism and the cogency of the trivium, but Restoration linguists were convinced that they had now found the obvious answer; adjust your words to the order of the things to which they refer, and you cannot go far wrong. The order of things was assumed to be a material order, verifiable by common sense and scientific method.

There are two sides to this question. It is probably better to write like Defoe than like Nashe, if it comes to a choice. L. C. Knights has argued that Elizabethan prose is too fluid to permit subtle effects of tone and modulation. But there is a certain loss in the achievement of a uniform style, a 'single vision', the imposition of anatomy and control. The loss may be represented in Stevens's aphorism: 'to impose is not to discover'. We think of the Restoration linguists as executive minds locked in one situation, the observer stationed before a scene which he must bring to focus; the subject, determined to control the object, at whatever cost. The deliverance of so many things almost in an equal number of words was an administrative ideal. That it changed the character of English prose is a familiar fact. But there were problems. The apposition of word and thing was fine until you questioned its basis and disclosed its insufficiency. It was embarrassing to discover that the correspondence soon dissolved. This discovery clouds Locke's great *Essay* and his *Thoughts on Education*; that the 'names of mixed modes' have no 'standards in nature', no 'things' to which they may be referred, 'whereby men may rectify and adjust their significations'. The structure of language and the structure of reality are not, alas, one and the same.

In the chapter 'Of the Imperfections of Words' Locke adverted yet again to 'the Doubtfulness and Uncertainty of their Signification' since 'Sounds have no natural Connection with our Ideas, but have all their signification from the arbitrary Imposition of Men.' He refers again to 'assemblages of ideas put together at the pleasure of the mind, pursuing its own ends of discourse, and suited to its own notions; whereby it designs not to copy anything really existing, but to denominate and rank things as they come to agree with those archetypes or forms it has made'.[1] Locke had in mind words like 'banter', 'sham', and 'wheedle', which stand for collections of ideas unknown to Nature: the mind is solely responsible for these words. Strictly speaking, of course, this applies to every word; because according to Locke himself words are signs not of things or of the nature of things but rather of the ideas within his mind who speaks them. Life would still be easy if the speaker could ensure continuous fellowship, however mysterious, between word and idea, but even this was impaired, because the doubtfulness of a word increased with the complexity of its idea; the word 'white' is easier to define than the word 'modesty'. All that Locke could suggest as a contribution to lucidity was that 'words standing for things which are known and distinguished by their outward shapes should be expressed by little draughts and prints made of them'. This is interesting as a commitment to the visual image, but it does not solve the problem. What it reveals is Locke's desire to confront the nature of things as directly as possible, if necessary by deleting words altogether. In the seventeenth century there were many projects for a real, universal language in which characters would express not words but the things themselves. Samuel Hartlib corresponded with Boyle on the matter in 1646. In 1668 the Royal Society published John Wilkins's *Essay towards a Real Character*, mainly because scientists thought that a universal language, like the ideogram, would facilitate the

[1] Locke, *Works* (London, 1727), vol. 1, pp. 218 ff.

development of a 'Philosophy of Mankind' and would put an end to religious bitterness and faction.[1] The question was pondered in different contexts by Bacon, Vossius, Herman Hugo, and Comenius. In Augustan literature, wherever we turn, we hear of 'the delusion of words'; as Pope in *The Dunciad* points to the imprisonment of thoughts in 'the pale of words'. Even Berkeley, who might have been expected to endorse the products of the mind more warmly than Locke, made the same complaint. In the *Alciphron* he admits the significance of words even when they do not stand in apposition to ideas; they may have a rhetorical function, for instance. But in the Introduction to the *Principles of Human Knowledge* he blames language for most of the current philosophical errors, especially for the pretensions of abstract ideas.

Swift's interest in the theoretical aspects of language was, of course, slight. He often discussed language, as in the *Letter to a Young Clergyman*, the *Proposal for Correcting, Improving, and Ascertaining the English Tongue*, the *Discourse to Prove the Antiquity of the English Tongue*, the *Polite Conversation*, *Hints towards an Essay on Conversation*, and *Tatler*, no. 230. But in these and other places he was mainly concerned with the relation between language and manners. Linguistic theory was not his concern. But I shall argue that he held language on a tight rein, and that when he thought of the relation between words and things he found himself preferring things themselves because they had the merit of silence. That he was alive to the absurdities in the question of *res* and *verba* is clear from the episode in the *Voyage to Laputa* when Gulliver visits the School of Languages. Three professors, he finds, are trying to shorten discourse by cutting polysyllables to monosyllables, 'and leaving out Verbs and Participles; because in Reality all things imaginable are but Nouns'. Another project was to abolish words altogether: 'since Words are only Names for Things, it would be more

---

[1] See Benjamin de Mott, 'Comenius and the Real Character', *Publications of the Modern Language Association*, vol. LXX (December 1955), pp. 1068–81.

convenient for all Men to carry about them such Things as were necessary to express the particular Business they are to discourse on'. Swift is ridiculing those who cannot see that a relation between *A* and *B* asserts difference as well as similarity. But the question itself, the status of words, is as serious to Swift as to Locke or anyone else; subject to the consideration that a shoemaker is well advised to stick to his last.

For the moment it is enough to posit in Swift the usual Augustan suspicion of words. His preference for things is part of a larger allegiance. We can put the matter quite simply. Value—such as it is—resides in things, because they have been given to man by God; rather than in words, which are man's invention and are likely to be tainted with his pride. It is one of Swift's fundamental assumptions that what man has received is better than what he has invented. This partly accounts for Swift's approval of the landed class rather than the moneyed class, a basic commitment in his Tory politics. Man has been given the land, but he has merely invented money. Given a primitive unity, man has invented faction, complexity, abstraction, lies. In *Further Thoughts on Religion* Swift contrasts man in this respect with the animals. 'Lions, bears, elephants, and some other animals', he says, 'are strong or valiant, and their species never degenerates in their native soil, except they happen to be enslaved or destroyed by human fraud: But men degenerate every day, merely by the folly, the perverseness, the avarice, the tyranny, the pride, the treachery, or inhumanity of their own kind.'[1] When Gulliver has spent his energy trying to explain European customs to his Houyhnhnm master, he reflects: 'It put me to the Pains of many Circumlocutions to give my Master a right Idea of what I spoke; for their Language doth not abound in Variety of Words, because their Wants and Passions are fewer than among us.'[2] A large

---

[1] *Irish Tracts, 1720–1723, and Sermons*, edited by Herbert Davis (Basil Blackwell, Oxford, 1963), p. 264.
[2] *Gulliver's Travels*, p. 242.

dictionary does not necessarily prove the range of imagination or the plentitude of life; it merely demonstrates the enormity of our desires. Some of this feeling in Swift, incidentally, may be explained by reference to the rhetorical tradition in which words are subordinated to things and facts. 'Rem tene, verba sequentur', Cato the Elder is supposed to have advised.[1] Admittedly, this may mean little enough; a speaker should take the precaution of having something to say. But when we meet Cato's counsel in Bacon, Hobbes, Locke, Cowley, Dryden, Defoe, Swift, and other writers, we find that it has acquired another implication, that words are often the choice instruments of delusion, that they are liberal to the degree of promiscuity, unless they are somehow restrained and fixed. The only available discipline, some writers hoped against hope, was the subjection of words to things, despite all the theoretical embarrassments. The best things were those that could be seen and therefore believed. Released, words were black magic.

This may account for Swift's suspicion of rhetoric, and especially his distrust of that part of rhetoric which is concerned with 'the moving of the Passions'. In the *Letter to a Young Clergyman* he argues that Demosthenes was luckier than Cicero. Demosthenes, 'who had to deal with a People of much more Politeness, Learning, and Wit, laid the greatest Weight of his Oratory upon the Strength of his Arguments offered to their Understanding and Reason: Whereas, Tully considered the Dispositions of a fiercer, more ignorant, and less mercurial Nation, by dwelling almost entirely on the pathetick Part'.[2] But Swift was so hostile to 'the pathetick Part' that he would not even give St Paul the right to consult it. Later in the *Letter* he insists that 'at least in these Northern Climates' the preacher who seeks to move the passions of an ignorant congregation is

---

[1] A. C. Howell, 'Res et Verba', *English Literary History*, vol. XIII (June 1946), pp. 131-42.
[2] *Irish Tracts, 1720–1723, and Sermons*, p. 69.

wasting his time. Swift does not say, what is clear enough, that he despises the rhetorician who addresses himself to the passions. The only rhetoric he allows is that of the simple style, the direction of sound arguments to the Understanding and Reason. The cultivation of a plain style is of course a rhetorical commitment in itself. Swift favoured it partly because he distrusted words and partly because his rhetorical aim was to provoke. He approved that style because it was the least of verbal evils.

But the point to make is that Swift was uneasy with anything that did not occupy space; so he treated words as if they were things. To ward off the ghosts he committed himself to the language of the eye, an administrative intention. Proper things, like land, are already in their proper places. The crucial questions are considerations of relation, position, the network of objects in space. If something is not in its proper place, move it, or get rid of it; this is the function of satire. *Gulliver's Travels* is designed to vex men into sanity, sanity being the proper 'commonplace' in which to reside. The good administrator puts things in a practical order, then leaves them alone. The human mind is not a particularly reliable instrument, it appears, so the best arrangement is the least pretentious, a simple diagram which helps to make life tolerable. Locke assumed that the best use of words was to distinguish the results of observation and to communicate them to other people. Swift assumed that the best use of the mind was to discern a simple, God-appointed arrangement of things, by which a man might live; the simpler, the better. Things themselves had the merit of arriving without human interference.

Inevitably, Swift thought that the English language, like everything else, was seriously corrupt. Much damage was the work of Court and the theatre. The chief evil was what he called in the *Tatler* 'false refinements', a Whig invention when propaganda was required. The best time in the history of the language was 'the peaceable Part of King Charles the First's Reign'; naturally, this was also the best time for politeness and conversation between the sexes. These conditions produce that simplicity which, as he says in the *Tatler* paper, is 'the best and truest Ornament of most Things in human Life'.[1] In matters of language, simplicity is the great standard. The Book of Common Prayer and the King James translation of the Bible are excellent in simplicity. Proper words in proper places may not be the most illuminating definition of style, but if we take it literally we find it relevant. We may translate it: few words, carefully chosen, each lodged in its proper place. Vices of style are always, in Swift's eyes, crimes against simplicity. In the *Letter to a Young Clergyman* he warns his pupil against 'hard words' and 'fine Language'. In *Remarks upon Tindall's Rights of the Christian Church* he makes fun of Locke for his 'refined Jargon', and in 1714 he complains to the Earl of Peterborough that everyone has become a 'refiner'. It is a Whig vice. Swift ridiculed Steele for attending to the cadences of words without consulting their meaning; as in *The Public Spirit of the Whigs* he sneers at the same victim:

He hath a confused Remembrance of Words since he left the University, but hath lost half their Meaning, and puts them together with no Regard, except to their Cadence; as I remember a Fellow nailed up Maps in a Gentleman's Closet, some sideling, others upside down, the better to adjust them to the Pannels.[2]

Swift links Steele with Burnet for similar reasons, referring to 'that peculiar Manner of expressing himself, which the Poverty of our Language forceth me to call their Stile'.[3] In the *Preface to the Bishop of Sarum's Introduction* he gives a more dramatic account of Burnet's style:

First, I would advise him, if it be not too late in his Life, to endeavour a little at mending his Style, which is mighty defective in the Circumstances of Grammar, Propriety, Politeness and

[1] *Bickerstaff Papers*, edited by Herbert Davis (Basil Blackwell, Oxford, 1957), p. 177.
[2] *Political Tracts 1713–1719*, edited by Herbert Davis and Irvin Ehrenpreis (Basil Blackwell, Oxford, 1964), p. 36.
[3] *A Proposal for Correcting the English Tongue, Polite Conversation, Etc.*, edited by Herbert Davis, with Louis Landa (Basil Blackwell, Oxford, 1964), p. 57.

Smoothness. I fancied at first, it might be owing to the Prevalence of his Passion, as People sputter out Nonsense for Haste, when they are in a Rage.[1]

When Swift praises Temple in the *Battle of the Books* and again in the Preface to Temple's *Letters*, he cites the master's style as proof of excellence. A man is known by the company he keeps and, with equal justice, by the propriety of his style. Swift once told Lord Orrery that he refused to sign a Report until 'the words *Mobb* and *behave* were alter'd to *Rabble* and *behaved themselves*'.[2]

This is not pedantry, since to Swift there is a direct relation between behaviour and style. To write well one must be, in Swift's estimate, a gentleman. If proof of merit is simplicity, proof of evil is 'singularity', wilful and eccentric vaunting, the personal equivalent of faction. There is one style which is better than any other; a simple style in which words are adjusted to facts and things. There is one style of behaviour which is better than any other. So there is a demonstrable relation between simplicity in style and propriety in life. Swift interpreted the correspondence with notable force. Blair maintained in his *Lectures on Rhetoric* that he had gone too far; Swift's manner was 'somewhat hard and dry', although for 'precision of style' and 'correctness' he was exemplary. But to Swift 'hard' and 'dry' are terms of praise. The best style in English was the equivalent of being an Anglican, a Tory, a monarchist, and so forth. Oldmixon and Mainwaring were right, then, in reading the *Proposal for Correcting, Improving, and Ascertaining the English Tongue* as a Tory pamphlet, not merely because it was addressed to Harley and Swift planned to pack his Academy with Tories; but because its linguistic assumptions were recognisably Tory. In the given case, Swift implied, there was a relation between political folly and bad writing; it

[1] *Ibid.* p. 82.
[2] *Correspondence*, edited by Harold Williams (Clarendon Press, Oxford, 1965), vol. IV, p. 396.

was possible to throw a crumb of praise to Steele in the *Proposal*, but the major attack delivered in *The Importance of the Guardian Considered* was based on the understanding that a bad man, a miserable Whig, is necessarily a bad writer, if he has the impudence to be a writer at all. Swift wanted, within reason, to ascertain or 'fix' the language; he thought that English was degenerating, changing too quickly, for the same reasons which were urging men to fall away from the Tory verities of character and opinion. When Matthew Arnold praised the French Academy and hoped for the development in England of a comparable force of opinion and taste, his concern was similar to Swift's; with this difference, that Swift's image of uniform excellence was based on a particular political conviction rather than a general sense of cultural health. To put the point a little more severely; Arnold was prepared to concede that the virtues of style were many and different, while he admitted a preference on his own authority; Swift thought that a good style was one style, uniform, and for that reason universally capable. For Swift, the character of a man's life was expressed in political and religious terms; for Arnold, it issued more variously in education, literature, and high culture, as well as in religion and politics. To write like Arnold it was necessary to fear for the continuity of civilised values in a world dominated by barbarians. To write like Swift it was necessary, genius apart, to dig a moat around politics and religion and there-after, with the greatest vigour, to hold the fort. There was always the risk of failure and, in his last years, the certainty of having failed.

There is a passage in Yeats's *A Vision* which offers relevant terms; the discussion of Phase 21 and the type which embodies that phase:

In phase he strengthens conflict to the utmost by refusing all activity that is not *antithetical*: he becomes intellectually dominating, intellectually unique. He apprehends the simplicity of his opposite phase as some vast systematisation, in which the will imposes itself upon the multiplicity of living images, or events, upon all in Shake-speare, in Napoleon even, that delighted in its independent life; for he is a tyrant and must kill his adversary. If he is a novelist, his characters must go his road, and not theirs, and perpetually demonstrate his thesis; he will love construction better than the flow of life, and as a dramatist he will create character and situation without passion, and without liking, and yet he is a master of surprise, for one can never be sure where even a charge of shot will fall. Style exists now but as a sign of work well done, a certain energy and precision of movement; in the artistic sense it is no longer possible, for the tension of the will is too great to allow of suggestion. Writers of this phase are great public men and they exist after death as historical monuments, for they are without meaning apart from time and circumstance.[1]

With this in mind we may look at a few sentences in Swift, including this passage from *A Short View of the State of Ireland*:

Now, if all this be true, upon which I could easily enlarge; I would be glad to know by what secret Method, it is, that we grow a rich and flourishing People, without Liberty, Trade, Manufactures, Inhabitants, Money, or the Privilege of Coining; without Industry, Labour, or Improvements of Lands, and with more than half the Rent and Profits of the whole Kingdom, annually exported; for which we receive not a single Farthing: And to make up all this, nothing worth mentioning, except the Linnen of the North, a Trade casual, corrupted, and at Mercy; and some Butter from Cork. If we do flourish, it must be against every Law of Nature and Reason; like the Thorn at Glassenbury, that blossoms in the Midst of Winter.[2]

Style functions here 'but as a sign of work well done', secreting itself in the work and finding itself there. We do not flourish, Swift urges; and if we did, it would be a freak of Nature, an act of extraordinary liberality on Nature's part. To the extent that we flourish, he suggests, we owe it to Nature's special care for us, a care evoked by the vision of our enemies systemati-cally destroying us. So the issue is joined: the laws of Nature and Reason transcend themselves as if by miracle, to operate

---

[1] W. B. Yeats, *A Vision* (Macmillan, London, 1962), pp. 156–7.
[2] *Irish Tracts 1728–1733*, edited by Herbert Davis (Basil Blackwell, Oxford, 1955), pp. 9–10.

in our favour, and are incited to do so by natural sympathy, a proper sense of justice. Cruel burdens are loaded upon us to prevent our natural growth; and so forth. So the power of Swift's sentence is in the first instance an achievement of structure: the facts are sharply blocked out, the edges finely cut, set off against their enemies. 'The tension of the will', Yeats says, 'is too great to allow for suggestion', for aura, atmosphere. Yet the sentence is full of surprise, especially where Nature's liberality is featured in the thorn at Glassenbury that blossoms, miraculously, in the midst of winter; like Ireland, when that poor country blossoms at all, but unlike Ireland, for the thorn's blossoms are perfectly formed. 'He will love construction better than the flow of life', Yeats says; because construction is what the writer does to life and the flow of life is what life does to us. We revel in the flow of life, or we do not: we yield ourselves to it, or we do not. In Swift's sentence the chief effect is an effect of construction as the mind imposes itself upon its material and the flow of life is acknowledged only where Ireland's masters have frustrated it and Swift takes up its cause. It is as if he were looking round the corners of his terminology and seeing there strange emblems of his loss. So the sentence, which at first sight seems nothing but construction, bristles with disclosure and gesture; these are its tokens of power. The decorum of the prose depends, of course, upon the 'tension of the will'; we call it irony when the will imposes the distance of its values.

In Swift's favourite constructions one fact is set off against another; often, one set of values in conflict with another. In the fourth Drapier's Letter he writes:

It is true, indeed, that within the Memory of Man, the Parliaments of England have sometimes assumed the Power of binding this Kingdom, by Laws enacted there; wherein they were, at first, openly opposed (as far as Truth, Reason, and Justice are capable of opposing) by the famous Mr. Molyneux, an English Gentleman born here; as well as by several of the greatest Patriots, and best

Whigs in England; but the Love and Torrent of Power prevailed. Indeed, the Arguments on both Sides were Invincible. For in Reason, all Government without the Consent of the Governed, is the very Definition of Slavery: But in Fact, Eleven Men well armed, will certainly subdue one single Man in his Shirt. But I have done. For those who have used Power to cramp Liberty, have gone so far as to resent even the Liberty of Complaining; although a Man upon the Rack, was never known to be refused the Liberty of roaring as loud as he thought fit.[1]

The paragraph begins by setting the Parliaments of England against Truth, Reason and Justice, embodied in Molyneux, the best Whigs and the greatest Patriots. A Parliament finding itself in that position should hesitate. But the 'Love and Torrent of Power prevailed', degeneracy being what it is. Swift is a master of surprise, for Yeats's good reason, 'because one can never be sure where even a charge of shot will fall'. The first surprise comes when he says that the arguments on both sides were invincible; this can only be the case where the issue is not joined. The two sides are called Reason and Fact but, alas, they have nothing to do with each other. Reason offers an invincible definition of slavery; 'But in Fact, Eleven Men well armed, will certainly subdue one single Man in his Shirt.' The poor man in his shirt, it then appears, is Right Reason itself, a pathetically accoutred figure in a degenerate age. 'But I have done', Swift says, and at once the distressed figure, the man in his shirt, becomes the speaker, M. B. Drapier, already accused. Both figures are now identified with Ireland on the rack, denied the liberty of roaring. The typical gesture of this paragraph is the swift movement from idea to image, especially where the idea must depend upon its own resources and the image is sustained by the degeneracy of the times. This dramatises the exposure of the moral idea which has nothing to defend it but its truth. Again, this is commanding prose; only one way of dealing with experience is allowed.

[1] *The Drapier's Letters, and Other Works, 1724-1725*, edited by Herbert Davis (Basil Blackwell, Oxford, 1959), pp. 62-3.

The implication is that all other ways are now in the possession of the Philistines.

These procedures are particularly rich in *A Modest Proposal*. Many features of the essay are at once obvious and important; the tone of the projector fending off human and moral considerations in his economic zeal and yet, now and again, stumbling upon a cliché which conceals an ironic truth—as when the projector varies his diction and calls the people of Ireland 'souls'; or the *tour de force* of out-Heroding Herod by parodying the Massacre of the Innocents. The basic technique is what Kenneth Burke calls 'planned incongruity', the imposition of a proper perspective by putting gross perspectives in lurid proximity. Much of Swift's irony is enforced by these discrepancies; the merit of incongruity is that a writer may capitalise upon it. In the face of much apathy—this is the first irony—the projector offers a highly organised programme at a time when highly organised programmes are much in vogue. Again, Swift's favourite discrepancies are those which destroy the relation between moral ideas and facts. People are the wealth of a nation, say the moral idealists and some economists; but not in Ireland, the facts reply. (In the *Proposal for Giving Badges to Beggars* Swift, all irony spent, says: 'As this is the only Christian Country where People contrary to the old Maxim, are the Poverty and not the Riches of the Nation...') Family feeling is the basis of unity and cohesion, the moralists say; but in Ireland this does not hold. Often Swift runs his sentence in the apparent guise of a syllogism, where the middle term spins the reader from one moral context to another and the conclusion is the last word in anarchy. 'I grant this Food will be somewhat dear, and therefore very proper for Landlords; who, as they have already devoured most of the Parents, seem to have the best Title to the children.'[1] The facts of the case are so perfect in their own terms that Swift allows them a correspondingly invincible ethic; or so the irony goes. The

[1] *Irish Tracts 1728–1733*, p. 112.

138

planned incongruity sets the idiom of rights and property against the sheer facts of the case, and the rout of the moralists is complete. Ostensibly, it is a question of title; reasonably enough, since this is the kind of mind at work. The right to devour children belongs, by the decorum of black poetry, to those who have already devoured the parents; a lurid propriety is suggested, by which the ethical consideration yields to considerations of perfection, completeness, the 'entelechy' of the case. Logic has a certain rhythm, shared with its travesty. This is how Swift's dominion works. The will imposes itself, as Yeats says, upon the multiplicity of living images by seeming to collapse before them. Swift says a moment later:

I have already computed the Charge of nursing a Beggar's Child (in which List I reckon all Cottagers, Labourers, and Four fifths of the Farmers) to be about two Shillings per Annum, Rags included; and I believe, no Gentleman would repine to give Ten Shillings for the Carcase of a good fat Child; which, as I have said, will make four Dishes of excellent nutritive Meat, when he hath only some particular Friend, or his own Family, to dine with him.

The sentence is a declaration of war; class war, with the beggars, cottagers, labourers, and farmers absurdly set against the gentlemen who will eat the children. No gentleman would repine to give ten shillings for the carcase of a good fat child; the point being that no gentleman intends to repine about anything he has done. Repining is not a gentleman's way. The incongruity works, this time, by offering a blatant euphemism so outlandish that the reader is bound to take it literally. The basic technique of the *Proposal* is to confound moral categories, to play off one set of categories against another, to contrive a situation in which words with rival allegiances collide and yet the sentence drives on to a conclusion beyond its contract. The cadence of cliché is always available as a banana-skin for the dense. When someone raises the question of old people, diseased or maimed, Swift answers: 'But I am not in the least Pain upon that Matter, because it is very well

known, that they are every Day dying, and rotting, by Cold
and Famine, and Filth, and Vermin, as fast as can be reasonably expected.' With the last phrase the projector's happiness
is complete; the complacency anticipated by the happy
repetition (dying and rotting) and the satisfying variety of
means (cold and famine and filth and vermin). Projectors
are always pleased when a single crude end is attainable by
any of several crude means. Most of Swift's sentences in the
Modest Proposal are moral exercises imposed upon the reader
for his discomfiture; hence the proliferation of incongruous
values where primacy is invariably ensured for the wrong one.
Enumerating the advantages of his proposal, he writes:

Sixthly, This would be a great Inducement to Marriage, which all
Wise Nations have either encouraged by Rewards, or enforced by
Laws and Penalties. It would encrease the Care and Tenderness of
Mothers towards their Children, when they were sure of a Settlement for Life, to the poor Babes, provided in some Sort by the
Publick, to their annual Profit instead of Expence. We should soon
see an honest Emulation among the married Women, which of them
could bring the fattest Child to the Market. Men would become as
fond of their Wives, during the Time of their Pregnancy, as they
are now of their Mares in Foal, their Cows in Calf, or Sows when
they are ready to farrow; nor offer to beat or kick them, (as it is
too frequent a Practice) for fear of a Miscarriage.[1]

Swift plays the game according to rules which he changes at
every turn; each rule obtains until the author's whim changes
it. It is like winning at chess by cutting off the opponent's
hands. The introduction of a new rule puts the projector
another step ahead. The passage begins as if it were a conventional plea for marriage and families, leading to the usual
endorsement of tenderness between mothers and children.
Then the rules are changed. Children are livestock, until
they are brought to market and killed. The reference to 'poor
Babes' seems to turn the sentence back to humanity, but only
for a moment in which we realise the absurdity of that direc-

[1] *Irish Tracts 1728–1733*, p. 115.

tion; then it spins in another direction, toward impoverishment and money. This is developed on the basis of the cliché that people are wealth: Swift treats it as if it were literally true; so mothers will vie with one another to show off the fattest child. This emulation is 'honest' because it is conducted in sanctioned terms; it is characteristic of such words that they lose their ethical meaning, under that kind of pressure, and assume the public tone; here the word is a political counter, shadow of its ethical self. The analogy is held at that point. Mothers would treat their children like calves; men would treat their wives like valuable cows, at least during pregnancy. This would make a significant improvement. The field on which this irony is played is the traditional view of the several levels of being extending from the vegetative level to Godhead; the point being that people are supposed to act more gracefully if they look up, emulating their betters, aspiring; but here they act decently by looking down. Animals are better than men. Mothers behave themselves as they should only if they think of their children as calves; and so forth. *Gulliver's Travels* is the most elaborate version of this device, playing off one level of being against another, confounding upper and lower; it works by confounding categories, becomes a powerful freak of nature by disclosing without particular comment the freaks already there. Meanwhile, projectors are not in the least pain.

In the *Modest Proposal* Swift uses many devices of irony, but chiefly one which he first discovered in *A Tale of a Tub*; to confound differences and blast similarities. It is the governing technique of the *Directions to Servants*. If people think certain things the same, you gain an effect by treating them as different; if they think things different, you suppress the difference. All the better if this involves, as in the *Directions to Servants*, a clash of values, poor ethics and the main chance. The eventfulness of Swift's prose arises from this procedure, where the detail of the writing, like harmonics in music, redeems the monotony of the denunciation. One of his recurrent problems was to persist in saying essentially the same few things, without frustrating his aim by repetition. The answer was: enliven the monotone by constant changes of pressure and dynamics. So changing the rules has the same effect, within the paragraph, as new chapters of incident in an extrovert novel. The stratagem is somewhat like the procedure in certain modern novels where the motif is boredom and the greatest human effort is seen to be expended on merely passing the time. One of the more entrancing discoveries of modern fiction is that even when nothing is happening, so far as reportage is concerned, the language which delivers this nothing may be eventful, lively with internal business. Flaubert is a master of this resource. Samuel Beckett has capitalised upon the tradition. In Beckett's later novels hundreds of paragraphs record ennui so engagingly that the reader asks, can it really be so boring if it yields these diverting sentences? The eighteenth-century masters are Swift and Sterne. What Swift is saying in the *Modest Proposal* is: 'You are murdering the Irish people; at least do it systematically, organize it for profit, don't waste such talents in carelessness. You are starving the people too quickly; fatten them up and sell them.' The difference between this synopsis and the essay itself is lively detail, variations upon the musical theme, incidents of language, verbal surprise and suspense. The essay as a whole is meant to strike the reader as monstrous and hypothetical, in fact, but he is not allowed to evade the feeling that it is not at all monstrous or hypothetical in principle. 'I do not do these things', he is allowed to feel; but, on a second thought, 'I do this kind of thing, admittedly.' The difference between fact and principle is allowed, at the price of acknowledging that the correspondence between them is outrageously exact.

We revert to words and things. Our impression of Swift's prose is that the words are always ready to be tested in the light of facts, things, Nature. His style is not wordy, it is thingy. Every change of key, every new direction, forces us to attend to a new thing on the way. We recognise this commitment when we say that his style is natural, meaning that it acknowledges Nature. The nearest equivalent in English verse is *Hudibras*, a poem Swift knew by heart. The chief quality of Swift's style is indeed simplicity, in the sense that it sponsors attainable objects and leaves nothing to chance. But the simplicity depends upon the peculiar form of his energy, which is constantly clearing away the debris of fancy and pride so that intelligible facts may have room to appear. This more than any other quality distinguishes Swift's style from Johnson's. Johnson was prejudiced against Swift and disapproved of his general style, but the reason is interesting. Under Boswell's pressure he conceded that Swift had 'a good neat style', and he allowed neatness as a merit. What he criticised was its dependence upon facts and things. This prevented him from admiring *The Conduct of the Allies*: 'it operates by the mere weight of facts', he said, 'with very little assistance from the hand that produced them'.[1] Professor Wimsatt has an excellent comment: Johnson disapproved of Swift's style because it was too heavily dependent upon 'a constant succession of different things, not different aspects of the same things'. Johnson's own aim, Wimsatt remarks, was 'to deal not in things but in thoughts about things'.[2] The difference is a matter of emphasis, but it is crucial. Johnson felt that attention to things was justified only by the grandeur of the generality they supported; the generality once achieved, the things could be dispatched. Swift did not object to generality, unless it appeared as speculative ambition; but he had no interest in it. In any case he knew, more painfully than Johnson, the gap between grand generality and puny deed. He was concerned to make a world as one builds a fort in time of need, by finding the things and putting them

[1] Johnson, *Lives of the Poets*, edited by G. Birkbeck Hill (Clarendon Press, Oxford, 1905), p. 48.
[2] William K. Wimsatt, Jr., *The Prose Style of Samuel Johnson* (Yale University Press, New Haven, 1941), pp. 99 ff.

together. He had no desire to think of the fort as separable from the things of which it was made. This is one reason for his nonchalance with metaphor. He had little need of metaphor, because he could attend to relevant things one at a time; so his chosen figure was the simile. The likeness imputed would always, in that figure, wait until he called it.

In language, it appears, Swift was extremely conservative. *A Tale of a Tub* is odd and special in his canon because it takes pleasure in the internal resources of language. Swift confounds his enemy by showing that two can play his loose game. The puns, far-fetched analogies, bogus comparisons, lexical freaks, and so forth are diversions to this end. But, as I have argued, the *Tale* cannot be completely understood in these terms. More generally, it should be remarked, Swift does not insist upon the constitutive resources of language; he is content with an instrumental role for words. Thought is one activity, speech another, and Nature is something else again. 'Proper words in proper places', yes, because the spatial idiom is congenial to Swift. The structure of language may not corres- pond to the structure of the mind, but it can be made to correspond, at least in one restricted sense, to the structure of the world. Each thing on this earth is given a place, presumably its proper place: the universe is a divine construction. Things which are out of place are scandalous. So also in language; to write well is to put proper words in their proper places, the propriety endorsed by common sense, Nature, and faith. Decorum is that sense of order. Swift's energy in language is not, except partially in the *Tale*, a self-delighting, self-engen- dering force; it is an instrument designed for ready use, in public.

II

We are told by Aristotle and reminded by Aquinas that 'man is by nature political, that is, social'; and we are to understand that this description establishes a hierarchy among the several modes of his life. A man will retain his private life, subject to the qualification that the retention is not extreme: he will not forget that he is a citizen, a member of society, the human fellowship. In the ideal human image a man will be active in the public way: if not, he lives his life at some cost to his humanity. Aristotle goes on to say that the essentially political modes of being are action (*praxis*) and speech (*lexis*);[1] we think of Cicero's compelling figure, the *doctus orator*, the learned speaker devoting his energy to the service of the commonwealth. As long as this tradition lasted, and as often as it was revived, a man's humanity was fully engaged, operative in its central force, when his life was declared in these terms; society, action, and speech. Bringing these together in one image, we say that he is fully human when he acts in a public world, speaking there on behalf of the commonwealth. The *Drapier's Letters* is a vivid occasion in this image. Concealed in the Drapier, Swift is speaking, taking action in a palpable world, on behalf of the integrity of the state. He is sustained by a terminology of long standing and great force. This explains why the Letters give such a vigorous impression of knowing what they are doing and where reality lies; as distinct from the *Tale of a Tub*, in which reality is obscure. Reading the *Drapier's Letters* we do not find occasion to say that Swift was merely negative; we do not invoke the lifelessness of the Houyhnhnms; we do not point to the insubstantial nature of Swift's values, the degree to which he undermines in practice the 'Augustan positives' he endorsed in principle.[2] The auspices are good. Swift, for once, has all the values in his favour; a great tradition, a public issue, and his own individual talent. In the *Drapier's Letters* he was guided by his sense of the classical

[1] For a discussion of these terms, see Hannah Arendt, *The Human Condition* (Doubleday, New York, 1959), pp. 24–5.

[2] F. R. Leavis, *The Common Pursuit* (Chatto and Windus, London, 1952). Also J. C. Maxwell, 'Demigods and Pickpockets', *Scrutiny*, vol. XI, no. 1 (Summer 1942), p. 35.

tradition in general, and—in particular—the forensic part of it as it was defined in Aristotle, Cicero, Seneca, and Quintilian. Acting as a public man, as a *rhetor*, he knew what was expected of him, and he knew that he could do it.

Part of this knowledge was his sense of an audience. In the *Tale of a Tub* we often feel that Swift is writing to himself, or to no one, and the hectic brilliance of the book is to some extent the result of that isolation. He did not know who was there, or whether anyone was there. In the *Drapier's Letters* he knew precisely who his readers were, and the spirit in which they were to read him. He did not admire that spirit, but he thought it might be shamed into movement. When he wrote the first Letter, intervening in a public dispute that had been proceeding fitfully for over a year, he spoke to Charles Ford as if the case were desperate: 'One can promise nothing', he says, 'from such wretches as the Irish people.'[1] Swift had not forgiven them for ignoring his pamphlet *On the Universal Use of Irish Manufactures*. But at least he knew who they were who read him. Indeed, there is a strange progression in the several Letters. In the first, he addressed himself to the Shopkeepers, Tradesmen, Farmers, and Commonpeople of Ireland, beginning 'Brethren, Friends, Countrymen, and Fellow-Subjects'. In the second, he speaks nominally to Mr Harding the heroic Printer, and therefore to readers of his *Weekly News-Letter*; a Dublin middle-class audience. The third Letter is more specifically addressed to the Nobility and Gentry of the Kingdom of Ireland. The fourth is addressed to the Whole People of Ireland. We may stop at that point and look at the pattern implied.

It is clear enough. The cogency of the *Letters* is largely the result of taking a few basic arguments and teasing out their implications. Swift commandeers the discourse on behalf of a few arguments and works these to the end of the line. The exhilaration of the *Letters* comes from the resourcefulness of

[1] *Correspondence*, vol. III, pp. 9–10.

this pattern; a few simple ideas, held apart, then brought together, and worked for all they are worth. The pattern is compelling because it is the internal equivalent of the external plan which Swift is proposing. Take a few sentences, work out all their possibilities, and thereby command the whole field of discourse: the public equivalent is to decide upon a single plan, hold to it with as much resource as you possess, and fend off all competitors. In Swift's case the public equivalent is Boycott; a simple position held with great hauteur and tenacity. A tragic version of this would be Martyrdom; a simple position held in the tragic spirit to the end of the line. Swift's political demands are best understood in these terms: he did not demand many things, but he demanded them totally.

The easiest version is the single word, taken up—it seems— quite innocently; but held until every implication in its vicinity is attracted to it. Swift gives it in principle in the *Letter to Viscount Molesworth*: 'And as it often happens at play', he says, 'that Men begin with Farthings, and go on to Gold, till some of them lose their Estates and die in Jayl: So it may possibly fall out in my Case, that by playing too long with Mr. Wood's Half-pence, I may be drawn in to pay a Fine, double to the Reward for betraying me; be sent to Prison, and not be delivered thence until I shall have payed the uttermost Farthing.'[1] This is in the spirit of gallows humour, itself a jest at the end of the line: it depends upon the fact that one has only to press words far enough to find them keeling over into the abyss. The richest jest comes when the word is innocent, to begin with, slipped into the sentence and, for the moment, ignored; then discovered, brought out into the light, and set to work in much more pointed sentences. In the seventh Letter, the *Humble Address to Parliament*, Swift picks up the word 'want' as a motif innocently provided by his enemies. 'Neither did our Case turn at all', he says, 'upon the Question,

---

[1] *The Drapier's Letters*, pp. 83-4.

whether Ireland wanted Half-pence or no. For there is no doubt, but we do want both Half-pence, Gold and Silver; and we have numberless other Wants, and some that we are not so much as allowed to name; although they are peculiar to this Nation; to which no other is subject, whom God hath blessed with Religion and Laws, or any Degree of Soil and Sunshine: But, for what Demerits on our Side, I am altogether in the Dark.' The wit that enables Swift to capitalise upon the innocent word, turning it into a monstrous noun, plural in its enormity, carries the joke to the point at which syntax has to stop; but until that point is reached, one clause incites the next as—by implication—one injury begets another. This is the pattern of the *Letters* as a whole: from small beginnings to large conclusions, widening circles of implication, from half-pence to everything. Swift is given an inch and makes an ell of it. No one can stop him, the sentences are his.

There is a corresponding development in tone. In the first Letter he intervenes in a note of some asperity, as if he were speaking of matters it should be unnecessary to discuss. He is the Drapier, partly to remind his readers that they have already let him down; partly to claim a commandingly objective position. It is well to recall some of the saltier jests on the theme of clothes; as when Swift urges, in *A Tale of a Tub*, that the only difference between a bishop and the next man is sartorial. Since the Drapier supplies these stuffs, he is in an excellent position to see the charade from the inside; he knows these animals before their transformation. Just as he has urged his citizens to dress plainly in Irish woollens, so he can claim for his own actions a corresponding simplicity. Against the silken rascals he can claim to speak in russet yeas and honest kersey noes. Dressed in russet and kersey he has every moral advantage: his 'style' is impeccable. So he says, in the first Letter:

Therefore, my Friends, stand to it One and All: Refuse this Filthy Trash. It is no Treason to rebel against Mr. Wood. His Majesty

in his Patent obliges no body to take these Half-pence: Our Gracious
Prince hath no such ill Advisers about him; or if he had, yet you
see the Laws have not left it in the King's Power, to force us to take
any Coin but what is Lawful, of right Standard, Gold and Silver.
Therefore you have nothing to fear.[1]

You need to be an impeccable Drapier to speak like that: but
Swift represents himself in this honest garb. He is a Protestant,
of English descent, utterly loyal to Hanoverian kings. Let others
look to their credentials.

In the second Letter Swift is already moving into the new
identity which will carry him to the end of the controversy.
He is still the Protestant loyalist, but he now begins to speak
as the Citizen of Ireland. 'How long, O Lord, righteous and
true', he intones; but he does so immediately after he has
called upon 'two or three Hundred principal Gentlemen of
this Kingdom' to sign a Declaration to refuse Wood's coin.
In effect, he has given up the nominal role of the Drapier,
and now finds his identity in membership of a race: he speaks
of the Gentlemen of the Kingdom, and the Papists are still
outside the Pale, but the identity he implies is, subject to that
qualification, national. This accounts for the fact that the
dominant style in the second Letter is the lampoon; and when
he reaches for a higher style, he speaks as if he were at the
head of a troop of yeomen: 'Be not like the deaf Adder', he
says, 'who refuses to hear the Voice of the Charmer, charm he
never so wisely.' And later: 'it is but saying No, and you are
safe'.

The third Letter is an ambiguous document. It is clearly
inferior to the rest, the edge somewhat blunt. The reason is, I
think, that the *persona* is now quite redundant, and Swift seems
to find it something of an embarrassment. To address the
nobility and gentry he has done his homework on the law, he
has been to school with Robert Lyndsay, his head full of prece-
dents and caveats. At one point he says: 'But, with all Deference

[1] *The Drapier's Letters*, p. 11.

be it spoken, I do not conceive that a Report of a Committee of the Council in England, is a Law in either Kingdom; and until any Point is determined to be a Law, it remains disputable by every Subject.' These are not the words of a Drapier, even one who has taken some pains to develop the mind God gave him; in the next sentence Swift raises the question to forestall the obvious objection. He claims that the matter stands to reason, and is obvious even to 'an illiterate Shop-keeper'. It is a neat trick, but the Drapier's limitations are beginning to oppress his inventor. At this point the circle of implication is beginning to extend itself beyond the strict limit of Wood's coin; we are touching the national nerve with talk of the Navigation Laws and other acts of severity performed upon a loyal Kingdom. The rhetorical manner is beginning to expand. But there is a certain uneasiness, a feeling of incongruity between the requirements of the Drapier, and the Voice of the Nation. There is a gap between the two. Swift tries to close it now by identifying the nation in terms of class. He drives a wedge between the King's officers in Ireland and the middle-class traders who are independent of the King's pay. Referring to the coin, he says: 'It is probable, that the first Willing Receivers may be those who Must Receive it whether they will or no, at least under the Penalty of losing an Office. But the Landed Undepending Men, the Merchants, the Shop-Keepers and Bulk of the People, I hope, and am almost confident, will never receive it.' Later, in the *Letter to Viscount Molesworth*, he identifies himself specifically with the 'middle Rank of Mankind': he speaks of 'an Opinion I have long entertained; That, as Philosophers say, Virtue is seated in the Middle; so in another Sense, the little Virtue left in the World is chiefly to be found among the middle Rank of Mankind; who are neither allured out of her Paths by Ambition, nor driven by Poverty'. But in the third Letter Swift is severely cramped by having to run so many decencies in one harness. The artistic symmetry of the work is endangered. Swift is addressing the nobility and gentry, but his argument requires him to dissociate himself from those who are holding jobs under the Crown. He is not yet prepared to speak for the whole People of Ireland; so he holds on grimly to his role as Drapier, however intractable it has become. The writing suffers.

I am implying, however, that the 'figure' of the *Letters* is driving Swift to go further, to go the whole way, by a certain momentum developing within the work itself. The internal logic of the work demands that he drop the identification with class and move into the centre of the national scene: the work itself is forcing upon him a role far larger than that of a Dublin Drapier. Swift is pushing the implications as far as they can go; but they are also pushing him further than his contract. He will wake up one morning to find himself a New Man: he will have the logic of the work to blame. This is one of the differences between Swift in the *Drapier's Letters* and Berkeley in *The Querist*. Many of Berkeley's queries, if brought together, would imply a fundamental reconsideration of Irish government and society; that, at least, if not public action. Berkeley had no wish to offend England and thought Swift's behaviour tendentious. His position, such as it was, is reflected with great precision in the form of the *Querist* itself; a sequence of isolated questions, abrupt sentences, every thought a new thought. His sentences are interjections; they have ended before they have well begun. So the work has no chance to develop internal energy: indeed, it is designed to protect Berkeley from the blow of his own implications. Giving the queries one by one, he restricts their range, curbs their generative force as soon as it has begun.

Already, in the *Drapier's Letters*, much of the energy is self-engendered. In the fourth Letter it releases Swift's frustration and at the same time forces him to go further. It propels him to become an identity. I use this word in the sense indicated by Harold Rosenberg when he distinguishes between an identity and a personality. A character in life or drama is an

identity when there is a role available to him and he is sufficient to take it up: he is merely a personality, however richly
endowed, when there is no role available to him or when he is
incapable of playing it. We find this situation so often in life
that we are not surprised to find it in the drama. Hamlet,
for instance, is merely a personality at the beginning of the
play, though a personality of the greatest interest. He has
qualities far in excess of his ability to use them. This would be
reason enough for his alienation even if he had no more specific
reason than his personality. There is no role for him to play;
and he is not prepared to take the first role he is offered, the
Avenger. So he remains a personality until late in the play,
after his return from England: then he is ready, the role is still
available, and in taking it up he becomes an identity. He and
his role are now one. To apply these terms to Swift: in the first
three Letters Swift is merely, however richly, a personality: as
he shifts from one audience to another, one tone to another,
he remains blind to the great role which is struggling to be
defined. But in the fourth Letter he becomes an identity, the
role is now visible, released by the pressure of an inner logic; and
Swift is now ready to take it up. He was not always ready.
In the first Letters his personality was bound to considerations
of class and religion. Now he is ready, and the role is there.

The immediate result is that he now addresses the Whole
People of Ireland and speaks in their name. 'The People
here', he says, 'being likewise left to themselves, unite as one
Man.' It is often argued that, even yet, Swift is addressing only
those within the Pale; not the Catholic peasantry. It is a poor
argument, as the tone of the Letter shows. Swift wrote this
Letter in October 1724, and in November he said, writing
to the Earl of Oxford:

There is a Fellow in London, one Wood, who got a Patent for
coyning Halfpence for this Kingdom, which hath so terrified us,
that if it were not for some Pamphlets against these Halfpence, we
must have submitted. Against these Pamphlets the Lieutenant hath

put out a Proclamation: and is acting the most unpopular part
I ever knew, though I warned him against it, by a Letter before he
came over; and thought by his Answer, that he would have taken
my Opinions. This is just of as much Consequence to your Lord-
ship, as the news of a Skirmish between two petty States was to
Alexander while he was conquering Persia. But even a Knot of
Beggars, are of Importance among themselves.[1]

This corresponds to the tone of the fourth Letter; the identity
is secure, the unity unmistakable. The knot of beggars is the
whole nation, and Swift is its voice. This is what uniting 'as
one Man' means. Now for the first time in the *Letters* Swift
associates himself with Molyneux, author of *The Case of Ireland's
Being Bound by Acts of Parliament in England*; and he links both
himself and Molyneux with Truth, Reason, and Justice. The
tone of this Letter moves freely between the lordly and the
impudent; the impudence often a mordant humour, an insolent
pedantry, the lordly tone invariably the voice of the Defender of
Liberty. 'The Remedy is wholly in your own Hands', he says;
'and therefore I have digressed a little in order to refresh and
continue that Spirit so seasonably raised amongst you; and
to let you see, that by the laws of God, of Nature, of Nations,
and of your own Country, you are and ought to be as free a
people as your Brethren in England.' The Voice here is at once
individual and representative. Swift allows himself a certain
quirky wit, and uses it mainly to punish the enemy, but his
high tone is the voice of an identity, who has lost and found
himself in his role. This is not the figure of 'Sibylline frenzy'
which Yeats invokes; but we recall that in the Preface to *The
Words upon the Window-Pane* Yeats links Molyneux and Swift
before going on to say that 'Swift found his nationality through
the *Drapier Letters*, his convictions came from action and
passion'.[2] We are accustomed to think that convictions come
first, if they come at all; and then action; and then passion, the
suffering. But Yeats is right. The convictions came to Swift

---

[1] *Correspondence*, vol. III, p. 41.
[2] W. B. Yeats, *Explorations* (Macmillan, London, 1962), p. 348.

from the inner logic of the action, as the end is implicit in the beginning and often a surprise to the inventor. Indeed, there is some historical evidence that Swift was carried, as it were, 'beyond himself' by the inner logic of the action. In the early stages of the fight his position was practically identical with that of, say, Archbishop King; opposition to the Half-pence, and if necessary a national boycott. But by the time the fourth Letter is reached, Swift has gone far beyond King. On 26 November 1724, King wrote to Southwell, referring to that Letter as 'ludicrous and satyrically writ'; and he speaks of the 'Seasonable Advice' as 'foolish enuff, and impertinent'. King's attitudes were governed by the morality of the occasion: Swift's were propelled by an internal logic in the *Letters* themselves which sent him far beyond the occasion. So it is Swift, not King, who raises the question of Ireland's 'dependency' upon England.

The relation between action and style is peculiarly close in the *Letters*. The matter of the occasion is not complex, but it is niggardly, requiring a detailed analysis of the coinage and the degree of its debasement. Swift does not want his readers to think about these questions; he wants them to do something and to keep doing it until the evil disappears: he wants them to refuse the coin. So he must counter the niggardliness of the detail by offering a few salient images notable for simplicity. As we might expect, his favourite device is to translate the alien argument into literal terms, often physical terms. When there is talk of Walpole and his intention to ram the coins down the throats of the citizenry, Swift deals with this by taking it literally; whereupon the citizens are encouraged by the fact that the physical impossibility operates in their favour:

As to Swallowing these Half-Pence in Fire-balls, it is a Story equally improbable. For, to execute this Operation, the whole Stock of Mr. Wood's Coin and Metal must be melted down, and molded into hollow Balls with Wild-fire, no bigger than a reasonable Throat can be able to swallow. Now, the Metal he hath prepared, and already coined, will amount to at least Fifty Millions of Half-pence to be Swallowed by a Million and a Half of People; so that allowing Two Half-Pence to each Ball, there will be about Seventeen Balls of Wild-fire a-piece, to be swallowed by every Person in the Kingdom: And to administer this Dose, there cannot be conveniently fewer than Fifty Thousand Operators, allowing one Operator to every Thirty; which, considering the Squeamishness of some Stomachs, and the Peevishness of Young Children, is but reasonable.[1]

We are back in Lagado. The principle of this rhetoric is Swift's favourite implication: trust the body, never trust anything that is alien to it, as the best laid schemes of Wood and Walpole are alien. His readers must do by will what their stomachs do by the wisdom of Nature: refuse the vile coin. The way to deal with the case is by boycott, as a shopkeeper refuses to sell a yard of cloth to a crooked customer who offers bad money. The cogency of Swift's rhetoric depends upon offering a simple bodily image as answer to a piece of planned chicanery. Since the case calls for a crude answer, it is taken up more effectively by crude men like drapers and citizens than by the Dean of St Patrick's. The immediate requirement is to write the kind of prose that gets things done. The passage involves, of course, a threat of war. That reference to 'Fifty Thousand Operators' is not merely an item of fancy: their failure is a challenge to Walpole. The threat is implicit in the image; it is never overt.

Naturally, some of the devices used are common to the *Letters* and to *Gulliver's Travels*; notably the juxtaposition of big things and little things. But there is an ingenious variant. From the first pages of the first Letter Swift degrades Wood by treating him as a wretched little thing: he is 'a mean ordinary man', to begin with, but as the case goes on he gets more and more diminutive, finally losing his humanity altogether. In the second Letter he is 'this little impudent Hardware-Man', on the next page 'this little arbitrary Mock-Monarch'. The

[1] *The Drapier's Letters*, p. 68.

indignity of submitting to such a wretched creature is then intensified: 'It is no loss of honour', Swift says, 'to submit to the Lion: But who, with the Figure of a Man, can think with Patience of being devoured alive by a Rat?' Wood remained to the end 'so little a Creature'. There is also a witty poem called 'Wood: An Insect' in which Swift pursues the comparison of his victim with a woodlouse and a woodworm. So he takes the sting out of Wood by sneering at him as if he were Skyresh Bolgolam in Lilliput. The procedure is common enough, especially where it capitalises on animal imagery. 'And if they Snarle now, they will Bite ere long', Sacheverell warned his 'High-Flying' colleagues in *The New Association*, a project for the extermination of Dissenters and Whigs. When Defoe parodied Sacheverell's *The Political Union* in his *Shortest Way with the Dissenters* he loosed the animals upon their master. The irony presents Dissenters as snakes, toads, serpents, vipers, contagion, 'viperous brood'. Threat by imagery comes before threat by sentence, since the 'natural' response to these vipers is extermination. No ethical argument is required. The sentence merely brings out, explicitly, what is already implicit in the images, that Dissenters are vicious animals and must be destroyed. Swift argues by sentence, but the argument is already given in the images; lice, worms, insects. Again in the brilliant *Letter to Molesworth* he makes a comparable threat by translating a cliché into literal terms:

The Provocation must Needs have been great, which could stir up an obscure, indolent Drapier, to become an Author. One would almost think, the very Stones in the Street would rise up in such a Cause: And I am not sure, they will not do so against Mr. Wood, if ever he comes within their Reach.[1]

But there is an engaging variant in this device of threat by image. In the third Letter, on the last page, Swift wants to present the quarrel between himself and Wood as a monstrously unjust occasion on which, nevertheless, right will

---

[1] *The Drapier's Letters*, pp. 88–9.

prevail. So he invokes the figure of David conquering Goliath. The analogies are even richer than those he troubles to specify. In the first Book of *Samuel* we are told of the war between Israel and the Philistines; that there were no workers in metal left in all Israel, because the Philistines had taken good care that the Hebrews should not be able to make swords or spears. So in times of battle Saul and his son Jonathan were the only men in the army of Israel who carried swords or lances. We are also told that Jonathan has nevertheless had a great victory over the Philistines by force of intelligence and sleight of hand. When, in all innocence, he breaks Saul's command by taking honey at a time of fasting, the people cry out, 'What, shall Jonathan die, who hath wrought this great salvation in Israel?' Tickell, Lord Carteret's secretary, wrote on 1 November 1724, that this quotation from *Samuel* 'has been got by rote, by men, women and children, and, I do assure you, takes wonderfully'.[1] Finally, we are told that David, the most unlikely candidate, is chosen King of Israel; that he is skilled in music and the harp; that he kills the uncircumcised Philistine with a stone and a sling; that he unites the tribes of Israel into a nation with its capital at Jerusalem. The relevance of the figure is not pursued beyond that happy point. The passage in the *Drapier's Letters* reads:

I am very sensible, that such a work as I have undertaken, might have worthily employed a much better Pen. But when a House is attempted to be robbed, it often happens that the weakest in the Family, runs first to stop the Door. All the Assistance I had, were some Informations from an eminent Person; whereof I am afraid I have spoiled a few, by endeavouring to make them of a Piece with my own Productions; and the rest I was not able to manage: I was in the Case of David, who could not move in the Armour of Saul; and therefore I rather chose to attack this uncircumcised Philistine (Wood I mean) with a Sling and a Stone. And I may say for Wood's Honour, as well as my own, that he resembles Goliah in many Circumstances, very applicable to the present Purpose: For Goliah

---

[1] *Ibid.* p. xx. Introduction by Herbert Davis.

had a Helmet of Brass upon his Head, and he was armed with a Coat of Mail, and the Weight of the Coat was five Thousand Shekles of Brass, and he had Greaves of Brass upon his Legs, and a Target of Brass between his Shoulders. In short, he was like Mr. Wood, all over Brass; and he defied the armies of the living God. Goliah's Conditions of Combat were likewise the same with those of Wood: If he prevail against us, then shall we be his Servants. But if it happens that I prevail over him, I renounce the other Part of the Conditions; he shall never be a Servant of mine; for I do not think him fit to be trusted in any honest man's Shop.[1]

The principle of this prose is to take command of the situation, to set up the conditions of discourse, so that you can move at your own whim from one mode to another. Swift gives the Biblical figure, and pretends to follow up its analogies with impartiality: he will take all the risks of the figure, now that he has invoked it. But in fact he is shameless in picking and choosing. He does not say, for instance, that Wood is like Goliath; he says that Goliath is like Mr Wood, thereby disgracing both parties. In the Bible the word 'shekels' is a neutral term of weight; later it became the name of the silver coin equal to that weight; Swift moves freely from one meaning to another. He can even choose to leave the connexions open. When he says, 'In short, he was like Mr. Wood, all over Brass; and he defied the armies of the living God'; there is no need to put in all the equations. The armies of the living God are at once the Israelites, the Irish, and all the ethical values implicated in the contest: Justice, Truth, and Nature. Swift begins with a profession of weakness: but soon the weakness is turned to divinely endorsed strength, David's weakness. If the enemy is Goliath, David is identified with 'the armies of the living God'. So Jonathan will win as David won. If David is defeated, he will become Goliath's servant; if Jonathan is defeated, he will become Wood's servant. But if Jonathan wins...and suddenly, the symmetry of the logic is wrecked. Jonathan–

[1] *The Drapier's Letters*, p. 48.

David becomes again the astute Dublin drapier, who would not have a trickster inside his shop.

This is a style for use rather than adornment, a style of russet and kersey. Its sole declared object is to get something done. This is the condition of its force. We often think that literature cannot be made under such conditions. Even if we acknowledge the activity of imagination in these Letters, and revel in their force and wit, we are somewhat scandalised by the roughness of their occasion. The relation between words and action seems too close for aesthetic comfort. I am afraid we must accustom ourselves to this relation while reading Swift. We do not read him as we read Valéry. The *Drapier's Letters* are rhetorical acts; in Aristotle's categories they are instances of 'Deliberative Rhetoric', pointed toward a future in which the audience will act as persuaded, in line with the 'gesture' proposed; as we say that the gesture proposed in the *Letters* is to hold hard, stick together. We should take this in our stride. If we do not, we are sophistical; as Cicero rebuked the Sophists for driving a wedge between wisdom and eloquence, action and speech. This is the happiest setting in which to read the *Drapier's Letters*. It is well to remind ourselves, too, that it is a condition of Swift's prose to be willing to abolish itself, when the job is done. There is a fine propriety in the fact that when Swift heard that Wood's patent was to be cancelled—the news came to him on 31 August 1725—he had already composed the last Letter, 'An Humble Address to Both Houses of Parliament'. Now he wrote at once to John Worrall to prevent the Letter from being printed. 'The work is done', he said, 'and there is no more need of the Drapier.'[1] The Letter was not published until the fourth volume of Swift's collected *Works* appeared, the Faulkner edition, ten years later.

[1] *Correspondence*, vol. III, p. 93.

CHAPTER 5

THE LAME BEGGAR

And hence it is, that in his fourth Voyage he discovered a Vein of Melancholy, proceeding almost
to a Disgust of his Species.

Memoirs of Martinus Scriblerus

Lemuel Gulliver travelled 'into several remote nations of the world'. Swift sent him there for reasons which are, I think, clear enough. The vogue of the neo-Elizabethan travel book (Dampier, Woodes Rogers, Defoe), was still strong enough to endorse the notion of man as a wondrous being, encompassing fantastic experience without breaking. After the publication of Newton's *Principia* in 1687 the tradition of the 'Extraordinary Voyage' was augmented by the addition of other planets besides the moon: man accepted this challenge to prove himself capable of doing so. The wonder of new experience awaited him as a test, a trial ancillary to the old trial set for Adam. The challenge of God and man was moved to new ground and the rules were changed; man no longer won by obedience, but by acumen. The new Adam was Robinson Crusoe. The dominant assumption in the travel books was that man is capable, Long Live Man; the sentimentalists implied that he would assimilate everything to his imagination. So *Gulliver's Travels* is, as everyone agrees, a parody of the optimistic travel book. To write it, one would have to do more than ponder the difference between big men and little men; one would exert continuous pressure upon the notion of man's capacity. The *Voyage to the Houyhnhnms* is a classic story of brainwashing: it shocks, not because Swift hates the human race, but because he shows a man's imagination and his values taken over by the citizens of his new experience. In Orwell's *1984*, at the end, we read of Winston: 'He loved Big Brother.' If we are no longer shocked by the rhymes of brainwashed soldiers, it is because we know they can be achieved so easily. In Houyhn-hnmland Gulliver is enchanted. This is part of Swift's irony. Another part is the demonstration, first arranged in *A Tale of a Tub*, that men can be enchanted more easily still by the products of their own fancy. The most arrogant products were those of the new science; so in the third Voyage Swift's peep-show reveals the Laputan scientists engaged with problems already published in Boyle's *Philosophical Works* and the *Philosophical Transactions of the Royal Society*.[1] The implication is clear: extravagance is so omnivorous that even the Laputans are slaves to it.

Swift's parody does not commit itself to one mode: it ranges widely. The object of attack may be man's intellectual pretension, his morality, his scholarship, his political institutions, his rage for Party, his travesty of religion. The second Voyage is mainly concerned with political absurdity; it is full of situations which reflect upon local political events. Swift stays with this line as long as he thinks it fruitful, but he is prepared to move off to another reflexion without notice. His formal requirements were very loose: he had no use for a tight, smartly organised scheme. He wanted the same degree of freedom which characterises *A Tale of a Tub*, where the digressions and the collapsing sentences are subject to the author's whim and to nothing else. Northrop Frye has resuscitated the name 'Anatomy' for this form, linking it with the loose tradition of the Menippean satire which turns looseness into a virtue. In this kind of writing, the looseness of the form allows for a constant succession of surprises. The chief pleasure of reading the *Anatomy of Melancholy* consists in wondering what can possibly come next; if the book lacks a tidy plot, it turns and twists so rapidly, sentence by

---

[1] Marjorie Hope Nicolson, *Science and Imagination* (Cornell University Press, Ithaca, 1956), pp. 110 ff.

sentence, that our desire for the interest of a plot is at once assuaged and transcended. The delight of reading *Candide* is caused by Voltaire's effrontery, his indifference to the requirement of a convincing story. It is a relief to feel, for once, that here is something about which we are not obliged to care. In the *Satyricon* Trimalchio elects to bring on the acrobats at one moment, and, at another, to contribute an elaborate aria about astrology: these events are related only because the same fancy spawns them. The Menippean tradition is capable of any eccentricity by fixing all eccentricities within the fancy of their inventors. The resultant world is in one respect like the comedy of manners, which depends upon the exclusion of certain feelings and the concealment of others. The missing feelings are important only because they are excluded; their presence in another work marks their absence here.

So it is irrelevant, I have already argued, to talk of Gulliver's character; he has no character, he is a cipher. Perspective is pertinent to our reception of Gulliver because the first law of his composition is that every relevant fact is available to the eye. To understand Gulliver it is only necessary to look at him, to see what he does; the fact that he is delivered so completely to one of five senses is the gist of the comedy. The eye is selective, a specialist. If, on the basis of what we see in Gulliver, we choose to guess what we do not see, that is our privilege. We cannot be prevented; but we can be discouraged. Beyond what is delivered to the eye, there is, in fact, nothing at all. Gulliver has a lively role, but its comic force consists in its limitation. He is what he does, what we see him doing, there is nothing beyond what we see. More to the point, there is nothing beneath what we see, no underground man to be sensed beneath the detail of his imprisonment. We are bewildered, then scandalised, by *Gulliver's Travels* because we expect depth and we are held to surface. Swift laughs at our sentimentality and frustrates it. Gulliver is a fraction, not a whole number. If the reader tries to gratify himself by completing Gulliver, tries to add intimations of character, soul, feeling, depth, then he convicts himself; he is a sentimentalist, Swift's favourite butt. It is Gulliver's condition to be a fraction; that is, the human average. The book challenges us to deny the equation. If we protest that we are represented by a cipher, Swift answers: 'of course'. Like everyone in England, Gulliver is a Yahoo with 'some small Pittance of Reason'. The Master-Houyhnhnm is right:

He seemed therefore confident, that instead of Reason, we were possessed of some Quality fitted to increase our natural Vices; as the Reflection from a troubled Stream returns the Image of an ill-shapen Body, not only larger, but more distorted.[1]

The critique is particularly apt if we take the hint of the pun and translate the comment into Locke's terms: the stream of sensory impressions, our reflexion thereon, and so forth. This is the average human condition. Gulliver carries nothing from one occasion to another; with every Voyage he starts again: no memories, no experience, no character. We are not invited to care what happens to him, as we care what happens to Moll Flanders: instead, we are encouraged to exercise, in response to everything that happens from the first word to the last, that alert attention for which care is often an easy substitute. To see Gulliver brainwashed by the Houyhnhnms is like seeing Malvolio gulled, the difference being that in Gulliver's place we ourselves should have succumbed. Bringing these affiliations together, we think of Swift's book as a travel book with the difference of parody; an anatomy; a comedy of humours; an evening of variety turns, in four parts; a spoof of the 'extraordinary voyage'; a new *Satyricon*, another *Golden Ass*.

Let us call it, for convenience, an anatomy of human pride; an evil for which the Houyhnhnms have no name because the evil is unknown among them. In the traditional chain of Being man is placed roughly half-way between animals and angels, but as the Laputans turn their heads either to left or right

[1] *Gulliver's Travels*, p. 248.

and have one eye in and one eye out, so man is convinced that he is an angel, possessed of pure angelic Intelligence. In 'Conjectures on Original Composition' Young accused Swift of blasphemy in *Gulliver's Travels*: 'he has blasphemed a nature little lower than that of angels, and assumed by far higher than they'. Obviously, you could speak in those terms only if you believed that the Incarnation of Christ changed the entire configuration of the Chain of Being. There is an interesting modern occasion in Heidegger; in the *Letter on Humanism* he expressed some resentment, on man's behalf, against the classical description of man as 'the rational animal'. The description is, he thinks, too low, an insult, since it confines man with the genus 'animal', whatever the degree of his attainments. Adjectives do not make up for nouns. Hans Jonas has taken up the argument in *The Gnostic Religion*: he makes the point that the Greek meaning of 'animal' refers not to 'beast', but to any animated being, 'including demons, gods, the ensouled stars—even the ensouled universe as a whole'. So man is not humiliated in this use of the word. But he goes on to say that the humiliation of man, to Heidegger, consists in placing man in any scale, 'that is, in a context of *nature* as such':

The Christian devaluation of 'animal' to 'beast', which indeed makes the term usable only in contrast to 'man', merely reflects the larger break with the classical position—that break by which Man, as the unique possessor of an immortal soul, comes to stand outside 'nature' entirely.[1]

The relevance of this to Swift is clear. Instead of allowing redeemed man to stand outside Nature, unique in the possession of his immortal soul, Swift pushes him back into Nature. He assumes that man is merely a particular kind of animal, meaning a particular kind of beast. Not content with this reduction, he implies that horses have a better claim to man's conventional status and should be promoted accordingly.

[1] Hans Jonas, *The Gnostic Religion* (Beacon Press, Boston, 1963 edition), p. 333 n.

It is idle to ask whether this is Swift's sober judgment or merely the direction his satiric fancy takes. We are to be vexed. But his Christian belief was not of the kind that implies a sacramental sense of man in the world. Despite the Incarnation, man has no special status in the world: in any event, his possibilities, however richly embodied in Christ, are increasingly neglected. This is the implication of Swift's satire. Man is cousin to the animals, distinct from them only by the possession of certain powers which he grossly exaggerates. Not only does he take an absurdly flattering view of himself, but he is encouraged to do so by benevolists, Deists, Freethinkers, scientists and sentimentalists. When Gulliver protests that he writes not for fame but for 'the Publick Good', he asks: 'who can read of the Virtues I have mentioned in the glorious Houyhnhnms, without being ashamed of his own Vices, when he considers himself as the reasoning, governing Animal of his Country?'[1] Swift is always careful to distinguish between the moral Universal and the particular version of it exhibited by each man: as he praised Reason, but despised each man's stock of it. When he thought of man, he turned the universal in the other direction: there are a few good men, but man himself is contemptible. In the famous letter to Pope written on 29 September 1725, he said:

... when you think of the World give it one lash the more at my Request. I have ever hated all Nations professions and Communityes and all my love is towards individualls for instance I hate the tribe of Lawyers, but I love Councellor such a one, Judge such a one for so with Physicians (I will not Speak of my own Trade) Soldiers, English, Scotch, French; and the rest but principally I hate and detest that animal called man, although I hartily love John, Peter, Thomas and so forth. this is the system upon which I have governed my self many years (but do not tell) and so I shall go on till I have done with them I have got Materials Towards a Treatis proving the falsity of that Definition *animal rationale*; and to show it should be only *rationis capax*. Upon this great foundation of Misanthropy

[1] *Gulliver's Travels*, p. 292.

(though not Timons manner) The whole building of my Travells is erected: And I never will have peace of mind till all honest men are of my Opinion . . .[1]

This is as close to a manifesto as Swift is prepared to go, and it is crucial in its bearing on *Gulliver's Travels*: all summers are bad summers, despite the presence of a few pretty swallows. Swift returns to this theme ('my disaffection to the World'), a few months later, again in a letter to Pope:

I tell you after all that I do not hate Mankind, it is vous autres who hate them because you would have them reasonable Animals, and are angry for being disappointed. I have always rejected that Definition and made another of my own. I am no more angry with —— Then I was with the Kite that last week flew away with one of my Chickens and yet I was pleas'd when one of my Servants shot him two days after . . .[2]

Ronald Crane has demonstrated that the key to Swift's manifesto and to the rhetoric of the book is the chapter in the old manuals of logic which dealt with the genus and the species.[3] I shall paraphrase his conclusion and add a few comments.

The argument begins with the definition of man as a reasonable animal: *Homo est animal rationale*. Up to the seventeenth century one of the great sources of logical teaching was Porphyry's *Isagoge*, his introduction to the categories of Aristotle. Porphyry, in opposing man as the only species of 'rational animal' to the mere brutes, chose the horse as his specific instance of an 'irrational' creature. It therefore became commonplace to say:

> *Homo est animal rationale;*
> *Equus est animal hinnibile;*

that is, it is characteristic of the horse to be a whinnying animal as it is characteristic of man to be a rational animal.

---

[1] *Correspondence*, edited by Harold Williams (Clarendon Press, Oxford, 1965), vol. III, p. 103.

[2] *Ibid.* vol. III, p. 118.

[3] R. S. Crane, 'The Houyhnhnms, the Yahoos, and the History of Ideas', in J. A. Mazzeo (editor), *Reason and the Imagination* (Routledge and Kegan Paul, London, 1962), pp. 231–54.

This was part of Porphyry's famous logical tree, reproduced in many of the contemporary manuals of logic. The manual closest to Swift, Narcissus Marsh's *Institutio*, repeats it and includes the usual distinction between the species *man* and the individual member of that species, John, Peter, Thomas. Swift turned Porphyry's tree upside-down, putting horses where the logicians put men, and men where they put horses. So the logicians are refuted, not for the first or the last time. This follows from the pressure of perspective which we have already considered. Crane argues, therefore, that we are to look upon the Yahoos and the Houyhnhnms as, quite simply, animals; existent to Gulliver but hypothetical to us. The point is that in Houyhnhnmland the normal distinction of species between rational creatures and irrational brutes is inverted. Horses, which Gulliver cannot help admiring, take the conventional place of men; and men-like creatures, the Yahoos, whom Gulliver cannot help detesting, take the conventional place of horses. The simplicity of the rhetoric is entirely characteristic of Swift, who liked to exhibit the resources of his favourite virtue. The plan is to prove, at one stroke, 'the falsity of that definition *animal rationale*'. What Swift recalled from his logical studies at Trinity College was sufficient; he saw in the logical manuals an inveterate complacency, fixed by definition and academic rote. He saw precisely the same complacency at work in theology, especially in those Anglican divines who persuaded their parishioners that God was revealing more and more of His truth to man every day; the gradual unfolding of Revelation. Swift thought otherwise. He thought that the early Christians were far closer to God's law than the pretenders of the seventeenth century: far from the revelation of God's truth increasing, it was more and more disastrously clouded by human pride. Like everything else, Christianity was degenerating.

Since it was too late for persuasion, he was driven to mockery. One vexation is answered by another. Swift's motive in writing

Gulliver's Travels was the same as Voltaire's in praising Chinese culture at Christian expense; to annoy the world and vex men into shelving their pride. Against the arrogance of the scientists and all the other virtuosi, he set up the claims of the layman, who was at least free from the most extreme pretension. This was not a mystique of 'the whole man'; or even a cult of 'the ignorant man' as we find it in modern poets like Yeats, Stevens, and Eliot. The satire against the scientists in the *Voyage to Laputa* would not be funny to scientists; laymen would find it engaging. Swift is capitalising upon the fact that laymen would find all scientific projects hilarious: he adds, 'And rightly so'. Whatever truth there is resides in the central man, free from pretension or extremity. But Swift knew that if you are dealing with moral or spiritual facts you cannot attack them on their own terms. The only hope of demolishing spiritual pride was by translating it into a physical equivalent. If you say, in keeping with the *Mechanical Operation of the Spirit*, that spirit is nothing but the sublimation of matter; or Soul nothing but the sublimation of Body; then a soul in the state of grace may be presented as a handsome body, and a soul in sin as a filthy body. One of the more reasonable projects of the scientists at Lagado is to uncover plots and conspiracies by examining the excrement of suspected persons:

Because Men are never so serious, thoughtful, and intent, as when they are at Stool; which he found by frequent Experiment: For in such Conjectures, when he used merely as a Trial to consider which was the best Way of murdering the King, his Ordure would have a Tincture of Green; but quite different when he thought only of raising an Insurrection, or burning the Metropolis.[1]

The general principle is the reduction of spirit to matter; as Bergson said that all comic effects are the result of the mechanisation of the organic. (Though, on second thoughts, comedy arises also from the reverse process. Men are funny when they

[1] *Gulliver's Travels*, p. 190.

168

act like machines, but machines are funny when they act like men; as when the computer said, 'Cogito, ergo sum.')

I have argued that the sources of Swift's comedy are chiefly two: similarity and difference. No terms could be more flexible. When we are told that the Lilliputians bury their dead with their heads downward, so that on the Day of Judgment they will be turned right-side up, we make what we like of this fact, but when we hear that they give their highest jobs to the best rope-dancers and the gymnasts most accomplished in leaping and creeping, we immediately think: so do we, if the truth were told. If the Laputans are argumentative in politics and yet can't keep their heads straight, we ask ourselves, 'can we?' William Empson has made the point: changes of size, in *Gulliver's Travels*, represent 'the impersonal eye':

... to change size and nothing else makes you feel 'this makes one see things as they are in themselves'. It excites Wonder but of a scientific sort. Swift used it for satire on science or from a horrified interest in it, and to give a sort of scientific authority to his deductions, that men seen as small are spiritually petty and seen as large physically loathsome.[1]

The poetic impression is that man is a misfit, however you look at him; if you give him the chance to prove himself in several contexts and if he fails in all, his case is hopeless. As for difference: when Gulliver offers to make gunpowder so that the King of Brobdingnag can destroy his enemies, the King refuses as if he were a peasant rejecting Foreign Aid. The effect is comic from both angles, though the moral advantage rests with the King. Most of the projects at Lagado are absurd, like building houses by starting at the roof; but some are not, like the plan to root out Party politics, or the notion of raising money by taxing people according to the merits they think they possess, every man his own assessor. The only complaint to be

[1] William Empson, *Some Versions of Pastoral* (Chatto and Windus, London, 1950), p. 267.

made against the projectors is that they take their insights too literally. Yeats said of Blake that 'the limitation of his view was from the very intensity of his vision; he was a too literal realist of imagination, as others are of nature'.[1] The scientists are too literal realists of fancy. In theory, it should be possible to restore human excrement to the food from which it began; to teach spiders to make silk; to abolish words by carrying the things for which they stand; or even to use upon the Body Politic the medicines found effective on the Body Natural. The common man is wiser than the scientist because he knows that such enterprises are not worth the candle; he is modest and therefore wise in proportion to his ignorance. The scientist is a martyr to the letter of his vision; he is his own tragic hero, affecting the Sublime, the heroic mode. His absurdity follows. If the rhetoric of *Gulliver's Travels* becomes more intense as it proceeds, it is because of these considerations; the moral of the *Voyage to Lilliput* is 'put not your trust in princes', the moral of the *Voyage to the Houyhnhnms* is 'put not your trust in man'.

But the main force of Swift's mockery is directed against man in relation to the animal. The sentimental theory says that man has the special power of making himself at home in Nature. The definitive version is given, many years later, in Wordsworth's Preface to the *Excursion* (1814) where he proclaims:

> How exquisitely the individual Mind
> (And the progressive powers perhaps no less
> Of the whole species) to the External World
> Is fitted:—and how exquisitely, too—
> Theme this but little heard of among men—
> The external World is fitted to the Mind;

There is nothing in Swift to support this. On the contrary, he implies that if the question is raised it will be found that animals achieve a much more equable relation with their environment. This is one aspect of Swift's modernity. Norman

[1] W. B. Yeats, *Essays and Introductions* (Macmillan, London, 1961), p. 119.

O. Brown has argued that 'Man is distinguished from animals by having separated, ultimately into a state of mutual conflict, aspects of life (instincts) which in animals exist in some condition of undifferentiated unity or harmony.'[1] One might add this: in *Gulliver's Travels* the Houyhnhnms are superior to man because they have achieved this harmony. From their point of view the achievement is so easy as to call for no comment; their harmony is axiomatic, like the air one breathes. From our point of view, it is done by eliminating the causes of discord: in Swift's view these are chiefly man's arrogance and pride. The Houyhnhnms have disposed of such encumbrances; this is the measure of their success. They do not lie, do not doubt, do not suffer from passion, do not waste in disease; they act reasonably by instinct. They converse, with the civilised decorum often ascribed to the Augustans. Gulliver's life in Houyhnhnmland is the good Epicurean life, 'Health of Body, Tranquility of Mind'. There is no reason to assume that Swift offers it to our derision. When modern critics say that the price is too high and life in Houyhnhnmland is unbearably dull, the answer is Freud's: we cling to our sickness and would not be without it. As Kenneth Burke's hero says: 'When people are both discerning and unhappy, they tend to believe that their unhappiness is derived from their discernment.'[2] This is one of several reasons for the prestige of worldly failure among those who would define their superiority in unworldly terms. It is an inveterate part of our pride: in our time to be holier-than-thou is to be unhappier than anyone else; flickerings of incipient content are read as danger signs, beckonings of temptation. This being so, Houyhnhnmland seems to us a desert of nothings; no this, no that; while in Swift's terms the things that it lacks are the things of which it is free. Absence is good, presence is doubtful. We try to read Swift as if he were

[1] Norman O. Brown, *Life against Death* (Vintage Books, New York, 1959), p. 83.
[2] Kenneth Burke, *Towards a Better Life* (Harcourt, Brace, New York, 1932), p. 13.

Conrad or Dostoevsky, but he refuses these attentions. Meanwhile, the animals are wiser than us. When Gulliver reaches England, his travels over, the sight of his wife and family disgusts him. He buys two horses and talks to them for four hours a day. 'They live in great amity with me', he says, 'and friendship to each other.' It is easy to say that Gulliver is now mad; but it is hard to deny that he was better off with the Houyhnhnms.

So the Houyhnhnms are better than men because they have less to confuse them. We tend to think of good fortune in terms of plenitude and store; we are capitalists of sensibility, collecting experiences as if they were money. We think of the fortunate as living a dense rich life. But Swift did not think of life in this way. It is a commonplace that he got along with less in the way of genuine conviction and commitment than any major writer of his time. The only force that held him back from nihilism was his own pride, the pride of self-assertion; one of the more engaging ironies is that he was preserved in his integrity by what he considered, in other men, the cardinal sin. In the same spirit one often has the feeling that Swift was not content merely to attack men; he wanted to rid the world of men. There was so much in himself that he was forced to deny, so he made denial his creed. But when he set out to imagine a race of beings genuinely acceptable and congenial, he thought of them as beings who didn't need to deny. The Houyhnhnms know nothing of disease, evil, pride, lying, the fear of death, verbiage, love, or sex. This happy condition is anticipated in Lilliput, where it is assumed that a child owes no duty to his parents and is therefore free from at least one of the inveterate sources of misery and guilt. If the Houyhnhnms live according to Reason and Nature, this means that they travel light. They do not doubt, or argue; they are chaste, friendly, benevolent. They think of illness as repletion; evacuation is their favourite device.

If the Houyhnhnms are fortunate in the number of things

from which they are free, the Yahoos are much closer to man in the measure of their burdens. Swift wrote to Thomas Sheridan in September 1725:

Therefore sit down and be quiet, and mind your Business as you should so, and contract your Friendships, and expect no more from Man than such an Animal is capable of, and you will every day find my Description of Yahoes more resembling.[1]

In the book the Yahoos are animals with a form in some respects resembling the human body. They hold their food between their claws and their forefeet; they are 'the most unteachable of all Brutes', having a 'degenerate and brutal nature'. But what they are is not as significant as how they appear to those who see them. Here again the pressure of perspective is maintained to curb pride. Gulliver thinks the Yahoos loathsome and in every way inferior to himself. The Yahoos think that Gulliver is the same as themselves. The Houyhnhnms, too, think that Gulliver is as near as makes no difference to being a Yahoo. They think that human beings have 'some Rudiments of Reason', which we use only to increase our natural corruptions and to acquire new ones; that we spend our lives extending our wants and desires; that we are defective in Reason and therefore in virtue, 'because Reason alone is sufficient to govern a rational creature'; that we resemble the Yahoos in hating one another, in appetite, greed, susceptibility to sickness, cunning, malice, spleen, and sexual desire. Where we differ from the Yahoos it is to our disadvantage; as, for instance, in our physique, where we are poorly equipped. In the last reckoning the majority opinion holds. When Gulliver thinks he is happily settled for life, with no thought of leaving Houyhnhnmland, the Houyhnhnms complain to their king that he is keeping a Yahoo in his household as if he were a Houyhnhnm rather than a 'Brute Animal'. So Gulliver has to leave.

Swift emphasises the similarity between man and Yahoos;

---

[1] *Correspondence*, vol. III, p. 94.

most dramatically in the incident in which Gulliver while
bathing is attacked by the female Yahoo, eleven years old:

> She embraced me after a most fulsome Manner; I roared as loud
> as I could, and the Nag came galloping towards me, whereupon
> she quitted her Grasp, with the utmost Reluctancy, and leaped
> upon the opposite Bank, where she stood gazing and howling
> all the time I was putting on my Cloaths.[1]

Like loves like, when likeness is recognised. It is agreed that in
the moral allegory of the book the Yahoos stand for 'natural un-
reason'; the point of the irony being, if this is so, what does
man stand for? If we consult Swift's master, La Rouchefou-
cauld, we find that in his description there is no difference
between man and Yahoo. In man, he says, moderation is only
pretence, Reason is always the dupe of the heart, the passions
are the only orators who always persuade.

Into this world marches Lemuel Gulliver, an innocent
abroad, a cipher. There has been a good deal of argument
about Gulliver's relation to his inventor: Gulliver as a dramatic
character, separate from Swift and therefore the object of
Swift's irony; or Gulliver as Swift's mouthpiece. The argument
is pedantic. There are many occasions on which Swift uses
Gulliver to enforce a point close to his own concerns; especially
in Book 2. Nothing in the tradition of plural form prevents him
from doing do. There are many occasions on which Gulliver
is exposed to Swift's irony. The fact is that Gulliver, who will be
brainwashed in Houyhnhnmland, has already been brainwashed in England: until he meets other values, his way of
life is entirely English. Gulliver is what the world and Emmanuel
College, Cambridge, have made him: this is a central point in
Swift's irony. If he were alive today, he would be a 'good
European', making trips to Strasbourg. So he is at once a
product of his time and a comic humour: if we ask how he could
be both, the answer is: how, being one, could he avoid being
the other? In Swift's eyes a representative man, if we consider

[1] *Gulliver's Travels*, p. 267.

174

what he represents, could not be anything but a comic humour. Nigel Dennis has suggested that Swift was incited to write *Gulliver's Travels* partly by the success of *Robinson Crusoe*. If we allow for the possibility that he wrote the *Travels* to turn *Crusoe* upside-down, the suggestion is attractive. Think of *Crusoe* as a chorale to the new man, self-reliant and resourceful: the point being that, given meagre materials, Crusoe makes himself at home, master in his own house. Then note that the chief characteristic of Gulliver is that he is at home nowhere; neither in England, nor in foreign places. Where Crusoe domesticates the scene in which he finds himself, Gulliver is always at sixes and sevens, too small or too big; he never fits, and he can never make a world fit him. Note, too, that he is never given a companion. He confronts beings who are bigger or smaller, weaker or stronger, but never anyone, not even Glumdalclitch or the sorrel nag, with whom he can form a relationship. He is neither a master nor a servant; he is not identified by the role he plays, because in that special sense he plays no role. But the alienation goes much deeper than this; it implicates Gulliver's entire relation to the world; or rather, the fact that he has no relation to the world.

We have been hearing a good deal about modern man in this predicament: surrounded by things to which he has no relation, except that of use. This is not 'man against the sky', but a much more humiliating image; man in solitude, where even his own form of loneliness does not strike an answering note in anyone else's. There are no echoes, auras, reverberations. At best, the objects which surround him are neutral, indifferent: at worst, they are sinister, every coat upon a coathanger becomes a Frankenstein. In recent years this image of man has imposed itself upon the French novel, notably in the work of Alain Robbe-Grillet. I will offer a brief paraphrase of this version before adding a few comments. The point to bear in mind is that if Gulliver is a 'modern' figure, his modernity is cast in these terms; not in the terms of Conrad or Dostoevsky.

The basic argument runs: 'The world is neither significant nor absurd. It *is*, quite simply.'[1] Its only characteristic is existence. Objects in the natural world are independent and alien. 'Man looks out at the world, and the world does not return his glance.' Heidegger says that it is the condition of man to exist, Robbe-Grillet has applied the aphorism to *Waiting for Godot*; Barthes has applied it to Robbe-Grillet's fiction. The object is 'sans hérédité, sans liaisons et sans références, un object têtu, rigoureusement enfermé dans l'ordre de ses particules, suggestif de rien d'autre que de lui-même...'[2] In the world at large, objects, scraped clean and seen afresh, 'relate only to themselves'. Things are things, nothing more or less. When we smear them with our mystery, they seem to reflect the modes of our soul and we think that they have 'depth' beyond the visible; we ascribe to them a soul of their own. This is delusion. We must give up the myth of depth, knowing that there is only surface. Man and Nature are distinct, one from the other, and separate in their identities. The gap between man and Nature is not a 'heartrending separation', it is merely a gap. Instead of entering into complicity with objects, we must refuse such complicity on the ground that it means self-delusion. This does not imply that we withdraw from the world of objects; but it means that we live in that world in a different spirit. We give no promises and we ask for none. We treat objects not as 'presences' but as utensils: 'a utensil is wholly form and matter—and use'. When we have finished with a hammer, we put it aside: it makes no demand upon us. Man no longer feels this absence of character as a lack, 'or an emotional distress'. 'His heart no longer requires a hollow place in which to take refuge'. He no longer yearns for the depth of things or the inner recesses which receive his feeling; because, having given up communion, he gives up

[1] Alain Robbe-Grillet, *Snapshots, and Towards a New Novel*, translated by Barbara Wright (Calder and Boyars, London, 1965), pp. 92 ff.
[2] Roland Barthes, *Essais critiques* (Éditions du Seuil, Paris, 1964), p. 31.

tragedy. Robbe-Grillet defines tragedy as 'an attempt to salvage, to "recuperate" the separation between man and things, and to make of that distance a new value'. But if we start by repudiating the sentimental treaty between man and things, the incitement to tragedy is thwarted. Besides, if we make of distance and separation an occasion of suffering, and if we elevate this suffering until it becomes an inescapable part of our dignity, we are merely 'loving our ills', and augmenting them so that we may love them more completely. So we must reject everything that makes us connive with objects: all the humanistic analogies whispering to us that the world is man. The only safe terms are terms of measurement: these are our best safeguard against words 'of a visceral, analogical, incantatory character'. The language of measurement helps us to make our passion stop at the surface, without trying to penetrate; the best words are words of measurement, location, size, and the like. We recall Gulliver's description of the execution in Brobdingnag:

The Malefactor was fixed in a Chair upon a Scaffold erected for the Purpose; and his Head cut off at one Blow with a Sword of about forty Foot long. The Veins and Arteries spouted up such a prodigious Quantity of Blood, and so high in the Air, that the great *Jet d'Eau* at Versailles was not equal for the Time it lasted; and the Head when it fell on the Scaffold Floor, gave such a Bounce, as made me start, although I were at least an English Mile distant.[1]

What Gulliver substitutes for the 'appropriate' feelings of pity and sympathy is merely a sense of the spectacular; a sense of the sheer scale of the event, measured against other events. He assumes that none of these events calls for any emotional response. This is very much in Robbe-Grillet's spirit. We are to decline every seeming invitation. If you say that a village crouches in the valley, you are giving no more information than if you said it is situated in the valley. But the word

---

[1] *Gulliver's Travels*, p. 120.

'crouches' is designed to transport the reader 'into the hypothetical soul of the village'; once there, the collusion of Nature
and man is complete. Genuinely to describe things, we must
refuse metaphor, hold ourselves intact outside the things
described. 'We must neither appropriate them to ourselves,
nor transfer anything to them.' Description is the only proper
mode of attention, because it fends off everything else, tragedy,
feeling, and desire. For this reason, sight is the most reliable
sense, and touch the most insidious; sight places the object
at a certain distance, touch incriminates. Smell is also dangerous, because 'it implies a penetration into the body by the
foreign thing'. To taste a thing is almost indecent; except for
one advantage, that at least you destroy what you taste, it can
no longer command your response. Sight has another merit; not
only does it reject the interference of the object, but it constantly reminds us that there is only one's own 'point of view':
we are restricted to that. 'The relative subjectivity of my view-
point', Robbe-Grillet says, 'serves to define my situation in
the world'; it is a constant admonition. The moral of Gulliver's
experience in Brobdingnag is that judgment, separated from
the persuasions of common sense, is dangerously exposed;
Gulliver himself never learns this lesson.

I have gone into this matter in some detail to enforce the
point that Gulliver's alienation from his context is not that of
'romantic irony' or the tragic hero. In a much more telling
sense it is the alienation of the modern ironist who lives on the
assumption that there is a gap between subject and object and
that the gap is permanent. In this respect the relation between
Gulliver and Swift is closer than we have allowed. It is a
commonplace that Swift has virtually no use for metaphor; the
reason is that he has little use for the collusions between man
and Nature which metaphor enforces. Again, when Gulliver
describes things, as we have seen, he is made to do so in such
a way as to rebuke more intimate approaches. His descriptions
keep himself away from the objects described and hold us

exactly where we are. His style is restrictive, disciplinary, administrative; it keeps things at bay. When Pope in *The Dunciad* commands his reader to 'awake' and fight against the enveloping Dullness, he means: 'let us commit ourselves to consciousness, against all the pressure and much of the evidence; let us bring to consciousness as much experience as possible, and keep the slagheap of unconsciousness as small as possible'. Swift's version is: let us bring things to the light of day so that we may at least see what they are doing. Instead of the 'fretful stir unprofitable', Swift opts for quietness; not the receptive quietness of Fanny Price in *Mansfield Park*, but a quietness wary and suspicious, always on guard. It was for this reason that he wrote his *Tritical Essay*; to get the most insidious pieces of trash into one bin, and then to deal with them. I am arguing that *Gulliver's Travels* takes for granted the alienation of man, and makes grim fun of it: fun, not pathos. It is a book of ossature rather than intestine, a distinction offered by Wyndham Lewis as congenial to the nature of satire. It is the kind of book Robbe-Grillet would write if he had Swift's genius and Swift's cause.

To show this in the book: we want a scene in which a relation between man and Nature is normally apprehended; a storm at sea, for instance. Most of the famous storm-scenes in English and American fiction present the storm as a mighty battle, an engagement of heroic proportions between forces deemed to be commensurate. This is based on the principle that, as Melville said, 'not the smallest atom stirs or lives on matter, but has its cunning duplicate in mind'. Here is a passage from Conrad's *Typhoon*:

The seas in the dark seemed to rush from all sides to keep her back where she might perish. There was hate in the way she was handled, and a ferocity in the blows that fell. She was like a living creature thrown to the rage of a mob: hustled terribly, struck at, borne up, flung down, leaped upon. Captain MacWhirr and Jukes kept hold of each other, deafened by the noise, gagged by the wind; and the great physical tumult beating about their bodies, brought, like an unbridled display of passion, a profound trouble to their souls.[1]

This passage says, as clearly as words can, that the world is man: all the analogies are human, the ship is a living creature, the storm is a mob, the forces at work are functions of human passion. 'There was hate in the way she was handled, and a ferocity in the blows that fell.' To confront a storm in this idiom is to turn it into a civil war, a war within the single state of man; the storm ceases to be water and wind and becomes human passion. Everything that touches man becomes man. If man is defeated, as in a storm, this means that he is beaten not by a force utterly different and alien but by a force of his own kind but greater; fifty times stronger, perhaps, but still a force of his own kind. Conrad often implies that man lives in an alien world, but the terms in which he makes the implication have the effect of qualifying it; more than any other modern novelist, he enters into collusion with Nature and forces it to receive man's soul. This is in keeping with the fact that language, as a human invention, tends to make everything in its own image: whatever is beyond or beneath human experience is assimilated to human terms. Some writers, like Conrad, connive with language in this procedure. Swift does not.

Here is a description of a storm in *Gulliver's Travels*, at the beginning of the *Voyage to Brobdingnag*. The language is often, I think, misconstrued:

Finding it was like to overblow, we took in our Sprit-sail, and stood by to hand the Fore-sail; but making foul Weather, we looked the Guns were all fast, and handed the Missen. The Ship lay very broad off, so we thought it better spooning before the Sea, than trying or hulling. We reeft the Foresail and set him, we hawled aft the Fore-sheet; the Helm was hard a Weather. The Ship wore bravely. We belay'd the Foredown-hall; but the Sail was split, and we haw'ld down the Yard, and got the Sail into the Ship, and

---

[1] Conrad, *Typhoon* (Dent, London, 1945 reprint), pp. 164–5.

unbound all the things clear of it. It was a very fierce Storm; the
Sea broke strange and dangerous. We hawl'd off upon the Lanniard
of the Wipstaff, and helped the Man at Helm. We would not get
down our Top-Mast, but let all stand, because she scudded before
the Sea very well, and we knew that the Top-Mast being aloft,
the Ship was the wholesomer, and made better way through the
Sea, seeing we had Sea room. When the Storm was over, we set
Fore-sail and Main-sail, and brought the ship to. Then we set
the Missen, Maintop-Sail and the Foretop-Sail. Our Course was
East North-east, the Wind was at South-west. We got the Star-board
Tacks aboard, we cast off our Weather-braces and Lifts; we set
in the Lee-braces, and hawl'd forward by the Weather-bowlings,
and hawl'd them tight, and belayed them, and hawl'd over the
Missen Tack to Windward, and kept her full and by as near as
she would lie.[1]

It has been assumed since Scott that Swift is parodying the
description of storms in the travel literature. Canon Knowles
has pointed out that the passage is taken almost *verbatim* from
Sturmy's *Compleat Mariner* (1669). But I am not convinced
that it is parody at all. It is too congenial both to the cast of
Swift's mind and to the implied relation, such as it is, between
Gulliver and his experience. Swift rarely makes fun of practical
skill, even if he does not worry very much about the details.
He writes like this not because he failed to write like Conrad
but because Gulliver's involvement in the events is quite
different from either Captain MacWhirr's or Conrad's. To
Gulliver the storm is merely a storm, the ship merely a ship.
The only demand he makes upon Nature is his own survival.
A comic humour asks to survive, he does not ask the wind
to receive his soul. He reports what happened, but the only
terms deemed relevant to the report are terms of event, terms
of use. The only time Gulliver comes at all close to translating
the events into more personal terms is when he says: 'It was a
very fierce Storm; the Sea broke strange and dangerous.' But
even here the effect is not to attribute ferocity to the storm but

---

[1] *Gulliver's Travels*, p. 84.

to estimate its force by comparison with other storms. 'Strange' means 'in a new guise' and 'dangerous' merely reports the fact. For the rest, the terms are those of description and measurement, nothing else. It is as if Gulliver were trying to achieve the 'alienation-effect' proposed by Brecht; an effect, incidentally, eminently congenial to humours. We are not invited to share Gulliver's experience; only to look at it. We are not, I think, invited to laugh.

Perhaps the most spectacular incident in *Gulliver's Travels* which marks the difference between the two attitudes to Nature is Gulliver's putting out the fire in the Empress's palace. The Empress lives by the symbolism of things, to the extent of ignoring the essential facts. Gulliver is prepared to convert anything into use. So he merely reports the facts; that he had drunk a lot of wine the night before, that it was very diuretic, that he had not discharged it during the night: since it was still available, it could be put to use. The symmetry is somewhat spoiled, I concede, by a later incident in the *Voyage to Brobdingnag* when Gulliver refuses to sit on the chair which he had made from the combings of the queen's hair; as he says, 'protesting I would rather dye a Thousand Deaths than place a dishonourable Part of my Body on those precious Hairs that once adorned her Majesty's Head'.[1]

Several things move together in the book. The Houyhnhnms are fortunate in having so little excess freight to carry; by contrast, we are bowed under the weight of our ills, like Lucky in *Waiting for Godot*. One of our absurdities is featured in the Struldbrugs, the fear of age: the Struldbrugs are in the book because Swift knew that fear and wanted to curb it in himself. The Houyhnhnms are passionless so they do not yearn; there are no tragedies in that country. Gulliver is meant to survey his own experience, not to grovel before it. The funniest thing about him is that his 'defeat' is so complete. In turn, we are meant to survey everything offered to us within the covers

[1] *Gulliver's Travels*, pp. 125–6.

of the book; not to share anything, but to look at it. This is
given in the style, which is designed to make one programme
easy and rival programmes impossible. To an unusual degree
the style of *Gulliver's Travels* and the admonitions upon which
it depends are one: the triumph of the book is the coherence of
its behaviour. Indeed, there is a sense in which the style can be
thought of as preceding the attitudes and virtually determining
them. Just as our muscles determine the direction and speed of
our movements, so we can speak, as Kenneth Burke does, of
'the musculature of a diction'. 'A gift is an imperative', he
says; 'a power is a command. It is the successful at love who
burn for women, and the articulate who are driven by the need
of statement.'[1] In Swift's case we need not burden ourselves
with the problem. Whether the style came first and raged
unappeased until it found attitudes and sentiments to its
liking, so that only those attitudes and sentiments could be
entertained: or whether the attitudes were strained and frustrated until Swift devised a style to liberate them; we need not
enquire. It is enough to observe that the style and the attitudes
drive imperiously together.

Of course it would be convenient if we could read *Gulliver's
Travels* as ironic from first to last. Hugh Kenner is not alone in
his determination to do so. Recognising that Gulliver speaks the
language of measurement, Kenner assumes that measurement
is bound to be comic. Thinking of Joyce and *Ulysses*, he offers
a comparison between Gulliver and Leopold Bloom. 'Gulliver's
Travels are those of a Bloom', he says; 'he is immensely impressed by the measurements of everything, and interested in
gathering tangible souvenirs.'[2] But the comparison will not
survive a moment's experiment. Kenner associates Bloom with
Lockean wit as distinct from judgment, where wit puts ideas
together merely for the pleasure of doing so, while judgment
distinguishes one idea from another. The 'superficially similar

[1] Burke, *Towards a Better Life*, p. 75.
[2] Hugh Kenner, *Dublin's Joyce* (Chatto and Windus, London, 1955), p. 143.

notions' which rattle around in Bloom's head are the materials
of loose association; the ironic distance between Bloom and
Joyce is implicit in the nature of those notions and the use,
such as it is, to which they are put. But there is no real comparison between Bloom and Gulliver in this respect; Gulliver's
head is not employed in gathering impressions in the service of
rumination. The point is that Gulliver is not, indeed, immensely
impressed by the measurements of everything; it is not his
fictive nature to be impressed at all. It is typical of Gulliver
to find, among the hundreds of different ways of life, that
only a few are useful and the rest are vain. This corresponds
with the Gutenberg discovery that spaces which are occupied
by certain black marks cannot be simultaneously occupied by
other black marks. Part of the achievement of the book is the
forceful elimination from its field of every rival intimation.
So we cannot be certain, at any moment, how far the irony goes
or whether it goes at all.

But our reading of *Gulliver's Travels* should allow for a fact
which is too rarely acknowledged, that it is a very funny book.
In one of the 'Intelligencer' essays Swift asked, 'whether I have
not as good a Title to laugh, as Men have to be ridiculous; and
to expose Vice, as another hath to be vicious'.[1] Arbuthnot wrote
to Swift on 5 November 1726: 'Gulliver is a happy man that
at his age can write such a merry work.'[2] As Swift said of *A Tale
of a Tub* in 'The Author upon Himself', it is 'a dang'rous
Treatise writ against the Spleen'. Some of the first readers of
the *Travels* were touched by the general satire, and Bolingbroke thought it a libel, but it was universally taken as a
merry work. The reason goes beyond the local political jokes,
hobbling princes and so forth. The work is merry because we
are discouraged from reading it according to any of the conventions which it mimes; travel book, philosophic *conte*,
extraordinary voyage. These conventions are invoked, only

---

[1] *Irish Tracts 1728–1733*, edited by Herbert Davis (Basil Blackwell, Oxford,
1955), p. 34.　　　[2] *Correspondence*, vol. III, p. 179.

to be set aside: the judicious reader must learn new rules as he
plays this game for the first time. Swift sets and maintains the
tone so resolutely by enforcing the assumption that no other
tone is relevant. But there is more. A comparison with *The
Beggar's Opera* may make the point.

One of the peculiar features of the *Opera* is that, issuing from
a life of daily frustration and inequality, Gay's tone implies
that, at some level, the differences between one man and
another are dissolved. In many respects Gay was so innocent,
so naive—Pope's epitaph says, 'In Wit, a Man; Simplicity, a
Child'—that he could hardly tell the difference between a
Whig and a Tory. But, in spite of that disability, he had a
remarkable feeling for the human continuities that persist
beneath or beyond difference. While his great contemporaries
deplored Party and called for unity, Gay was the man who did
the trick; in *The Beggar's Opera*, where for sixty nights he had
London singing the harmony of rich and poor. The theatre
cannot do better than this, if this is what it wants to do. William
Empson was the first to see the point of *The Beggar's Opera* in
that way:

Clearly it is important for a nation with a strong class-system to
have an art-form that not merely evades but breaks through it,
that makes the classes feel part of a larger unity or simply at home
with each other. This may be done in odd ways, and as well by
mockery as admiration. The half-conscious purpose behind the
magical ideas of heroic and pastoral was being finely secured by
The Beggar's Opera when the mob roared its applause both against
and with the applause of Walpole.[1]

The same motive works in the poems. Gay's *Fables* cuts across
differences of social class to emphasise differences of nature
and character. In the second Book of *Trivia* the magnificent
lines about the brutal coachman invoke the transmigration of
souls to insinuate, for the sake of ordinary decency, a critical
perspective. In *The Beggar's Opera* the moral is that 'the world

---

[1] Empson, *Some Versions of Pastoral*, p. 199.

is all alike', whether we take this in Macheath's vein or another. At the end the Beggar points the moral:

Through the whole piece you may observe such a similitude of manners in high and low life, that it is difficult to determine whether (in the fashionable vices) the fine gentlemen imitate the gentlemen of the road, or the gentlemen of the road the fine gentlemen. Had the play remained as I at first intended, it would have carried a most excellent moral. 'Twould have shown that the lower sort of people have their vices in a degree as well as the rich: and that they are punished for them.

Punished, that is, unless they are reprieved; as here they are reprieved. The last words of the play point up the same mobility: 'the wretch of today may be happy tomorrow'. This is the mark of Gay's comedy; we are all human. Macheath's courage declines as the liquor falls to the bottom of the bottle, but we are all in the same state. Gay gives Macheath the lordly note in his rakishness because he has earned it. The classes and categories remain, but some of their stiffness is gone. We are all lame beggars, as on the seal of the King of Luggnagg.

Still, it was a precarious balance, out in the streets, even before the sixty nights were over. Dr Herring, the king's chaplain, condemned the *Opera* for presenting crime in a glamorous light. Swift had to come in with his *Vindication*. The new play, *Polly*, was banned by the government in 1729. The public success of Gay's *Opera* means something, but it does not dispose of a general point which Empson makes, that after the Restoration the notion of national unity lost ground to the notion of manly independence, self-reliance. Even Gay had to spend his declining years trying to get used to the idea that you can only depend on yourself.

Gulliver's Travels achieves by mockery what *The Beggar's Opera* achieved by good humour, the feeling that we are all human together. Gay wanted to comfort people with this reflexion: Swift had a different purpose. But it was one effect of the

Travels to bring people together, if only in a sense of their folly. The perspective imposed by the work implies that at some level our militant differences are trivial and we should be ashamed to pursue them:

Difference in Opinions hath cost many Millions of Lives: For Instance, whether Flesh be Bread, or Bread be Flesh: Whether the Juice of a certain Berry be Blood or Wine: Whether Whistling be a Vice or a Virtue: Whether it is better to kiss a Post, or throw it into the Fire: What is the best Colour for a Coat, whether Black, White, Red or Grey; and whether it should be long or short, narrow or wide, dirty or clean; with many more. Neither are any Wars so furious and bloody, or of so long Continuance, as those occasioned by Difference in Opinion, especially if it be in things indifferent.[1]

This is part of Gulliver's report to his Master in Houyhnhnm-land, but it is also part of Swift's counsel to his readers; both reports are possible because of the height from which they are delivered. The human comedy is best seen from above; couched in a merry work which revels in oddities of perspective.

[1] *Gulliver's Travels*, p. 246.

CHAPTER 6

THE SIN OF WIT

I

When we say that Swift was an occasional poet and an amateur, we mean that he took his poetry with less gravity than his prose. But we mean a little more than that. There is more to his verse than 'Simple Topics told in Rime'. It is true that many of his poems give the impression of being vacation exercises: he carried his verses lightly, and put them aside with equal nonchalance. The most useful service offered him by the very existence of poetry was that it helped him to deal with several modes of experience in a relatively undemanding spirit. There are a few poems in which he is as severe as ever, full of indignation and rebuke, but these are exceptional occasions. Most of Swift's poems are more equable than his prose: they have the effect of releasing him, now and again, from his quarrel with the world. Even when the quarrel persists, it is free from the vexation of the prose. Indeed, there were many burdens which Swift could hardly have borne at all, but for the amateur nature of his poetry.

It is clear that many of the poems were written for fun. But fun, to Swift, was an athletic exercise to keep the mind in trim. A riddle, a lampoon, anything would serve. If he could turn a local irritation into verse, he could rid himself of the bitterness attending it: 'In a Jest I spend my Rage'. When Thomas Rundle was appointed Bishop of Derry in February 1735, Swift resented the appointment largely, it appears, because Rundle was sponsored by the Lord Chancellor. So he wrote a skit on the Bishop, and disposed of his resentment in sixty lines. A few months later he wrote a warm account of Rundle's merits in a letter to Pope. In turn, Pope exempted Rundle from the strictures of the *Epilogue to the Satires*.

In 1934 Yeats told Oliver Edwards that in poetry he took his later manner from Swift: and, for proof and illustration, he read the third stanza of the 'Ode to the Honourable Sir William Temple':

> But what does our proud Ign'rance Learning call,
>   We odly Plato's Paradox make good,
> Our Knowledge is but mere Remembrance all,
>   Remembrance is our Treasure and our Food;
> Nature's fair Table-book our tender Souls
> We scrawl all o'er with old and empty Rules,
>   Stale Memorandums of the Schools;
>   For Learning's mighty Treasures look
>   In that deep Grave a Book,
>   Think she there does all her Treasures hide,
> And that her troubled Ghost still haunts there since she dy'd;
> Confine her Walks to Colleges and Schools,
>   Her Priests, her Train and Followers show
>   As if they all were Spectres too,
>   They purchase Knowledge at the Expence
>   Of common Breeding, common Sense,
>   And at once grow Scholars and Fools;
>   Affect ill-manner'd Pedantry,
> Rudeness, Ill-Nature, Incivility,
>   And sick with Dregs of Knowledge grown,
>   Which greedily they swallow down,
> Still cast it up and nauseate Company.[1]

This comes from one of the earliest poems. We are accustomed to think of it as mere 'prentice work. But if we read the 'Ode' again with Yeats in mind, we see that Swift is not shamed by that relation. There are many rough patches, but there are other places in which the poem has something of that vigour, that directness, which we admire in Yeats's later work. Yeats did not say what he admired in the 'Ode'. When he quoted the same stanza again, in *On the Boiler*, he gave it without

---

[1] Swift, *Poems*, edited by Harold Williams (Clarendon Press, Oxford, second edition, 1958), vol. I, p. 27.

comment. But we may guess that what he admired was a certain tone; we hear it in the juxtaposition of 'common Breeding, common Sense'; before that, in the invocation to Learning's 'troubled Ghost'; further back still, in the scrawling of Nature's table-book. If we think of this as a Yeatsian tone, we mark the strength of the tradition Yeats invoked: to a large extent it is Swift's tradition, tuned for a new context. The values to which Swift appeals in the 'Ode' are Yeatsian values; Nature, civility, courtesy, a certain independence of spirit. The poem implies that they are still available, though they are increasingly under attack. Swift invokes these values, and the tradition of *sprezzatura* in which they are defined, but if necessary he will speak upon his own authority. One of the most compelling marks of his poetry is its commitment to one thing at a time. The poet does not claim to say everything at once, in one poem, one book, one word. He confronts every occasion as it arises. Much of nineteenth-century poetry is so grandiose in its intention that it is unwilling to say one thing at a time. Swift takes this limitation as a matter of course. To give one example: in September 1727, he was delayed for a week at Holyhead while coming back to Dublin. He was troubled about Stella, who was ill. During those days, while he had nothing better to do, he kept a diary and scribbled verses as they occurred to him. One of them begins:

> Lo here I sit at holy head
> With muddy ale and mouldy bread
> All Christian vittals stink of fish
> I'm where my enemyes would wish.[1]

It is easy to say that this is doggerel, but it is more important to recognise the continuity between Swift's doggerel and his finest work, that the imaginative resilience of the one depends upon the strength of the other, the readiness to speak out. There is something of this continuity in Joyce, too, a movement of feeling which joins *The Holy Office* to *Ulysses*. The sense of

[1] Swift, *Poems*, vol. II, p. 420.

'muddy ale and mouldy bread' animates the great occasions in *Gulliver's Travels*, the *Modest Proposal*, the *Description of the Morning*, and the other choice things. There are certain tones in poetry which depend upon that sense; as Yeats discovered when he wrote the occasional poems in *Responsibilities* and *The Green Helmet*.

Of course Swift did not strike this note as soon as he took to verse. Largely under the influence of Cowley, he stuck to the Ode for his first poems and the Ode proved an intractable form. He had very little feeling for it, and as long as he clung to it, he established only a fitful relation with his true concerns. To hear him going through the motions of an Ode is to mark a certain ventriloquism in his style. Henri Focillon speaks of a vocation of form corresponding to a vocation of mind. There is a technical destiny in these matters.[1] The form of the Ode was intractable to Swift because it had little to do with the chief qualities of his mind. The Ode spreads itself over a long stanza, the lines unequal, the rhythm resisting definition at any point. It delights in postponement. If the lines are not to flag, they must aspire, and the poet must accept the excelsior note and whatever it entails. It is hard to be your own master in the Ode: Swift is uncomfortable in this restriction, even allowing for the splendid stanzas in the 'Ode to Temple'. His mind works best in the juxtaposition of small units, in balance and adjudication, where every change of direction is under minute control. He does not like to wait to see what is going to develop. As a poet he distrusts the vague, transitional moments, when a thing is neither fully itself nor something else. He is restless with things that do not maintain their own identity. In *The Day of Judgement* he speaks of 'the World's mad Business', and to Swift the main forms of that madness were abstraction, formlessness, bogus visions, clouds of pride. Poems were worth-while because they were receptacles of sense, specific things,

---

[1] Henri Focillon, *The Life of Forms in Art*, translated by C. B. Hogan and G. Kubler (Wittenborn, Schulte, New York, 1948), pp. 44, 48.

ways of getting things done. In 'Verses on the Death of Dr. Swift' he praises Pope for putting an uncommon amount of sense into his lines:

> In Pope, I cannot read a Line,
> But with a Sigh, I wish it mine:
> When he can in one Couplet fix
> More Sense than I can do in six.[1]

'Fix' is a spatial term; a thing is fixed in position and related there to other things. The relation is all the better if it is static, definitive; all the worse if it is tentative, problematic; worse still, if it is arbitrary, imposed by human will or whim. What Swift means by 'Sense' is clear enough; thoughts that have survived the trial of experience. It is clearer still when he puts it beside a word like 'true'. In the Imitation of Horace's *Hoc erat in votis* he writes:

> And let me in these Shades compose
> Something in Verse as true as Prose;
> Remov'd from all th' ambitious Scene,
> Nor puff'd by Pride, nor sunk by Spleen.[2]

So the 'sin of wit' which he invoked in another poem means the unpopular force of intelligence, truth, sense, the sharp edge of discrimination. Swift is not interested in daring flights of fancy on which new meanings may be discovered. He distrusts every ambiguous cloud of significance. He is content with the old meanings and angry that they are denied: poetry is a way of maintaining their force. This is what he means by 'fixing' the sense.

Clearly, among the available literary forms, he needed the couplet. The couplet allowed him to direct a flow of energy through single meanings and finite relationships. This is a prior condition before there can be any general significance at all; general significance, to Swift, is merely the sum of specific acts of intelligence. The facility provided by the

---

[1] *Poems*, vol. II, p. 555.   [2] *Ibid.* vol. I, p. 199.

couplet is that it requires the deployment of specific meanings, moment by moment, every shot has to count. The result is that the double vocation of mind and form enabled him to hold at bay themes which, in the prose, threatened to run wild. In poems like 'The Beasts' Confession' and 'On Poetry: A Rhapsody' he curbs the same themes which, in prose, drive him to violence. The couplet gives him the assurance that control, embodied in a formal tradition, is still possible:

> What Reason can there be assign'd
> For this Perverseness in the Mind?
> Brutes find out where their Talents lie:
> A Bear will not attempt to fly:
> A founder'd Horse will oft debate,
> Before he tries a five-barr'd Gate:
> A Dog by Instinct turns aside,
> Who sees the Ditch too deep and wide.
> But Man we find the only Creature,
> Who, led by Folly, fights with Nature;
> Who, when she loudly cries, Forbear,
> With Obstinacy fixes there;
> And, where his Genius least inclines,
> Absurdly bends his whole Designs.[1]

If the tone is rueful, it is still safe. One reason for this urbanity, in a writer to whom urbanity comes hard, is that in English literature the tradition in which such comment is securely made is largely a verse tradition. The serious part of the tradition issues in the satires of Dryden and Pope; the burlesque part in Butler and John Philips. Swift could choose; the conventions were well established. In prose fiction the lines were not at all clear: it was much harder to conceive how the work might be done. The tradition of English verse satire, going back from Pope and Dryden through Donne, Raleigh, and Greville to Lyndsay, the Scottish satirists and beyond, was a more complete accomplishment: it was in close relation to the great

---

[1] *Ibid.* vol. II, pp. 640–1.

dramatic tragedies, for one thing. The satiric couplet in the early eighteenth century is the direct inheritor of this tradition; hence its vitality in the hands of Pope, Gay and Johnson. True, the tradition had changed between Raleigh and Pope: changed, and narrowed. Even in Pope there is little sense of the tragic dimension within which, in Raleigh, the individual reflexion is made. The context of feeling in Pope is narrower than in Raleigh, mainly because the religious sense, the stress of that kind of implication, is weaker. There is nothing in Pope, or even in *The Vanity of Human Wishes*, to set beside Raleigh's 'Even such is Time':

> Even such is time, which takes in trust
> Our youth, our joys, and all we have,
> And pays us but with age and dust;
> Who, in the dark and silent grave,
> When we have wandered all our ways,
> Shuts up the story of our days,
> And from which earth and grave and dust,
> The Lord shall raise me up, I trust.

By the time we reach Swift and Pope, this sense of age and dust has been replaced by a sense of social error and absurdity; if the cast is larger than ever, the screen is narrower than before. It is, in another form, the difference between the sermons of Donne and Swift; Donne in the sermons is a voice in the night, heavy with mortality; Swift's sermons are digests, the daily dozen of sensible exercises, 'what every Englishman should know'.

But Swift confronts the incorrigible themes, in the poems, with vigour and resource which are partly personal and partly traditional. The themes are those which irritate the prose: it is still the old, inescapable story—the vanity of human delusion, the decay of intelligence. The concern which reverberates through the poems is the fear that intelligence is beaten, that the enemies are already at the gate. The chief enemy is 'the slagheap of the unconscious', the realm of Chaos and 'old

Night' invoked in Pope's *Dunciad*. Pope and Swift are deter
mined to force things into the light of day. Swift goes even
further than Pope in exposing whatever is dark or subliminal:
so that even when he writes an occasional poem, he always
keeps his mind focused on the object: to push things into the
daylight of common sense, to force them into definition.

Already in Swift's day this seemed a last-minute attempt to
hold the fort. One of the most remarkable developments in
eighteenth-century literature is that within twenty-five years
after the publication of the *Dunciad* the unconscious was
considered the chief source of poetic vision. The slagheap
became a mine. The crucial term in the story is Imagination:
in the first years of the eighteenth century it was still considered
a wild and unreliable power. But by the middle of the century
it had been promoted. Thomas Warton objects to Pope's
poetry because it lives in sunlight, the world of the understanding, rather than the more subtle twilight of the imagination. Indeed, when Pope used images of darkness and night to
represent the loss of clarity, form and intelligence, he stood on
ground which was already shifting beneath his feet. Within a
remarkably short time these images, despite the ridicule
visited upon them in *Peri Bathous* and elsewhere, acquired a
new and paradoxical 'radiance': the most profound visions
were now available, it seemed, at night, and the moon took the
place of the sun as the visionary power. The new text is Addison
on the Pleasures of the Imagination. The suggestion is that the
effect of the white light of Reason is to enforce the separation of
man from Nature. The light of reconciliation is twilight, when
the pleasures of imagination are available without rational
effort. Along with this, there is a new assumption, that the
crucial events take place within the mind; not outside. Admittedly, the materials, the sensations, come into our minds from
outside, but as long as we agree with Locke that these sensations
are the primary data, nothing in their origin is as important
as their history within the individual mind. Psychology replaces

politics.[1] It is easy to see why Swift would not speak the new language: to him, what happened inside the mind, in most cases, was delusion; the important events were public, social, political; administrative acts performed to make the world a more tolerable place. Swift had the deepest suspicion of those who would have the great dramas enacted within the mind; much of his work is a demonstration of this absurdity. But he was the last great writer to maintain that position. The new feeling was expressed, at least in part, by Addison's insistence that many things which cannot pass the test of right reason are still eminently legitimate materials for poetry. Again, the new feeling took great stock in the notion of process. Since the chief value of life was to be found within the individual mind and was therefore a psychological matter, the whole process was considered crucial. Writers like Swift had little or no interest in process; they judged by results. But the new psychology fastens upon the individual psyche from the first arrival of a sensation and traces the graph of its history through all its stages. Swift regarded most of this history as trash and its devotees as fools: nothing was interesting until it revealed itself in form or until it could be forced into that degree of definition. The new law reads: anything on which the imagination can work is legitimate. As Reason is supplanted by Imagination, it becomes natural to rescue the unconscious from Pope's denunciation, because sensations and associations come vividly from that source. When this is done, the split between Reason and Imagination is complete. Reason is handed over to the scientists, the merchants and the philosophers. Imagination is retained and promoted as the strictly creative power, the only power which can see things in all their variety. In the middle years of the eighteenth century the notion of a direct engagement between man and Nature in a clear white light was considered too blunt, a harsh confrontation in which man's spirit

[1] See Ernest Lee Tuveson, *The Imagination as a Means of Grace* (University of California Press, Berkeley and Los Angeles, 1960).

was bound to suffer: besides, this had been tried. The new psychology invites man to much more diffuse experience, blurring the sharp edges: as, a century later, Mallarmé, appalled by the naked confrontation of man and sky, finds ease in a London fog. The price of this ease was high: one of the disadvantages of the new psychology was that it eventually drove the poet from society altogether. When Yeats pondered the fate of the 'Tragic Generation', he marked as one of the main causes of their catastrophe the morbid effort to create a new purity and beauty from 'images more and more separated from the general purposes of life'. These general purposes are the aims of man in society; to a writer like Swift they are virtually the only important aims; or at least the only aims at once important and tangible. Pope and Swift spent their lives attending upon those aims; choosing, discriminating, adjusting. They worked on the assumption that if only the social purposes of man are clarified and tested, his private condition can be left to his own devices. The immediate necessity was to enlarge the domain of mind and intelligence. If something has to be rejected, well and good, let it be rejected; but keep the slagheap as small as possible.

We can consult these new assumptions in the aesthetic of darkness, the 'school of night' which urged that darkness is the true place of the sublime. Young's 'Night Thoughts' is the first major poem in this tradition, Burke its most accomplished critical sponsor. These follow the new psychology. The old feeling is to be found mainly in Pope, Swift and Gay. When Gay writes 'A Contemplation on Night' he tolerates night only by reminding himself that when it is night in one hemisphere it is day in the other. But even while rehearsing this pleasant truth, his images give him away: night is the place of 'gloom', he repeats 'the gloomy reign of night', the stars are the only proof that God's in His Heaven. The poem ends:

> When the pure soul is from the body flown,
> No more shall night's alternate reign be known:

The sun no more shall rolling light bestow,
But from th'Almighty streams of glory flow.
Oh, may some nobler thought my soul employ,
Than empty, transient, sublunary joy!
The stars shall drop, the sun shall lose his flame,
But thou, O God, for ever shine the same.

We can list the chief enemies of day and mind: the unconscious, sleep, dreams, visions of fancy, delusions of pride, the passions. Swift tried to rid himself of these and to perform the same service for the world. He seeks this object in many poems, including 'On Dreams':

Those Dreams that on the silent Night intrude,
And with false flitting Shades our Minds delude,
Jove never sends us downward from the Skies,
Nor can they from infernal Mansions rise;
But all are meer Productions of the Brain,
And Fools consult Interpreters in vain.

For, when in Bed we rest our weary Limbs,
The Mind unburthen'd sports in various Whims,
The busy Head with mimick Art runs o'er
The Scenes and Actions of the Day before.

The drowsy Tyrant, by his Minions led,
To regal Rage devotes some Patriot's Head.
With equal Terrors, not with equal Guilt,
The Murd'rer dreams of all the Blood he spilt.

The Soldier smiling hears the Widows Cries,
And stabs the Son before the Mother's Eyes.
With like Remorse his Brother of the Trade,
The Butcher, feels the Lamb beneath his blade.

The Statesman rakes the Town to find a Plot,
And dreams of Forfeitures by Treason got.
Nor less Tom-Turd-Man of true Statesman mold,
Collects the City Filth in search of Gold.

Orphans around his Bed the Lawyer sees,
And takes the Plaintiff's and Defendant's Fees.

His Fellow Pick-Purse, watching for a Job,
Fancies his Fingers in the Cully's Fob.

The kind Physician grants the Husband's Prayers,
Or gives Relief to long-expecting Heirs.
The sleeping Hangman ties the fatal Noose,
Nor unsuccessful waits for dead Mens Shoes.

The grave Divine with knotty Points perplext,
As if he were awake, nods o'er his Text:
While the sly Mountebank attends his Trade,
Harangues the Rabble, and is better paid.

The hireling Senator of modern Days,
Bedaubs the guilty Great with nauseous Praise:
And Dick the Scavenger with equal Grace,
Flirts from his Cart the Mud in Walpole's Face.[1]

It is characteristic of Swift to put the blame on man himself;
dreams are not sent either from Heaven or from Hell, we ourselves manufacture them, they are functions of our own
corruption. In 'A Beautiful Young Nymph Going to Bed' there
is the same suggestion, that dreams are in strict accord with
the nature of the dreamer. Again in the early poem 'To Mr.
Congreve' Swift writes:

Thus are the lives of fools a sort of dreams,
Rend'ring shades, things, and substances of names;
Such high companions may delusion keep,
Lords are a footboy's cronies in his sleep.[2]

So dreams delude our minds by setting before us our own
memories, fancies, and desires; an unwholesome compound
from which we extract our visions. The only difference between
the dream and the reality is that in the dream-world we pursue
our evil desires with impunity: in society, at least up to now
and for the moment, there are a few obstacles in our way.
This tension between the real world, where our corruptions are
at least held at bay, and the dream-world, in which we live as

---

[1] *Poems*, vol. II, pp. 363–4.   [2] *Ibid.* vol. I, pp. 47–8.

viciously as our desires, accounts for the weight of Swift's
satire. The satire works by finding similarity beneath overt
difference; as the dreams of soldiers and butchers are shown to
be identical. It is the same force that presses together, in the
one stanza, the physician and the hangman. But in this stanza
the satire goes deeper still. 'The kind Physician grants the
Husband's Prayers'; plays God, granting and withholding. 'Or
gives Relief to long-expecting Heirs.' This God conspires with
the evil of men. If the physician's act is within the world of
dreams, it is not clear that the husband's prayers for the death
of his wife have even that much excuse; they are palpable
facts, with which the diseased imagination plays. To find anything comparable in early eighteenth-century poetry we must
go to Pope, to couplets like

> The hungry Judges soon the sentence sign,
> And wretches hang that jurymen may dine

—where the double hunger, a compounded outrage, is an
effect on the same scale. Pope counts on the spread of words like
'appetite' and 'hunger' from the bodily to the ethical dimension; as Swift counts on the fact that sentences often find themselves reversed; if the theologians say that man is made in the
image of God, here is a physician who can make God in the
image of a diseased man. Swift is demonstrating, in this remarkable poem, effects of adjustment and juxtaposition which are
possible only in the light of day and mind. What is possible in
dreams, he has already made clear. Over the course of the
next century poets invested a great deal of capital in dreams.
De Quincey proposes to help people to dream productively.
'Habitually to dream magnificently', he says, 'a man must have
a constitutional determination to reverie.' Thereafter, the main
trouble is that one's dream is constantly interrupted by social
event. De Quincey thinks this a disaster.[1] The faculty of dream-
ing, he says, 'in alliance with the mystery of darkness', is the

[1] See Bonamy Dobrée (editor), *Thomas De Quincey* (Batsford, London, 1965),
pp. 66–7.

'one great tube through which man communicates with the shadowy'. There, in one sentence, we have Swift's defeat; for Swift regarded 'the shadowy' as a highly dubious world, and all attempts to communicate with it as self-delusion. Dreams represented a mode of life he detested and, against his best official efforts, feared.

Swift's poem is an imitation of a very beautiful poem by Petronius, 'Somnia quae mentes ludunt uolitantibus umbris'. If we compare the original with the imitation we can see the parts of the poem which are entirely Swift's, and consider the pressure which incited them:

> Somnia, quae mentes ludunt uolitantibus umbris,
> non delubra deum nec ab aethere numina mittunt,
> sed sibi quisque facit. Nam cum prostrata sopore
> urget membra quies et mens sine pondere ludit,
> quicquid luce fuit, tenebris agit. Oppida bello
> qui quatit et flammis miserandas eruit urbes,
> tela uidet uersasque acies et funera regum
> atque exundantes perfuso sanguine campos.
> Qui causas orare solent, legesque forumque
> et pauidi cernunt inclusum chorte tribunal.
>
> Condit auarus opes defossumque inuenit aurum;
> uenator saltus canibus quatit; eripit undis
> aut premit euersam periturus nauita puppem;
> scribit amatori meretrix, dat adultera munus;
> (et canis in somnis leporis uestigia latrat).
> In noctis spatium miserorum uulnera durant.[1]

Here there is no question of blame. Petronius's tone is sympathetic: whatever we do by day, we continue to do by night in our dreams, not because we are evil but because we are held in the grip of things. It is like Yeats's vision of necessity in *Purgatory*, where the Old Man is held in a chain of consequence which he cannot break. Petronius does not say, as Swift says by

---

[1] *Pétrone: Le Satiricon*, texte établi et traduit par Alfred Ernout (Société d'édition, 'Les belles lettres', Paris, 1962), pp. 191–2.

implication: 'Know Thyself.' He is acknowledging the force of things, and the price our own nature has to pay. Swift cannot leave matters in this neutral realm; if he has a gift for rebuke and invective, he is driven to exercise it. 'A gift is an imperative.' So his poem is all blame. Memory of the things his characters have done is mixed with desire of things yet undone, the mixture an inventory of vice. In the stanza about the soldier the question of remorse is raised only to mark its absence. The soldier smiles when he hears the widow's cries, and to round out the symmetry of the occasion waits for the mother to see him before he stabs the son: there are possibilities here of a grisly decorum. The butcher's performance lacks an audience of this splendour, but he makes up for it by animating the preliminary gesture; nothing as detached as seeing his victim, he 'feels' him beneath the blade. By the time we reach this stage in the poem the participants have become emblematic figures, as in a grim tryptych or an allegory.

Clearly, there is a close relation between the insistence with which these emblem-figures are fixed in their settings and the vigour of the couplets themselves. The steady phalanx of Swift's couplets has the effect of ensuring that a certain perspective is maintained. Focillon has discussed two orders of shapes, two different relations between forms and their environments. In the first, the space which is liberally allowed to surround the form has the effect of keeping it intact and permanent. In the second, the forms enter into dynamic engagement with their environment to such an extent that the strict beginning and end of the forms are hidden. The first, Focillon calls the 'system of the series'; the second is the 'system of the labyrinth'. The system of the series is composed of 'discontinuous elements sharply outlined, strongly rhythmical, and defining a stable and symmetrical space that protects them against unforeseen accidents of metamorphosis'. The system of the labyrinth is a later exigency, where the labyrinth 'stretches itself out in a realm of glittering movement and colour'.[1] Swift's poem is a remarkably vivid example of the 'system of the series', where the elements, the couplets, are 'sharply outlined', holding a stable environment in place: the relation between these particular couplets and the forces pressing against them is so strong, so tense, that it indeed protects them 'against unforeseen accidents of metamorphosis'. Swift's equilibrium, indeed his sanity, depends upon the resilience with which this relation is maintained: if it were to shift, veering to a 'labyrinth', he would be defeated. His vocation for the enclosed couplet allows him to fix things in their places, with some confidence that they will stay there. In prose he was much more exposed. Wylie Sypher has remarked something along the same lines in Pope. Pope, he says, 'carefully sets all his scenes at a certain distance from his own feelings so that a sufficient interval is kept between himself and his poem, himself and his reader'. The focus 'does not shift'; but within the unchanging focus he can shift as much as he wants, varying the tone as much as he pleases because there is always that saving distance.[2] To revert to Swift; it is a condition of his poetry that the reader is kept outside: he is never allowed to break in, or to secrete himself in the folds. What holds the reader's attention is the force with which Swift commands his own vision, his own perspective, and the space that surrounds it.

II

We can see Swift trying to hold this perspective, and to command the surrounding space, in the 'boudoir' poems. If the note of these poems is strident, this is partly explained by his involvement in the relevant passions, and partly by the difficulty of holding the surrounding space in check.

A motto is given, by implication, in a passage from 'The Lady's Dressing Room':

[1] Focillon, *The Life of Forms in Art*, p. 18.
[2] Wylie Sypher, *Rococo to Cubism* (Vintage Books, New York, 1960), p. 46.

The Virtues we must not let pass,
Of Celia's magnifying Glass.
When frighted Strephon cast his Eye on't
It shew'd the Visage of a Gyant.
A Glass that can to sight disclose,
The smallest Worm in Celia's Nose,
And faithfully direct her Nail
To squeeze it out from Head to Tail;
For catch it nicely by the Head,
It must come out alive or dead.[1]

At this point poor Strephon has inspected the contents of Celia's bedroom; when he comes upon her glass and looks into it he sees the 'Visage of a Gyant'. What stares back at him is his own terrified face, monstrously enlarged. But when Celia uses the glass to root out a worm in her nose, the glass is a commanding frame of reference; it holds its images within a determined frame and refuses to release them or—just as important—to allow anything else to enter. When the glass is in place, nothing can leave, nothing can enter, until the inspection is complete. This, however gruesome, is the technique of these poems. Nothing is allowed to leave, the tight form of the couplet encloses everything, the 'system of the series'. Nothing is allowed to enter, because it is prevented by the frame of the couplet as by the frame of the glass. The glass holds its image in this fixed position: it withdraws the image from its context only to fix it according to a more commanding perspective. The couplet withdraws an image from its context, that is, from all the things in its setting which might well modify our interpretation of it; and it puts the image in a setting of Swift's contrivance, where it will be subject to pressure of a much starker kind. This work is often done in Augustan literature by the great impersonal terms, Wit, Sense, Nature, and so forth. The object is to render impossible the formless or the labyrinthine sprawl, to hold everything at bay. If we add that the theme of these poems is, as I have suggested, the vanity of

[1] *Poems*, vol. II, p. 527.

human delusion, we can see how that vanity is held or, in the best of these poems, transfixed.

In 'The Progress of Love' the bashful Phillis, due to marry, runs away with the butler John, becomes a whore, contracts venereal disease. Swift's poem is a parody of the traditional romantic ballad: the falling in love, elopement, the maiden's letter to her father, the gay lover, pain, sadness and the tender death are held up against the facts. The 'system of the series' operates by crushing entire chapters of incident into a few couplets to dramatise the speed of Phillis's decay:

> Fair Maidens all attend the Muse
> Who now the wandring Pair pursues:
> Away they rode in homely Sort
> Their Journey long, their Money short;
> The loving Couple well bemir'd,
> The Horse and both the Riders tir'd:
> Their Vittels bad, their Lodging worse,
> Phil cry'd, and John began to curse;
> Phil wish't, that she had strained a Limb
> When first she ventur'd out with him.
> John wish'd, that he had broke a Leg
> When first for her he quitted Peg.[1]

It is a technique of speed; incidents are given so swiftly that the faintest suggestion of pathos is swept aside. Where a sentimental novelist would spend several chapters describing how John lost his job and Phillis, to support them, had to sell herself on the streets and there picked up the disease, Swift tosses these chapters into a few lines:

> How oft she broke her marriage Vows
> In kindness to maintain her Spouse;
> Till Swains unwholesome spoyld the Trade,
> For now the Surgeon must be paid;
> To whom those Perquisites are gone
> In Christian Justice due to John.

[1] *Ibid.* vol. I, p. 224.

205

So he commands the space in which his couplets are set by fending off the conventional response to romantic ballads. It is entirely in keeping, for instance, that he does not even let Phillis die: the last lines of the poem leave her and John transfixed, running a public house in Staines, where even the rhymes tell against them:

> They keep at Stains the old blue Boar,
> Are Cat and Dog, and Rogue and Whore.

Normally, when Swift holds up a magnifying glass against a situation, it is to look at it more closely than convention requires or allows. Often this takes the form of reading literally what is meant figuratively: in 'The Progress of Beauty' he makes fun of beauty by taking literally the poetic comparison between a beautiful face and the Moon. As the Moon wanes, Celia declines into a whore. If you insist upon living by sentimental analogies, you must pay Swift's price, their consequence. He compares a woman's face to a piece of China-ware, because both can be repaired by the application of white lead. But the basic technique is an elaborate parody of the philosophical discussion of Form and Matter:

> Matter, as wise Logicians say,
> Cannot without a Form subsist,
> And Form, say I, as well as They,
> Must fayl if Matter brings no Grist.

If the diseased Celia loses her nose and her teeth, the form is ruined, and the best she can do is to make sure to appear, like the stars, only at a distance and by night:

> Two Balls of Glass may serve for Eyes,
> White Lead can plaister up a Cleft,
> But these alas, are poor Supplyes
> If neither Cheeks, nor Lips be left.

The procedure here is to 'translate downwards'. Treat the Soul as if it were Body, then treat the body as the mere sum of its parts; work up the picture of an ideal body as a structure of replaceable parts, so that when one part wears out by disease you can replace it. Then advert to the fact that this, alas, is impossible. So the only recourse is to discard the worn-out body. This is hard on women, but they have only themselves to blame. As for their men; they can only pray to get a new woman every month:

> Ye Pow'rs who over Love preside,
> Since mortal Beautyes drop so soon,
> If you would have us well supply'd,
> Send us new Nymphs with each new Moon.

This is eminently Swiftian; to treat the organic as if it were mechanical. He does it again, more systematically, in 'A Beautiful Young Nymph Going to Bed'. Corinna is a machine, her bedroom a factory; when she goes to bed, the factory is shut down. It is essential to this device that all the moving parts of the body are detachable:

> Then, seated on a three-legg'd Chair,
> Takes off her artificial Hair:
> Now, picking out a Crystal Eye,
> She wipes it clean, and lays it by.
> Her Eye-Brows from a Mouse's Hyde,
> Stuck on with Art on either Side,
> Pulls off with Care, and first displays 'em,
> Then in a Play-Book smoothly lays 'em.
> Now dextrously her Plumpers draws,
> That serve to fill her hollow Jaws.
> Untwists a Wire; and from her Gums
> A Set of Teeth completely comes.
> Pulls out the Rags contriv'd to prop
> Her flabby Dugs and down they drop.

In the morning Corinna finds the machine destroyed; the crystal eye is gone, a rat has stolen the plaster, all the other parts are in a mess. But she is a resourceful mechanic, and the merit of mechanical things is that they can be replaced:

> The Nymph, tho' in this mangled Plight,
> Must ev'ry Morn her Limbs unite.

How she does this, Swift does not say. Or rather, he implies that the Muse is too 'bashful' to look very close; the Muse speaks a different idiom. The poem ends with the factory still in chaos, but Corinna is about to put herself together again. Lovers should not investigate factories. As Swift says in 'Strephon and Chloe':

> Why is a handsome Wife ador'd
> By ev'ry Coxcomb, but her Lord?
> From yonder Puppet-Man inquire,
> Who wisely hides his Wood and Wire;
> Shews Sheba's Queen completely drest,
> And Solomon in Royal Vest;
> But, view them litter'd on the Floor,
> Or strung on Pegs behind the Door;
> Punch is exactly of a Piece
> With Lorraine's Duke, and Prince of Greece.[1]

This is Swift's country by general assent, but he was not the first to discover it. Close at hand, it figures largely in Rochester's poems, especially in 'A Letter from Artemisa in the Town, to Chloe, in the Country'. Artemisa is telling her country cousin the ways of men in the city. Anticipating a famous sentiment in Swift, she says:

> They little guess, who at our Arts are grieved,
> The perfect Joy of being well deceiv'd.

If 'Wonder', which Swift calls delusion, is to be preserved, the lover must fend off 'clear Knowledge':

> Woman, who is an arrant Bird of Night,
> Bold in the dusk, before a Fool's dull sight,
> Must fly, when Reason brings the glaring Light.[2]

The glaring light is also Swift's recourse, to protect himself from his own passions, from the unconscious, and now the human rage for delusion. But it is a severe test. In several poems Swift

---

[1] *Poems*, vol. II, p. 592.
[2] Rochester, *Poems*, edited by John Hayward (Nonesuch Press, London, 1926), p. 29.

shows us the lover who insists upon the truth of things and goes in search of it; but invariably he is blinded by what he sees, and, unless he is already overwhelmed, settles for the perpetual possession of being well deceived. The motto of these poems is: live with illusion, but know that you are being deceived; beguile yourself with the image before you, but know that it is a pleasant fiction. In 'The Lady's Dressing Room' Strephon steals into Celia's bedroom while she is out. He is determined to seek the truth. Swift warns us, by a pun on Milton's lines in *Paradise Lost*, that we would be wiser to leave uninspected the 'secrets of the hoary Deep'. As the culmination of Strephon's vision, there is the discovery that Celia excretes. Strephon's folly is a new original sin, an insistence upon man's right to go 'to the end of the line', disobeying God, Nature, and common sense. Strephon's sin is the presumption of Knowledge: he insists upon penetrating to the truth of Celia, and his only reward is the acquisition of a 'foul Imagination'. The chief characteristic of this imagination is that it translates Celia 'downward': she is equated with her stink, and in that respect she becomes Everywoman. Celia's bodily nature is 'original' in the sense in which Strephon's sin is original. Swift says:

> But Vengeance, Goddess never sleeping
> Soon punish'd Strephon for his Peeping;
> His foul Imagination links
> Each Dame he sees with all her Stinks . . .[1]

But it is Strephon's 'vicious Fancy' which generalises in this way. The poem ends with the return of the prudent narrator, apostle of the reasonable middle-way. This man lives with the public show of things, and he never questions further. If Celia looks like a goddess, well and good, enough is enough; celebrate her as if she were a goddess. Common sense is the philosophy of 'as if', maintained with prudence. If we do

---

[1] *Poems*, vol. II, p. 529.

this, we easily get over the problem of Celia's 'ointments, daubs, and paints and creams', these are merely her votive accompaniments. Strephon's foul imagination cannot see these things without blaspheming; foulness is the price he pays for the truth. If he could bring himself to rest in the appearance of things, Swift says,

> He soon would learn to think like me,
> And bless his ravisht Sight to see
> Such Order from Confusion sprung,
> Such gaudy Tulips rais'd from Dung.

Middleton Murry has argued that this last part of the poem is an attempt to take the harm out of the earlier, excremental part. It has the air of being tacked on as an afterthought. 'The Lady's Dressing Room' is yet another version of Swift's invariable theme, the question of Form and Matter, Spirit and Body. In other places Swift tends to show that spirit is 'nothing more than' body. Here he says: accept the fact that the spirit of beauty is implicated in the matter of body; accept it, live with it, get used to it, and live with corresponding prudence. But this is just another way of saying that we must in this case 'sublimate', cling to the pleasing delusion if we are not to go mad, like Strephon, with our foul imaginations.

The story is complicated in 'Strephon and Chloe', a parody of those fables in which a goddess, like Thetis, comes to earth and marries a man. Chloe, seemingly a goddess in human form, marries Strephon but on her wedding night reveals herself just as mortal as he. Their love duet becomes a collusion of obscenities. Swift's feeling is not so much horror at the 'excremental vision'; but rather, hatred of everything in life that depends upon the absurd delusions of pride and pretence. Often the pride is spiritual or even aesthetic; hence the parody of the Grand Style with its world of 'fine Ideas'. The implication is that the only way to hold ourselves safe is by ensuring that our passions are subject to the test of common sense. To achieve this reduction Swift is willing to answer one

extremity by another. This complicates the argument of
'The Lady's Dressing Room', where we are admonished to
rest in beguiling appearance. Now we are to seek our safety
by modifying our passions: for this urgent purpose Swift is
willing to confront the facts. The narrator tells Strephon that
if he had been fortunate enough to see the excremental truth
of Chloe before he was too deeply sunk in passion, he would
now be easy in heart:

> Your Fancy then had always dwelt
> On what you saw, and what you smelt;
> Would still the same Ideas give ye,
> As when you spied her on the Privy.
> And, spight of Chloe's Charms divine,
> Your Heart had been as whole as mine.

This implies that even Strephon's foul imagination might be a
small price to pay for ease of heart and indifference. Meanwhile
the advice is: prudence and limitation:

> On Sense and Wit your Passion found,
> By Decency cemented round;
> Let Prudence with Good Nature strive,
> To keep Esteem and Love alive.
> Then come Old Age whene'er it will,
> Your Friendship shall continue still:
> And thus a mutual gentle Fire,
> Shall never but with Life expire.[1]

It is interesting that Swift does not subvert either the emotion
of love or the institution of marriage; only insisting that both
be pursued in reasonable terms. Love is a function of friendship, and passion rises no higher than 'a mutual gentle Fire'.
In 'The Phoenix and Turtle' Shakespeare speaks of the lovers'
passion as a 'mutual flame'; Swift's flame is still mutual but it
is to burn gently. The tone of the poem is rueful. Swift is
rebuking women for ignoring, after marriage, the considerations by which the marriage was achieved:

[1] *Poems*, vol. II, p. 593.

They take Possession of the Crown,
And then throw all their Weapons down;
Though by the Politicians Scheme
Who'er arrives at Pow'r supreme,
Those Arts by which at first they gain it,
They still must practise to maintain it.

The reference is to Marvell's 'Horation Ode upon Cromwell's Return from Ireland'; to the last stanza, where Marvell advises Cromwell to press on, and now that he has achieved power, to maintain it by the same arts. Swift is bringing to the situation of love and marriage the same considerations, and the same attitudes, which Marvell exhibits toward Cromwell; as if to say: whatever moral reservations I might have about your actions up to this point, I must concede that you have been successful; so, proceed, this must be done and there is nothing else to do. The tone common to Swift and Marvell arises from the force of fact, judiciously acknowledged. Norman O. Brown has argued that in 'Strephon and Chloe' sublimation and awareness of the excremental functions are presented as mutually exclusive; the conclusion being that sublimation must be cultivated even at the cost of repression. But this assumes that Swift is dealing with a force of passion which is constant. In fact, Swift urges Strephon to keep the horror to a minimum by cutting back the passion, to begin with: start by looking hard and long at the facts of the case, this will have the effect of curbing your passion. Then if you wish, proceed. You do so with impunity, because the force of your passion is now small, there is little to repress. This is in line with Swift's prayer for Stella, that she be granted happiness by the reduction of her desires. It follows naturally from his assumption that happiness, a ratio between one's desires and one's possessions, can be preserved either by increasing the possessions or by reducing the desires.

This interpretation is supported by 'Cassinus and Peter'. Strephon's error consisted in his failure to curb his passion

when he had a chance; a sharp vision of the facts would have
done the trick. But Strephon did not take this opportunity. In
the present poem Cassinus has made the same mistake; now
it is too late. He has loved the illusion of Caelia. Now when
the facts collide with his passion, they turn its force into disgust,
hatred, foul imagination. Hating Caelia, Cassinus hates all
women and therefore life itself. So he is the type of Swift's
victims. In these poems lovers who did not take the first
opportunity of modifying their passions are for ever lost, and
they must pay the price in universal disgust. Cassinus is driven
mad by his vision of omnivorous excrement. Even now, mad,
he thinks that Caelia's excreting is a unique sin against her race
and sex. He can hardly bring himself to tell Peter his frightful
secret, and he warns him never to tell anyone else:

> To force it out my Heart must rend;
> Yet, when conjur'd by such a Friend—
> Think, Peter, how my Soul is rack'd.
> These Eyes, these Eyes beheld the Fact.
> Now bend thine Ear; since out it must:
> But, when thou seest me laid in Dust,
> The Secret thou shalt ne'er impart;
> Not to the Nymph that keeps thy Heart;
> (How would her Virgin Soul bemoan
> A Crime to all her Sex unknown!)
> Nor whisper to the tattling Reeds,
> The blackest of all Female Deeds.[1]

Brown thinks that this poem shatters the solution reached in
'Strephon and Chloe'; the life of civilised sublimation is
destroyed because the excremental vision cannot be repressed.[2]
But this would be so only if we were to identify Cassinus with
Swift himself. This is out of the question. For one thing, it
would mean forgetting Peter. In the first lines Cassinus and
Peter are 'Lovers both'. But Peter is a sensible fellow, he
never runs to extremes. When he visits Cassinus and finds him

[1] *Poems*, vol. ii, p. 596.
[2] Norman O. Brown, *Life against Death* (Vintage Books, New York, 1959), p. 188.

in distraction, he cannot understand what has happened. When Cassinus says 'Caelia', Peter can only think that she has been killed, or she has 'played the whore', or caught the pox. These are the thoughts of a solid man. This, Swift implies, is the way to take one's passions, with rough common sense. Poor Cassinus is an idealist, a naif, compounding fictions and giving them names. No wonder he goes mad. I am suggesting, of course, that this tragical elegy is richly comic: the comedy is 'black', but it does not require us to assume that Cassinus is Swift or that the poem is Swift's last letter to the world. That passion can be kept on a close rein is Peter's message; that we go mad unless we keep it so is the point of Cassinus. But the poem gives us both idioms.

These poems are not, in fact, obsessed; their 'excremental vision' is held in check by other forces. Swift is merely pursuing the logic of his terms: soul and body, soul in sin, body in disease. If the motto of Swift's prose is: Negate; the motto of the poems is: Modify your desires and passions. Better still if we can substitute friendship for love. In 'Cadenus and Vanessa' Swift says:

> But Friendship in its greatest Height,
> A constant, rational Delight,
>   On Virtue's Basis fix'd to last,
> When Love's Allurements long are past;
> Which gently warms, but cannot burn;
> He gladly offers in return.[1]

If friendship is safer than love, this underlines the general advice to live by modest desires; it is given in several poems, particularly in 'Desire and Possession'. Reduce desire: then hold what remains with all the resources of perspective and force. If something appears intractable, translate it downward; if it is organic, treat is as if it were mechanical. If it is human, be on the watch for animal imagery which will intimidate it,

[1] *Poems*, vol. II, p. 711.

thereby releasing you. It is not enough to hold the object; you must command the space surrounding it and live by that command.

III

These are the chief terms of Swift's poetry. Clearly, they are strong enough and flexible enough to sustain many kinds of poem. But if we think of them in loose association, they point toward the poetry of invective. The greatest example is 'The Legion Club'.

The poem is an attack upon the Members of the Irish House of Commons after they had voted to deprive the clergy of certain tithes legally due. But although it has an object and a local occasion, it is invective in the further sense that it develops energy and momentum from its own resources, once it has started. Kenneth Burke has discussed invective as a kind of Pure Poetry, which needs little external stimulus to keep it going. Once started, it can work up a fine head of steam with only occasional assistance from its object. It is like the *encomium*, the essay in pure praise, panegyric turned upside-down. It may be argued that Swift was happy in this form because he delighted in carrying things to the end of the line, exploiting purely internal resources far beyond the requirement of the occasion. This would account for his most extreme riddles and puns and, in this poem, for the virtuosity of the rhymes. The poem is called 'The Legion Club' because of the answer of the unclean spirit in *Mark* (v.9): 'My name is Legion; for we are many.' This prompts Swift to develop the notion that the Members are all mad, that the House is Bedlam, that when they speak they rave. Or, again, that the House is Hell, full of evil shadows and spirits. Or a cage for weird animals. Each of these visions is driven by energy which is engendered as one line is generated from another; nothing else is required. In one stanza he dreams of destroying the House, with the

215

Devil's aid, on the understanding that God often uses the Devil as His scourge. But then he thinks of letting the House stand, and using it as a lunatic asylum:

> Since the House is like to last,
> Let a royal Grant be pass'd,
> That the Club have Right to dwell
> Each within his proper Cell;
> With a Passage left to creep in,
> And a Hole above for peeping.
>   Let them, when they once get in
> Sell the Nation for a Pin;
> While they sit a picking Straws
> Let them rave of making Laws;
> While they never hold their Tongue,
> Let them dabble in their Dung;
> Let them form a grand Committee,
> How to plague and starve the City;
> Let them stare and storm and frown,
> When they see a Clergy-Gown.
> Let them, 'ere they crack a Louse,
> Call for th' Orders of the House.[1]

It could go on indefinitely. The chief effect of the couplets is to ensure that they command whatever they touch. Often this is a matter of bringing images into startling relationships, by *fiat* and insistence. The relation between 'picking Straws' and 'making Laws' is a brilliant parody of choice and chance, achieved with the connivance of an accommodating language. The same feature in the language makes it possible for Swift to suggest the quality of speeches in the House of Commons by adding an appropriate accompaniment:

> While they never hold their Tongue,
> Let them dabble in their Dung.

This is, presumably, what Swift meant when he referred to 'my own hum'rous biting Way', in the 'Verses on the Death of Dr. swift'. In the poem 'To Mr. Delany' he distinguishes between

[1] *Poems.* vol. III, pp. 830–1.

raillery and abuse, and he attaches the adjective 'obliging' to the nouns 'ridicule' and 'jest'. The distinctions are never clear. In prose, Swift recommended Voiture; in verse, Delany—at least on this occasion. We may accept his terms; raillery, jest, with the addition of invective. There is also Humour, which he described in the same poem:

> Humor is odd, grotesque, and wild,
> Onely by Affectation spoild . . .

This is clearly Swift's possession in such poems as 'The Legion Club'. Rochester seems to have thought of it as 'pointed Satire'. Under whatever name, it is an achievement of style.

I should not imply that Swift's poems are all in these keys. He had his light moments, when the easy occasion called for the other kind of wit; as in 'Mrs Harris's Petition'. Indeed, to go through Swift's entire poetry is to be astonished by its variety, the range of feeling invoked. We often think that of all the different kinds of poetry, he wrote only two or three; but we forget the occasions when the writing of a poem served him instead of a letter, a pun, a conversation, a journey, a postcard, or a public speech:

> By Faction tir'd, with Grief he waits a while,
> His great contending Friends to reconcile.
> Performs what Friendship, Justice, Truth require:
> What could he more, but decently retire?

If we did not know, it would be hard to ascribe that to Swift, at least with any conviction. The tone seems more delicate, more charitable, more Johnsonian than our standard impression of him. He wrote the poem, 'The Author upon Himself', in the summer of 1714, distressed by the growing bitterness between his great contending friends Oxford and Bolingbroke. We must allow for this tone; we find it again in the birthday poems to Stella.

Indeed, Swift's finest poems are remarkable achievements of style: his handling of tone, for instance, is never random or awkward. The 'Satirical Elegy on the Death of a Late Famous

General' is a case in point. Marlborough died on 16 June 1722 but his defeat was already achieved on 30 December 1711, when he was deprived of all appointments, an event celebrated in Swift's 'The Fable of Midas'. The Elegy reads:

> His Grace! impossible! what dead!
> Of old age too, and in his bed!
> And could that Mighty Warrior fall?
> And so inglorious, after all!
> Well, since he's gone, no matter how,
> The last loud trump must wake him now:
> And, trust me, as the noise grows stronger,
> He'd wish to sleep a little longer.
> And could he be indeed so old
> As by the news-papers we're told?
> Threescore, I think, is pretty high;
> 'Twas time in conscience he should die.
> This world he cumber'd long enough;
> He burnt his candle to the snuff;
> And that's the reason, some folks think,
> He left behind so great a stink.
> Behold his funeral appears,
> Nor widow's sighs, nor orphan's tears,
> Wont at such times each heart to pierce,
> Attend the progress of his herse.
> But what of that, his friends may say,
> He had those honours in his day.
> True to his profit and his pride,
> He made them weep before he dy'd.
>   Come hither, all ye empty things,
> Ye bubbles rais'd by breath of Kings;
> Who float upon the tide of state,
> Come hither, and behold your fate.
> Let pride be taught by this rebuke,
> How very mean a thing's a Duke;
> From all his ill-got honours flung,
> Turn'd to that dirt from whence he sprung.[1]

The elegiac genre is mocked, its skeleton retained for that purpose. The form of the poem enacts the burial arrangements

[1] *Poems*, vol. I, pp. 296–7.

as if to make the reported death doubly sure. Marlborough is to be put into the grave, the 'dirt from whence he sprung', because this is required by decency. The poem begins in astonishment; registering the receipt of news by one who is merely surprised to hear it. This note marks one limit beyond which the feeling will not go, and it implies other limits in other directions. The individual stages in the development of the poem are therefore the occasions on which the surprise is, in one degree or another, assimilated: 'Well, since he's gone, no matter how...' The event is treated as news, so that no other treatment may be allowed. Just as the body is to be put into the grave, the discourse is also to be reduced from the first note of astonishment. Swift's way is to use the conventional figures—the candle of life, the trump of doom, the procession of weeping mourners—but to pursue them beyond the limit of decorum until their conventional glories drop away; then, in their literal state, they collapse. He holds these poor figures aloft until the venal attributes which they conceal have time and force to drag them down; the stink of the snuffed candle, the trump which cannot be ignored, the widows and orphans who wept while Marlborough was alive. Pope's version is quite different in its significance:

> Behold him loaded with unreverend years
> Bath'd in unmeaning unrepentant tears
> Dead, by regardless Vet'rans born on high
> Dry pomps and Obsequies without a sigh.[1]

Ronald Barthes has remarked that in the ages which he calls classical the language was a common property and 'thought alone bore the weight of being different'. To Pope and Swift language is a system of signs embodying relations; exercises of the system may be different in detail because they are the same at large. All poetic couplets are the same in one respect;

---

[1] 'A Character', in Pope, *Minor Poems*, edited by Norman Ault (Methuen, London, 1954), pp. 358–9.

hence their difference in every other respect. In the Marlborough poems the weight of being different is a matter of
tone. Pope's magnificence is the force of solemnity which
refuses, even on this occasion, to sink beneath itself: the values
which sustain the solemnity have been humiliated in Marlborough's life, so they are potent in absence and denial, 'un-
reverend', 'unmeaning', 'unrepentant', and 'Obsequies without
a sigh'. Swift begins the corresponding part as if solemnity
might be in question: 'Behold his funeral appears...'; again,
absence is the sign. Pursuing this line, he makes an abrupt
change to the colloquial: 'But what of that, his friends may
say'; until the general is condemned by his wretched advocates.
The solemn note is admitted, only to enrich the mockery.
In Swift and Pope we are to watch an action: 'Behold'. But
in Pope we are to mark its moral solemnity; in Swift we are
to attend an event corresponding to the mean accountancy by
which it is described. 'True to his profit and his pride'; the
two are one, as the language allows. This is Swift's method,
when he attacks someone who is omnivorous and impartial in
vice. In the *Short Character of the Earl of Wharton* he adverts to
politics, religion, and lechery, but only to say that in this case
they are all one; there is no point in differentiating where the
acts are indistinguishable:

He is a Presbyterian in Politics, and an Atheist in Religion; but he
chuseth at present to whore with a Papist.[1]

In the Satirical Elegy the definitive gesture comes at the end,
heaving the body into the grave. Alluding to the events of
1711, Swift pursues the figure ('From all his ill-got honours
flung') until life itself is seen as one of the ill-got honours; as
Marlborough rightly lost his offices, so now he has rightly
lost his life. Belatedly, justice is done: 'Turn'd to that dirt
from whence he sprung'. 'Sprung' and 'dung' make one of

---

[1] Swift, *The Examiner, and Other Pieces Written in 1710–11*, edited by Herbert
Davis (Basil Blackwell, Oxford, 1957), p. 179.

Swift's favourite rhymes; 'sprung' and 'flung', another. Grim propriety is ensured when the body cannot be distinguished from its origin. The relief is audible when mighty things are brought low. 'Come hither, all ye empty things': meaning the readers, too, if we are tempted to high vice, and in any event all the little Marlboroughs who have not yet been caught. The last lines are an *exemplum*, a demonstration of a process in the world at large, Marlborough's inglorious death the proof of the case. The act of Fate is given in the last two lines as a process at once majestic and impersonal; personal only by analogy. Most of the action is done by 'flung' and 'turn'd': they are poised together for precisely this reason. Syntax is working here to ensure that one part of the action is immediately followed by another: flung from his honours, Marlborough is then flung further, beyond all considerations of this transitory kind, into death and corruption. The turning, the transformation into dirt, is already accomplished, as if the spectators' outraged feeling could not wait.

THE AUTHORSHIP OF
'A TALE OF A TUB'

Robert Martin Adams has revived the old question of Thomas Swift's part in the composition of *A Tale of a Tub*.[1] 'This worthless story has long been disproved', Sir Harold Williams asserted in a brisk footnote to the *Correspondence*. The question is not, however, at rest.

Mr Adams's case for Thomas Swift as part-author of the *Tale* is based upon two copies of the first edition, one in the Columbia University Library, the other in Cornell University Library. Both are annotated. Briefly, the argument is that the Cornell marginalia are in the hand of Thomas Swift and that they sustain the claim that Thomas was largely responsible for *The Mechanical Operation of the Spirit* and the narrative sections of the *Tale* itself. This would leave Jonathan with the credit of *The Battle of the Books* and the great Digressions. Mr Adams argues that Curll's *Key* (1710) was printed from the Cornell and the Columbia annotations. He also claims that the case for Thomas is supported by stylistic analysis. The argument, in detail, is extremely impressive. If we agree, as we must, that the handwriting is Thomas Swift's, we find great difficulty in setting aside the implications. To mention a single detail: on page 67 the annotator of the Cornell copy glosses a reference to gold lace: 'By this Gold lace I intended to sett forth the Processions & vain Pomp of the R.C. Religion, but He has inserted it here in a wrong place.' He then changed this to read, 'By this Gold lace it is intended . . . '. Either way, the note is mad delusion unless it is based upon a pretty intimate experience in the early planning or composition of the work. Indeed, in the new light of Mr Adams's essay, it is impossible to deny to Thomas Swift some part in the work. But the question is: what part? Curll's *Key* speaks of 'a couple of young Clergymen in the Year 1697 . . . ' as authors of the *Tale*.

[1] Robert Martin Adams, 'Jonathan Swift, Thomas Swift, and the Authorship of *A Tale of a Tub*', *Modern Philology*, vol. 64, no. 3 (February 1967), pp. 198–232.

The strongest arguments against Mr Adams come from Jonathan Swift. There is, first, the letter to Benjamin Tooke, dated 29 June 1710, referring to the recently published *Key*:

I believe it is so perfect a Grub-street-piece, it will be forgotten in a week. But it is strange that there can be no satisfaction against a Bookseller for publishing names in so bold a manner. I wish some lawyer could advise you how I might have satisfaction: For, at this rate, there is no book, however so vile, which may not be fastened on me. I cannot but think that little Parson-cousin of mine is at the bottom of this; for, having lent him a copy of some part of, &c. and he shewing it, after I was gone for Ireland, and the thing abroad, he affected to talk suspiciously, as if he had some share in it. If he should happen to be in town, and you light on him, I think you ought to tell him gravely, that, if he be the author, he should set his name to the &c. and rally him a little upon it: And tell him, if he can explain some things, you will, if he pleases, set his name to the next edition. I should be glad to see how far the foolish impudence of a dunce could go.[1]

We cannot take this at its face value. Mr Adams has commented somewhat damagingly upon it. On the other hand, the challenge it offers is repeated, publicly, in the Postscript to the Apology in the fifth edition. Referring again to the *Key* and the assigning of names, Swift says:

The Author farther asserts that the whole Work is entirely of one Hand, which every Reader of Judgment will easily discover. The Gentleman who gave the Copy to the Bookseller, being a Friend of the Author, and using no other Liberties besides that of expunging certain Passages where now the Chasms appear under the Name of Desiderata. But if any Person will prove his Claim to three Lines in the whole Book, let him step forth and tell his Name and Titles, upon which the Bookseller shall have Orders to prefix them to the next Edition, and the Claimant shall from henceforward be acknowledged the undisputed Author.[2]

The challenge could hardly be more positive. Already in the 'Apology' itself Swift had claimed full independence; 'he has not borrowed one single Hint from any Writer in the World.' So if Thomas were to put in a bid, he had his chance now. There is no evidence that he ever raised the question again.

Jonathan's challenge is remarkable. Clearly he resented any suggestion that his parson-cousin had a hand in the affair. It is

---

[1] *Correspondence*, edited by Harold Williams (Clarendon Press, Oxford, 1965), vol. I, pp. 165–6.
[2] *A Tale of a Tub*, edited by A. C. Guthkelch and David Nichol Smith (Clarendon Press, Oxford, 1920), p. 21.

very difficult to reconcile the challenge with Mr Adams's argument. My own view is that the original plan for the *Tale* probably came from Thomas when the cousins were together in Sir William Temple's library. By May 1694, Thomas may have blocked out some parts of the work. Jonathan took these materials and developed them; extending, revising, recasting, working up the detail. Indeed, he may have changed the whole thing until not even three consecutive lines remained intact. At that stage, naturally enough, he regarded Thomas's part in the work as superseded; a few loose suggestions, receding in memory. After seven years, very little remained unchanged. Thomas, on the other hand, would have retained his first materials fresh in the mind; poor things, perhaps, but his own. So he would always be able to recognise familiar places when he saw the first printed edition. But the work had changed so much by then, being revised perhaps in every line, that he could not force a claim, at least in public, even when challenged.

The evidence based on style, incidentally, is not convincing. At one point Mr Adams quotes a passage from *The Mechanical Operation of the Spirit* which is similar, in many respects, to the passage in the *Tale* where Jack offers a treatise on Providence. The argument is that the passage in the Fragment is demonstrably inferior to that in the *Tale*, as Thomas is inferior to Jonathan. But Dipak Nandy has observed, in an essay shortly to be published, that according to Mr Adams's disposal of relevant sections, Jack's oration comes in a section (xi) ascribed to Thomas. Stylistic arguments are often deceptive.

The question is not settled, one way or the other. On balance, the evidence still seems to concede to Jonathan the verbal detail, the minute arrangement of words, sentences, and paragraphs. That Thomas had a hand in the early discussions is clear enough; that he drafted some parts I would be willing to concede. But it is difficult to allow Thomas's part in the affair to go much beyond that point. The real disappointment is that Thomas's annotations do not throw much new light on the notoriously dark places. In some few cases his note is more accurate than the version in the *Key*; but his gloss upon the 'camelion' passage, for instance, is not necessarily better than the explanation in the *Key*. There is no obvious reason why the camelion should be the Deists rather than the priests of the Church of England; here the *Key* seems right. It is also disappointing that Thomas, who is supposed to have special information, does not solve the old problem of Moulinavent; though of course he does not claim to have written that section (VIII). Thomas's gloss and the *Key* at this point are equally unsatisfactory, leaving Barrett's suggestion in the *Essay on the Earlier Part of the Life of Swift* (1808) the best guess available. Most of the difficulties arise in sections which Mr Adams ascribes to Jonathan. He is still our problem.

ONE OF SWIFT'S MARGINALIA IN BARONIUS

In the final volume of the Herbert Davis edition of Swift (*Index to the Prose Writings*, compiled by William J. Kunz, Steven Hollander, and Susan Staves under the supervision of Irvin Ehrenpreis; with Addenda, Errata, Corrigenda edited by Herbert Davis and Irvin Ehrenpreis (Basil Blackwell, Oxford, 1968) Professor Ehrenpreis prints for the first time a selection from Swift's marginalia on Baronius's *Annales Ecclesiastici* (twelve vols., 1612 edition). The annotations are dated, in Swift's hand, 'A.D. 1729'. The selection includes (p. 35) a comment which appears in volume VII, p. 728: 'Confessio fidei barbaris digna'. In the relevant part of Baronius's text the theme is the return of the Russian Church to communion with the Church of Rome. Baronius gives the address of the Russian Hypatius to Pope Clement VIII, the specific declaration of faith and communion. The first main article in the entire Nicene Creed, recited by Hypatius as the primary matter of the common faith. Professor Ehrenpreis prints the 'Confessio fidei' remark as applying to the first words of that Creed, 'Credo in unum deum Patrem omnipotentem, factorem caeli & terrae . . .', etc. In this he follows the late Herbert Davis.

Davis raised the question on 2 April 1966 at a seminar in the Clark Memorial Library, Los Angeles. Discussing Swift's use of irony, he referred to the seventh volume of Baronius:

In the appendix to that volume, Baronius prints the document accepted by the Russian Church as the statement of the Christian Faith when they were received into communion with the Church of Rome. This included the *Credo* text of the Nicene Creed in Latin, exactly as it is translated in the English prayer book, then in use at the cathedral of St. Patrick's. Over against the opening words Swift has written:

> Confessio fidei
> barbaris digna

which I suppose must be translated, 'A creed worthy of the barbarians', or, perhaps, 'fit for the Russians'.

Davis comments:

Does this mean that, after all, Swift had become a creature of the Enlightenment, a real contemporary of Voltaire, or at least so much an Augustan as to find the source of his morality in Republican Rome rather than among the Christian barbarians? This, I suppose, would be easily acceptable to many of Swift's modern readers, probably to all his admirers in Russia and in Asia. But might there be another remote possibility, that he was here indulging himself for a moment in a sort of Pauline irony, where he admits that having had to give up all hope of the world—that Augustan civilized world his friends still believed in (he separates himself from them in that phrase in a letter to Pope—*vous autres*)—nothing now was left for him but the faith of the barbarians, that primitive Christianity which he had once said it would indeed be a wild project to offer to restore?[1]

These are important ideas. But I propose to argue that the 'Confessio fidei' gloss does not refer to the Nicene Creed at all.

The Baronius volumes are the property of Christ Church Cathedral, Dublin. Recently, however, they have been transferred on permanent loan to the Archbishop Marsh Library, Dublin. In volume VII the pencil gloss at p. 728 is perfectly clear, but it is not placed 'over against the opening words' of the Nicene Creed. It is placed somewhat higher on the page. When I first saw the gloss I took it as referring to the sentence immediately preceding the Creed; the more I examine it, the more convinced I become that my first assumption was right. The sentence reads:

Firma fide credo & profiteor omnia & singula quae continentur in Symbolo fidei, quo sancta Romana Ecclesia vtitur, videlicet:

Credo follows at once. If Swift's gloss refers to this sentence rather than to the Creed itself, it means that he is sneering at the Russian Church, so abject now in its belated grovelling before Rome. The Russian sentence is not a mere formula, it is a commitment, a blank cheque drawn in favour of Sancta Romana Ecclesia. The fact that payment was soon to be stopped makes the grandeur of the Russian profession the more ludicrous. The 'fidei' of Swift's gloss then parodies the 'fide' and the 'fidei' of the Russian avowal. So the question of Swift's faith or despair in 1729 does not arise. Certainly it cannot be raised on the basis of this gloss. He has not said anything about the Nicene Creed.

[1] *The Uses of Irony*: Papers on Defoe and Swift, by Maximillian E. Novak and Herbert J. Davis (Clark Memorial Library, University of California, Los Angeles 1966), pp. 62-3.

INDEX

INDEX